Remember, I am coming soon! . . .

I bring with me the reward that will be given to each man as his conduct deserves. I am the Alpha and the Omega, the First and the Last, the Beginning and the End! Happy are they who wash their robes so as to have free access to the tree of life and enter the city through its gates! Outside are the dogs and sorcerers, the fornicators and murderers, the idol worshippers and all who love falsehood . . .

The Spirit and the Bride say, "Come!" Let him who hears answer, "Come!" Let him who is thirsty come forward; let all who desire it accept the gift of life-giving water . . .

(Rev. 22:12-15, 17)

Tribulations and Triumph
Revelations on the Coming of
THE GLORY OF GOD

"The Heavens declared His Justice:
and all people saw His glory"

(Psalm 96:6)

St. Dominic's Publishing Co.
109 Executive Drive, Suite D
Dulles, Virginia 20166
703-742-3939

I

DEDICATION

*To the Immaculate Mother, Mary,
Queen of Peace
and to Jesus Christ,
Prince of Peace,
King of Kings, and Lord of Lords.*

Tribulations and Triumph
Revelations on the Coming of
THE GLORY OF GOD

"Be silent, I wish to speak. . .

Call the book **The Glory of God.** *The glory of God shines forth as the light in the darkness. Let all of my children who read these words recognize in them the glorious God who lights the true path to love, peace, and eternal glory.*

This is my wish. So say I the Lord God."
(8-18-92)

Messages for all God's children
From the Lord God
and Mary, the Mother.

(Given by Inner Locution)

According to a decree of the Congregation for the Doctrine of Faith, approved by H. H. Pope Paul VI, (1966), it is now permitted to publish and distribute without an Imprimatur books about new apparitions, revelations, prophecies, or miracles. In accordance with the regulations of the Second Vatical Council, we who publish and distribute this book state that we do not wish to precede the judgment of the Church in this matter, to whose authority we humbly and obediently submit.

With reference to private revelations, H. H. Pope Urban VIII, 1623-44 has stated:

> "In cases which concern private revelations, it is better to believe than not to believe, for, if you believe, and it is proven true, you will be happy that you have believed, because our Holy Mother asked it. If you believe, and it should be proven false, you will receive all blessings as if it had been true, because you believed it to be true."

NOTE: The messages in this book are recorded exactly as they were received. It will be noted that many times not all of the message is included. These are private instructions for Joanne and in no way change the public message. Where the private message is included in the text, it is enclosed in brackets and is included because it clarifies the message or is a call to action. Also, you will note that quotation marks are not used because it is meant to be understood that all of the messages are believed to be the words of the Lord God or Mary our Mother.

All Biblical references are taken from the Douay-Rheims Bible, Tan Books and Publishers, Inc.

Published by: St. Dominic's Publishing Company,
109 Executive Drive, Suite D
Dulles, Virginia 20166
Phone 703-742-3939
Fax   703-742-0808

ISBN 0-9636640-0-X

ACKNOWLEDGEMENT

It is with deep gratitude that I acknowledge those special people whom the Lord God has provided for the publication of this book.

This book would not have been possible without David Haug who willingly and wholeheartedly accepted the responsibility of directing all the aspects involved in publishing the book, and Amy Piehler who spent many hours in the typing and layout of the manuscript. Their help, their advice, their expertise, their prayers, and their devotion to the project have been invaluable.

I wish to thank the members of my family who have been a special source of strength for me. They have unfailingly supported and encouraged me in all that the Lord asks of me. Their love sustains and uplifts me in the good times as well as the difficult times.

A most special thank you and heartfelt gratitude to my spiritual director for his sure wisdom, his steady hand guiding me around many pitfalls, and his great patience in leading my stumbling steps along the path the Lord has chosen for me.

There are so many others -- the members of my prayer groups who have encouraged me and offered many prayers on my behalf; my dear and special friend Barbara who knows exactly when I need a kind word or helping hand; and my new and old friends who have responded generously in times of need.

To all of these I am deeply indebted.

"Extinguish not the spirit. Despise not prophecies. But Prove all things; hold fast that which is good. From all appearance of evil refrain yourselves." (1 Thessalonians 5:19-22).

v

EDITORIAL NOTE

The messages in this book are believed to be prophetic private revelations given by inner locution for the present time and circumstances, and for future events. However, while "divine interventions are considered normal gifts given whenever God sees fit to give them" (Dubay 246), certain norms must be considered for guiding the reader of these words.

1. Only the complete and entire public revelation which came through the Divine person of Jesus Christ is "free from substantive distortion by the power of the Holy Spirit" (Groeschel, 29).

2. As in many scriptural prophecies such as Amos 5:1-2, certain messages in this book speak of events as having already occurred, such as those of 10-17-90, 12-7-90, and 1-26-91. In this case it is well to recall the answer given by God to the prophet Habakkuk who questions the ways of God regarding the internal evils of Judah and social abuses of his day: "For the vision still has its time, presses on to fulfillment, and will not disappoint; if it delays, wait for it, it will surely come, it will not be late" (Hab 2:3). Therefore, these messages in this book spoken of as having already occurred may be understood as representing a future reality although they are stated in the present tense.

3. While locutions are normal gifts of God, whose revelation is sure and solid in the divine light in which it is communicated, there is no assurance of infallibility for ordinary people. It is possible for what is received to be recorded incorrectly, and to be misunderstood, misinterpreted and misapplied (Dubay, 261). Thus, no private revelation should be considered an infallible guide for present or future events.

Therefore, as you read these words, it is advisable to seek for enlightenment in prayer through the power of the Holy Spirit, and wait for the "visions", locutions in this case, "to press on to fulfillment" in the light of God's purposes.

Sources:

Dubay, Fr. Thomas, S.M., FIRE WITHIN. Ignatius Press: San Francisco, 1989.

Groeschel, Fr. Benedict J, C.F.R., A STILL SMALL VOICE. Ignatius Press: San Francisco, 1993.

Table of Contents

Notes IV

Acknowledgement..V

Editorial Note VI

Preface IX

Part I - 1990 1

Part II - 1991 53

Part III - 1992 121

Part IV - 1993 165

Part IV - 1994..205

Appendix 232

Index 235

Preface

"It shall come to pass in the last days, (saith the Lord), I will pour out of my Spirit upon all flesh: and your sons and your daughters shall prophesy, and your young men shall see visions, and your old men shall dream dreams. And upon my servants indeed, and upon my handmaids will I pour out in those days of my spirit, and they shall prophesy." (Act 2:17-18) .

✣ ✣

*T*he contents of this book which you are about to read contain private revelations given by means of inner locutions. These messages are consistent with an urgent call to conversion, a gracious invitation to holiness, and God's merciful warning of an impending judgment if we do not heed His call to **conversion and repentance**. In general, these messages call for proper understanding and prayerful discernment. Therefore, as you read and reflect upon these writings, you are invited to pray for these two gifts and to retain what is good from the messages. They are not meant to cause confusion or to disturb a person's peace with the spirit of fear, rather they are an encouragement to greater zeal in responding to the love and mercy of God. Because of the nature of these writings, they have been submitted for review to the proper Church authorities who, while not endorsing them, recognize my right to publish them and are not opposed to their publication.

You may now be asking who I am, how I came to receive these messages, and why another publication of private revelations when there are already so many available? A brief autobiography may help to answer these questions.

I was born in Pennsylvania the oldest of five children, and I am of Polish ancestry. We were poor though not poverty-stricken. Life in our home was difficult. My father was a strict authoritarian and, many times, an aggressive disciplinarian. My mother was a timid and gentle woman who served as a buffer between my father and us children. Still, our home life was basically stable, and we knew that we were loved and well cared for. As I grew older, however, it became apparent that my father was becoming more and more dependent upon alcohol, and as his behavior became more directly influenced by his drinking, life became even more difficult for all of us. The wise course was to try to avoid being seen or heard, and I turned to reading as a refuge. Thus, I became introverted and introspective, and so I am a reserved and quiet individual.

In spite of our family problems my parents, without fail, insisted upon a strict observance of our Catholic faith and our Polish religious traditions. I attended Catholic schools from first grade through high school then worked until I was married and had my first child. It was not until 1983 that I was able to realize my dream of a college education when I entered a local university. It was a long difficult endeavor that was hampered by the need to work for part of the time I was in school, the shared care of an elderly relative in the last years of his life, severe illnesses for my husband and myself, and the responsibilities of home and family. However, I graduated Cum Laude in 1991 with a BA degree in the Humanities and with minors in English and philosophy.

During this period, in the fall of 1987, I first heard about the events taking place in Medjugorje in the former Jugoslavia where it is believed that Mary, the Mother of Jesus Christ, has been appearing daily since 1981. I have always had a great love for Mary and a great attraction to the Fatima apparitions, so when I heard about the Medjugorje apparitions there was never any doubt that I would go there. I made my first trip in March 1988. It was a difficult trip because I did not anticipate certain events which led to my profound conversion. On my first day in Medjugorje I became very ill. The illness brought bitter disappointment because I was isolated from my group and I could not participate in the activities of the pilgrimage. I was so sick that I had to sleep in a sitting position so that I could breathe. That first night, I prayed to Mary that I would not die in Medjugorje (I truly believed this was a possibility), and that she could do anything with me if she would just let me get home.

At that time I did not understand the necessity of this situation. However, out of it came the single most important event of my

Preface

entire life. As I sat in my room on my last day in Medjugorje, I was overcome with a terrible and intense disappointment compounded by my struggle to understand the pain and hardships of my life, and I began to cry. As I cried out "why is this happening to me?", I became aware of a presence in the room, although I did not see anyone. To this presence, from the depth of my being, I poured out my whole heart and soul. This went on for most of the afternoon until I was so exhausted I no longer had strength to speak. I had cried out a lifetime of disappointments, rejections, pain, sorrow, confusion, doubts, anger, hatred, everything that I could not understand. And as I sat there exhausted all I had the strength to do was whisper "what do you want of me?" At that moment I was enveloped in the most beautiful peace I have ever experienced. I can truly say, that from this experience my life changed to such a degree that I am no longer the same person I was then.

This was not the end of it though because when I returned home my illness brought more suffering, yet it was the means of further spiritual development. Within twelve hours after my return home, I was rushed to the emergency room and spent several days in the hospital with a severe attack of asthma (which I had never had before) complicated by pneumonia and bronchitis. I am now an asthmatic. The illness was so severe and debilitating I was unable to do much of anything for several months except to read and pray. I set aside my novels and began to read everything I could find on the Church, Mary, spirituality, prophecy, divine mercy, the saints, even going so far as to write to publishers in order to find the books I was led to read. Prayer was intense and meditations so deep that many times I was not aware of my physical surroundings or the amount of time that had elapsed. I began to put into practice the Medjugorje message of prayer, fasting, peace, conversion, and penance.

It was after my second trip to Medjugorje in the fall of 1989 that I was led to participate in a Life in the Spirit seminar at my parish. I was hesitant about participating because of negative articles I had read about the charismatic movement and, because of my introverted nature, I did not want to participate in anything that might make me look foolish. Nevertheless, I did participate, hesitant at every step of the way, and praying that I would not

Preface

receive the gift of tongues, again because I thought this to be too out of the ordinary for one who is so very ordinary. Prophecy was so far beyond my comprehension I never even considered it as a possibility. In the end I prayed -- "I really don't want the gift of tongues but I will accept whatever it is your will to give me." Not only did I receive this gift but within two weeks I began to receive these messages, which I continue to receive to this day.

When I first began receiving the messages I experienced a great deal of consternation and was my own worst skeptic. However, as the messages continued, I came to realize that what I was recording was information and theology of which I have no knowledge in a style that is totally different from my own. In the beginning I was instructed by the Lord God not to speak of these messages to anyone until He commanded me to do so. The first command to speak came on November 29, 1990, and the command to publish came on August 23, 1991. These commands have been repeated on several occasions since then with an increasing urgency. Therefore, under the guidance of my spiritual director and with the cooperation and support of my family, I made the decision to publish the messages in response to the direct command of the Lord God and to what I believe with my whole being is the will of God.

Growth in spirituality and one's relationship with God is an ongoing process, and my growth and testing continues. God calls each one of us, and His graces are for all. If we open our hearts, minds, and souls; if we accept His call and return love for love; if we pray for His gifts and graces, He leads us on the path of holiness. He leads us to peace, and joy, and to a love beyond human understanding. Our spiritual growth continues until that moment when we are received into the heart and the arms of our God who gently teaches us the way, if we let Him. Let these messages then, through the intercession of Mary our Mother, bring those who read them to the loving embrace of Jesus our Lord, our King, our Saviour.

Joanne Kriva
December 1994

Tribulations and Triumph
Revelations on the Coming of
THE GLORY OF GOD
1990

"Delay not to be converted to the Lord, and defer it not from day to day. For his wrath shall come on a sudden, and in the time of vengeance He will destroy thee."

(Eccl. 5:8-9).

9-10-90   FIRST MESSAGE RECEIVED

The day is coming when the Lord your God shall reign. Rejoice and be glad. The time will come when the world shall be as one.

This is the Lord your God most high speaking. Tell My people I love them . . . It is I who am speaking. What must be will be. Bring My people home . . . Praise be to God, eternal Father, eternal Son, and eternal Spirit. Amen.

9-20-90 The Lord your God shall act. Get ready.

9-27-90   THE WORLD IS IN GREAT DANGER

Speak in My name. Say: The world is in great danger. Hear the word of the Lord who wishes to save His people. Hear the word of your Lord Jesus Christ who says come back to me My people. I love you. Hear My voice. Come back to My sacraments. Love each other as I love you. Call My name in your every need. I will hear and answer you. Become once again My people; people of faith. Do not respond to the call of the secular world. Come to me instead. I am here for you. Do not deny me My right to care for you. Thus says the Lord, your God, most high.

1

9-28-90 *HEAR THE WORDS SPOKEN THROUGH MY PROPHETS*

Say in My name: Peace to My people. I love you. Hear the words that have been spoken through My prophets. They speak the truth. If you do not heed My words I shall be forced to act. The world is in dire situation. Only My grace can save it. Pray for conversion. Conversion must come from your heart. I hear My people's cries and will not leave them destitute. I am their loving Father. Their prayers will be answered.

10-1-90 I DESIRE TO SAVE ALL MY CREATION

Say in My name: Come to Me My children. Too many are far from My loving heart. I desire to save all My creation from the dire consequences which now threaten it. If you do not respond to My call for conversion, prayer, and penance, I will act against those who refuse My mercy. I am your loving God, but My patience is at an end. Come to Me all you who hear, and I will grant you My protection from what is to come . . . The number of days is counted. I will act swiftly in the glory of My power. I will reign supreme over all My creation, and all will give glory to the Lord, your God. Hear My words. I speak the truth. Only a few will remain to love and serve their God. Pray, My children, and repent, for the time is near when your God shall come in all His glory, and power, and majesty to reclaim His rightful place in His creation. *There is no time left.* The punishment will be severe for those who do not hear. I wish to save all My people.

My Holy Mother will no longer be allowed to intercede for you. Her time on earth is coming to an end. *Do not delay, but do as I command.* I will grant mercy to all who ask for it. Your time is short. If anyone hears My voice, I will save him, but to those who do not hear, I will send to eternal damnation. Please respond to My pleas, My children. The Lord, your God, is a loving and forgiving God, but My justice

2

shall rain down on My creation. I shall no longer tolerate the abomination that My creation has become. I speak in a loud voice: **Repent all you who inhabit My creation!** God, your Lord, has spoken. . .

10-2-90   RETURN TO YOUR GOD — COME TO ME

Say in the name of the Lord God most high: You are all so far away from Me, My children. Return to your God who loves you. Believe in My mercy. Confess your sins. Read the words of the prophet Isaiah. His words speak to you today. The Lord, your God, is just. His love endures forever. Hear Me, My people. Why must I beg you to return My love? You are My brothers and sisters.

Speak in My name. Say, I love you. What more is there to give for your salvation? I gave you My life. My Mother pleads for you. My message is before all people. Still you do not hear. Oh My people, what more do you want? Isn't My love enough for you? There are signs and wonders throughout My creation. Still you do not see. What more can I do? Your time is short. Come then, oh My children, back to the arms of your loving Father, Son, and Spirit. Trust in the mercy of your Lord. Come back, My people, before it is too late. So many will perish in the fruitless conflict. Come, My people, I call you once again to the truth and the light. Hear Me, oh My people. Be faithful to your God, most high. **Come to Me! Come to Me! What more can I say.** That is all.

10-3-90   PROCLAIM THE NAME OF THE LORD

Say in My name: The Spirit of the Lord shall come upon all those who ask for it. In the name of the Lord God most high say: My Spirit shall renew the face of the earth. Hear, oh My people, the words of the Lord your God.

Say in My name: I love you. Holy is the name of your Lord God Almighty. Do not blaspheme against His

3

name. His name must be on every tongue. His name must be proclaimed throughout the earth. All glory and honor must be given to His holy name. Raise your voices and give glory and praise to your Almighty God. Sing out your praises with joyful hearts. The Lord God Almighty is coming in all His glory.

Hear My words and rejoice. All on earth shall know that I am their God. Rejoice My people, for the kingdom of God is at hand . . . I am the God of love. Let all My people hear My words and raise their voices in praise and thanksgiving. May their souls rejoice in the goodness of the Lord . . .

10-4-90 I COME TO LEAD YOU BACK TO EVERLASTING LOVE

Say in the name of the Lord Jesus Christ: Hear Me My people. I speak to you in love. I come to lead you back to My everlasting love. The Lord your God loves you. His name must be in all your mouths. Proclaim Him as your Lord and Savior. Speak in My name. Say: You are My beloved children. Pray and convert your souls. Open your hearts to My abundant graces. Oh hear Me, My people. Let My Spirit fill your souls with peace . . . That is all.

10-4-90 YOU WILL ANNOUNCE MY JUSTICE

What will be will be. So be it. You (Joanne) will announce My justice to the world. I spoke, they did not listen. Their hearts are closed. The time of My justice is at hand. Let those with ears hear. There will be death and destruction. The earth will groan in its agony. Few will be saved. Repeat My words: The time of My mercy has come to an end. The time for your conversion is at an end. The day of the Lord is at hand. Thy will be done throughout the earth. Infinite God of power and majesty, how mighty are your works . . . Now say in the name of the Lord, Jesus Christ. Holy is the name of God. Bow down in adoration to the Lord your God . . . In all the earth My glory reigns. Shout with joy all My people for My kingdom comes.

4

You shall reign with Me forever. All that is in the earth and on the earth shall be renewed. The power of God most high will come upon you. Give glory to God for His goodness . . . Go in peace.

10-6-90 RECEIVE MY LAST WARNING

In the name of the Lord your God say: All glory and honor and praise to our Almighty God. In His name say: Woe to you who dwell on the earth. The wrath of God is at hand. You have made a mockery of His love and His mercy. Receive My last warning through My instrument. She speaks in My name. Her words are My words. No one who does not hear My word will be saved. *My justice shall come upon the whole earth. Your crimes cry out to heaven. I can no longer let the cries of My people go unanswered. Their prayers fill My heavens.* I will answer them. Their time has come. Remain steadfast in your faith. My loving heart will protect My own . . . The Lord your God has spoken. That is all . . .

10-7-90 MY MOTHER IS MY PERFECT CREATION - LIFE IS A SACRED TRUST

Say in the name of the Lord your God: My peace I give you. Oh holy people of God, your time is at hand. The victory will be yours. The powers of heaven will defeat the powers of hell. Satan and his followers will no longer hold sway over the world. Satan's power is at an end. *My most Holy Mother is succeeding in loosening his hold on the world. Her victory is imminent. Her glorious triumph is accomplished in obedience to My will.* Her Immaculate Heart has triumphed over the forces of evil. Her light shines forth throughout the earth. My people call her blessed; My people venerate her pure heart. She is the glorious Queen of heaven and earth. All on earth shall sing her praises. All shall bow and honor their Mother whom I have given them. She is our triumphant and loving Mother. All who venerate her honor Me. My Mother is love. Love her and My graces

5

will descend upon you in abundant measure. My Mother is My perfect creation; unchanged in her purity, glorified in heaven, and loved beyond measure. Her pure soul reflects the glory of the one God who created it. She reigns in splendor in the kingdom of the Father. She performs My will in perfect obedience. Her glory lights the heavens; her reign is eternal. Praise her in all her beauty and majesty for she is supreme in all My creation. Our love for her is without end. . . She is unequalled in all creation. Love her with unlimited love. Let her presence radiate in your lives. Let her love flow from your hearts. Let the glory of My Mother shine throughout the earth. Through her My peace will come to My people. Come, My people, give My Mother the honor and the love that is due her sovereign majesty. Follow Me in honoring her. I give My blessing and protection to all those who hear these words and do My will. Oh hear My words, My people, your loving God has spoken. That is all.

Now say: My people, your lives are in My hands. Respect the life I have given you. All life is My creation. I, who have created life according to My infinite power, will no longer permit the destruction of what is My creation. I alone know the time and the circumstances granted to each life. Mankind no longer lives according to My commandments. They have turned away from their God. They live in the misery of their own emptiness. Without Me they are walking sepulchers. Without Me they have no hope. Without hope they cannot be saved. Their souls are dead in their bodies. Their bodies have no purpose. They are nothing without Me. My life is not the life of the world. The world cannot retore life. Come to Me My children lost in your own darkness. Let Me give you back the life you have rejected. Let Me return you to the light of My love. Give Me back My creation. Turn the life I have created back to My love and care. Life is a sacred trust. Uphold that trust. The Lord your God has spoken. That is all . . .

Say in the name of the Lord your God most high: My peace is a gift. When you live in My love you shall have peace. When you live according to My Word, you shall have peace. My Word is My truth. All who have My truth live in My peace. There is no peace in the world; the world has rejected My truth. There is no peace in My Church; the Church has perverted My truth.* There is no peace in your hearts; you do not pray to know the truth. *I am the truth!* When you have Me you have truth. Truth does not come from the world. The world corrupts My truth; it rejects My truth, it wallows in its own self-delusion. Hear Me My people. I have spoken through My prophets. They speak the truth. My truth is for all people. Hear the voices of those who speak in My name; they speak My truth. Hear My voice, oh My people, and live in My truth. The Lord God is calling in a loud voice - **Come Back To My Truth!** Come back to Me, My children. Come back to the God who loves you. These are the words of the Lord your God most high. That is all.

Now say in the name of the Lord God most high: The world's peace is false peace. There is no peace where there is no love. My brothers and sisters have forgotten how to love. Love does not lie in the things of the world or of the flesh. It comes from My Spirit living within you. If you do not have My Spirit, you are empty shells. You are hollow people filled with useless pursuits. Your souls are dead; your passions rule you. You sin and have no thought of everlasting life. The fires of hell await those who reject My mercy. Come to Me My people and ask My forgiveness. *You must repent of your sins; they are many. You must convert your souls. You must live in the light of My truth. You must live in My love. My love can transform your hearts. My love can bring you peace.* Ask for it and it shall be given to you. Ask, My people, because I love you. Ask through My Holy Mother. I will grant what she asks. She intercedes for you, but her time is now short. After

7

that it will be too late. Pray, My children, for My love and My mercy. The time is late. I wish salvation for all My people. Hear the voice of the Lord your God, for He speaks the truth. Hear and respond, My children. My justice shall soon come upon the world. Do not delay. These are the words of the Lord your God most high. Hear and believe. That is all.

(* Specific issues are dealt with in other messages.)

10-9-90 LET ALL THE EARTH REJOICE

Now say in the name of the Lord your God: Glorious is the name of the Lord. Glory and Hosanna to our God. Say in My name: The day of the Lord is upon us. Call out His name with loud voices. Proclaim His word throughout the earth. The name of the Lord shall be exalted; Holy is His name. Let the earth rejoice in the coming of the Lord. All in heaven and on earth rejoice! All power and majesty is His. Come My people, rejoice, your God is at hand. His glory will endure forever. Join with Me, My people, in the triumph. Walk with Me My people. Your reward is great. Sing songs of praise and glory to your Almighty God. The Mystery of the kingdom is yours . . . Hear, oh My people, the words of the Lord your God. Your reward is great. Your faith has saved you. You are mine. Come to Me now and enter into your reward. Come! Come to your God who loves you. Come, My faithful people. My voice cries out with shouts of joy — *Come! Come! Come!* I welcome you into My kingdom. Come to My love. Come to My light. Come into your eternal inheritance. My plan for you is now completed. Rejoice My people. Your time is now ended. From the fullness of your hearts give praise and honor and glory to the Almighty God who has saved you. REJOICE! SING! Shout out the glorious triumph. Oh My people, how I love you. I embrace each of you in My loving arms. My joy knows no bounds. Come, My children, celebrate with Me. Let the joyous cries fill My kingdom. Your God reigns! That is all.

10-10-90 DO NOT DELAY IN RESPONDING TO YOUR GOD

Now say in the name of the Lord, your God: I love you, My people. In the name of the Lord your God say: Do not delay in responding to your God. My mercy is My love for you. I am Love. Say: Oh you who hear My words, come to love. Share My love with each other. My love fills the hearts and the souls of those who love Me. I am the source of love. If you have Me, you have love. My mercy endures through all ages. Do not be afraid, My people, to come to the mercy of your God. Your sins will be forgiven when you come to My mercy. Life is short. That is all.

10-11-90 MY MESSAGE IS URGENT — PRAY FOR MY MERCY

I wish to speak to you. My message is urgent. Many will die soon. Pray for them. They are lost. My poor children! Pray for My mercy. The world is in grave danger. *My justice is about to descend upon the earth. The Mystery of iniquity is at hand. His scourge will devastate the earth. He is pure evil. My Mother's time is ended. Now only death and darkness shall reign on the earth.* The word of God is true. The spirit is upon My servant. She writes My words. My words are true. Prepare, My children, for My chastise-ment is upon you. *My people will be protected. You must pray the rosary. You must light your blessed candles. You must stay in your homes. I will give you My light.*

Now say: *Do not be afraid.* The terror will be great but you who hear My word will be safe. Trust in Me. I love you, My own. No harm will come to you. You are marked with My seal. I know My own. You need not fear. Your response to My Mother's messages has saved you. I hear her pleas on your behalf. I love her. We love you.
(Go in peace My child. Pray for My people. They must be strong in their faith. They must pray. They must not despair. They will be protected from what is to come . . . These are the words of the Lord, your God. That is all.)

9

10-12-90 MY JUSTICE CANNOT BE DENIED

In the name of the Lord your God say: My time has come. All who dwell on the earth shall know their God. My wrath is overflowing. My people no longer know their God. Their sins cry to heaven. My justice cannot be denied. All who live in My love are My chosen ones. They comfort Me. They live My words. They speak in My name. My mercy is for all, but only a few come to Me. So few return My love. So many are lost. My Mother's heart sorrows for her lost children. Our love falls on cold hearts. Open your hearts. Let our love light the darkness in your souls. Almighty God and Father we adore you. Thy will be done. These are the words of the Lord, your God. That is all . . .

10-13-90 PRAY FOR MY POPE — BEWARE OF THE EVIL ONE

Say in the name of the Lord your God: Pray for My Pope (John Paul II). He endures great suffering. His enemies surround him. He teaches My truth to the world. *There is one who plots against him. This is the Evil One.* The Pope is in great danger. Evil surrounds him. His days are numbered. He is My *faithful son. He has served Me well. There will be great turmoil in My Church. Beware of the Evil One. Many will suffer because of him.* He will fill My heaven with many faithful souls. He will bring destruction upon the face of the earth. His power is from the Spirit from hell. Do not be deceived by him. The stench of his sins will cover the earth. My Mother's voice is now stilled in My ears. What has been foretold will now be accomplished. Have courage My people. My Father's will be done . . . Thus says the Lord your God.

Second message received 10-13-90 is a continuation of the first message. Say in the name of the Lord your God: I speak in a loud voice. My Spirit is upon those who hear My voice. My faithful servant Pope John Paul II is in My loving arms. He has entered into My kingdom. Know by My holy words that My judgment is upon the earth. All My faithful ones, have faith in Me, your Almighty God. Your faith will save you. You shall enter into My kingdom. You shall live in the light of My love in the kingdom of My Father. He stands at the door to welcome you. The Almighty God stands upon the firmament and gathers you in His loving arms. Remain steadfast My people. Blessed be Almighty God forever. Holy is His name.

Now say: Repent you who still have time. The days that remain are few in number . . . The Lord, your God, has spoken. That is all. * see Editorial note p. VI #2.

10-14-90 THE GLORY OF GOD RADIATES THROUGHOUT THE UNIVERSE

Say in the name of the Lord your God: Hear Me My people. Rejoice in the glory of your God. All glory and honor and praise are His forever and ever, Amen.

Say in My name: The glory of God radiates throughout the universe. It shines forth to light the universe. All creation is the handwork of the glorious God of heaven and earth. The souls of men conformed to the glory of their creator radiate the glory of God. Their spirits unite with the God who created them. They share in the everlasting oneness of their God. They are united in the Mystery of the Trinity, one God in three persons: the Father, the Creator; the Son, the Redeemer; and the Spirit, the Truth. Come to the Spirit, come to the Redeemer, and come to the Creator, and you shall be renewed. Unite yourselves to your salvation.

In the name of your Almighty God say: *You are My glorious creatures. You are the image of My glorious nature. My glory shines forth in pure souls. My glory is the reward of the pure of heart, the humble of spirit, and those of simple faith.* Oh glorious people of God, in the glory of your one

11

God renew the Church of the Son. Unite in the one truth and bring to the Father the radiant gift of His holy and purified creation. Rejoice oh glorious people of God, your gift is sanctified in the eternal unity of the Mystery of redemption. Oh holy people of God, you are redeemed by the united cooperation of the Father, the Son, and the Spirit. Your God is one. Your God saves. Your God loves you in the unity of the three; Three-in-One who is, was, and ever shall be without beginning or end. Thus says the Lord your God, He who *is* in time and eternity.

10-16-90 MIGHTY SPIRIT OF GOD INFLAME US

Now say in the name of the Lord your God: Oh wisdom of the most high God infuse our souls with your presence. Enter into our intellects. Reveal to us our limitations as the imperfect creatures of God. Lead us to God's light in the knowledge of His truth. May we come to know our God in our whole being; in our hearts, and minds, and souls.

Now Say: Mighty Spirit of God inflame us with love for the wisdom of God. Let our souls thirst for the truth. Let us drink to the full the power of God's holy Word. Guide our steps to the seat of perfect knowledge that we may know and understand the perfect truth that is our God. Almighty and everlasting God, we place ourselves in your loving hands. Teach us oh Lord. Strengthen us, keep us free from the errors of the Evil One. Thy truth be ever in our minds, our hearts, and our mouths. Let us live the truth of our Lord, Jesus Christ.

Pray, oh people of God, for an unyielding faith in the knowledge of the whole truth that is our God. Remain steadfast and uncompromising in your fidelity to the Almighty God of heaven and earth. Come to the Lord God Almighty in complete trust in His wisdom and His mercy. ***Pray, My people, for perseverance, for the time of your witness is at hand. Speak the praises and the wonder of the glory of the***

Almighty God. Bow down in adoration at His holy feet. Venerate His Holy Mother. She is the sacred, but all human perfection of the love of God. With God, in perfect obedience to His will, each person can reach perfection in the eyes of God. Come to His wisdom, come to His truth, come to His love. Come to your joy in the eternal perfection of His kingdom. Hear the words of the Lord your God most high; your reward will endure forever in your eternal perfection. Thus says the Lord, your God. That is all.

10-17-90 IT IS DONE

I, the Lord your God, now wish to speak. Say in My name: Oh heavenly Father, the Spirit of your Son lives in the hearts of the chosen ones. The plan is accomplished. All who have been called have come. All who have ears to hear, hear. All who have eyes to see, see. All who have tongues to speak proclaim My message throughout the earth. My faithful ones have been gathered. All has been accomplished according to thy will. Your faithful ones are sealed. They live under the protective mantle of My Mother's love. I bring to you your loyal servants, your royal people. *It is done!*

Now say: Rejoice, oh holy people of God, our God is mighty. Oh holy and Almighty God we, your people, worship and adore you. Your ways are Mysterious, oh Lord. Thy will be done.

In the name of the Three-in-One say: Oh holy people of God, your great sacrifice fills the heavens with the sweet aroma of your love and faithfulness. It is filled with the incense of the sacrifice of My innocent lambs. They follow in the footsteps of their Shepherd. They fill the heavens with the perfume of their holiness. Theirs is the sweet odor of sanctity. Oh holy people of God, what grandeur awaits you. Oh holy ones, I call you to your reward. Come, claim what is yours. Thus says the Lord your God. That is all.

CHANGE YOUR HEARTS

Now say in the name of the Lord your God: I speak through My instrument. Her words are My words. My time is come . . . The struggle for God's truth is won in the hearts of those who love Him. So few love Him. Hate reigns in the hearts of men. Hate will come to know its own. Hate spreads over the face of the earth. You destroy each other because you do not love. Look at your brothers and sisters with the eyes of My love. See yourselves in My love. Change your hearts. Give up your hatred. Turn to each other and forgive. Pray for forgiveness. Reach out in brotherhood. Clasp your hands together and give to each other pardon. Give each other the gift of peace. Share in your common humanity. Look at each other through the eyes of your Almighty Creator and recognize how precious you are. See with His eyes the goodness in what He has created. Do not look with just your physical eyes, but look with your soul. See the soul of your neighbor. You are My brothers and sisters. When you look at each other with the eyes of your souls, you see Me in each other. If you hate your brother or your sister, you hate Me. If you hate Me, you are the followers of evil. I am love. If you hate, you cannot possess love. Love brings peace. Why then do you choose hate? When you come to love, you will find peace. Hear these words, oh My people, they are My truth. Thus says the Lord your God most high. That is all.

I AM WHAT YOU SEEK

Say in the name of the Lord your God most high: Evil runs rampant throughout the earth. Evil controls the souls of most men and women. Evil brings the scourge of My chastisement. *I am the Almighty God of Heaven and Earth!* I have commanded you to love one another. Instead, you love only yourselves. You do not love your God; you reject Him. You deny Him. I cannot come to those whose hearts and minds are closed. They are orphans with no one to care for them. They are empty wanderers in an empty world. They cannot bring peace without love. They cannot have love without God. They are nothing without God. Each looks to his own pleasure and finds it not. The pleasures of the senses are not the pleasures that come from loving God. *I Am!* Do not deny Me. *I exist!* Come to Me. Put aside your pride. Put aside your self that you have molded and let My love recreate you into My image. I bring you peace. I bring you love. I bring you joy. Come to that which is far better. Come to Me, My people, and find what you seek. *I am what you seek!* These are the words of the Lord, your God. That is all . . .

. . . Say in My name: Our Holy Mother must be so pleased with your response to her call. Let us continue to love and honor her. She is our purest Mother fashioned to bring all honor and glory to our Almighty God. Let us all continue to respond to her urgent call to conversion and continue to live according to the directions she gives us in her messages. She has each of us in her loving care, and gently leads us and walks with us to the receiving arms of our holy God. Let us each recognize the wondrous gift of her loving work and return her love in our response to her call. She is the perfection of God's love. Let us follow her example; let her lead us to perfection in God's love. That is all.

10-20-90 I HAVE WAITED SO LONG FOR YOU — MY WRATH OVERFLOWS

In the name of the Lord your God say: Come, My children, into the place I have prepared for you. Come to the everlasting light. Come with your pure hearts into My kingdom. I have waited so long for you. Rejoice that your journey is ended. Come to My peace. Here there is only joy, only love, only the sweet odor of sanctity. Enter into the family of My saints. Join your voices with theirs and sing your praises to the Almighty Father. Your God has brought you to salvation. His wondrous deeds are praised by every

15

tongue. Every heart is joined in the love of its Almighty Creator. All is peace. All is fulfilled. The glory that is God shines forth. It fills the heavens. There is no darkness; there is only light and peace. There is no suffering; there is only love. What came before is no longer. You, My people, have triumphed. There is now for you your eternity in the unending and unchanging love of your Almighty God. Your eternity is to live in the eternal light enfolded in the love that never ends. Oh My people, come! You have won for yourselves peace. Your God never forgets His faithful ones. You are now gathered in the loving arms of your God who has never forsaken you. Rest now, My children, yours was a difficult battle. The battle is over; the war is won. My justice is ended. **God Reigns!** Thus says the Lord your God.

Now say: My wrath overflows. The power of My wrath is ferocious. It strikes out to the very core of My creation. Woe to those who dwell on the earth. Woe to the earth. It shall be shaken to its very foundation. My wrath is immense. It cannot be contained. I, the Almighty God, in all My power deliver upon the earth the mighty judgment. Fear not My chosen ones. But you Evil Ones, you will fear. You will tremble at the awesome power of the one who now brings His justice against you. You will cower before the Almighty majesty. You will despair as you look into the fires of eternal damnation that await you. Then you shall know that I am your God. Receive then the reward for the path you have chosen. You are committed to the eternal fires of hell. The Lord God Almighty and eternal has spoken. That is all.

10-21-90 **YOU HAVE NO OTHER NEED BUT ME**

I, the Lord your God, speak. Say in My name: Oh glorious people of God, My light shines in your hearts. There is no darkness where I am. Dispel the darkness; let My light shine forth from your hearts. Bring My light back into the world. Pray with open

16

hearts. Seek always the will of your God in all that you do. Seek only what is good and holy. Look always to Almighty God for help. Continue to pray the rosary. Receive My sacraments often. Attend daily mass and receive My body and blood with pure hearts. I am your strength in the battle. I am your salvation. Be guided in all things by your God. I lead you in truth. I lead you in hope. I lead you to everlasting joy and harmony. Oh My dear people, you cannot begin to understand the depth of My care for you. Trust in My care. I do not leave My children even when they abandon Me. I am with you always in all ways. Come, My children. Come and find your God who cares for you. Your days will be serene, your hearts filled with peace. Why do you find it so difficult to accept what is for you to take? Come to My compassionate heart, My merciful heart, My loving heart. You have no other need but Me. Thus says the Lord your God.

Now say in My name: I bless you, My children. My peace is upon you. I, your loving God, come to you with arms outstretched to receive those who respond to My call. I await your coming. Thus says the Lord, your God. That is all.

10-22-90 I AM THE COMMANDMENT OF LOVE

Now say in the name of the Lord your God: I call you, oh holy people of God, to enter into My peace. All who come to Me shall have peace. All who live in My love affirm the goodness of the Lord. He is the source of all good. Evil comes from the source of all evil. Where there is love, there can be no evil. Evil does not come from love. Evil that is done in the name of love is evil. Only good follows from love. Know that love, My love which I give you, is not the false love of so many of My creatures. Love without My foundations that I taught in scripture is not My love. My love cannot be separated from My commandments. Love one another as I have loved you. I am the Commandment of Love. Follow Me and you shall love as I love in the Father,

17

the Son, and the Spirit, one love in the three, given for your salvation. Receive from the Triune God the one, holy, and sanctifying love. The power of My love transforms each soul, and each soul becomes a glorious light in the darkness. Light up My world, oh My chosen ones, and let My light fill the universe. Thus says the Lord your God. That is all.

10-23-90 BECOME MY HOLY PEOPLE

Now say in the name of the Lord your God: Happy is the holy person. Let holiness be your goal. Become My holy people. Pray, fast, receive My holy sacraments. Make your peace with your God. Love Him with your whole heart. Rejoice in His presence in the tabernacle of your churches. Come to your holy God. Give Him praise and thanksgiving for His mighty power. Let your hearts receive His loving goodness. Kneel before him in adoration. He provides for your every moment. Forget your cares and let the presence of God enfold you. Let it happen, My children. Let Me care for you. Let Me lift you up. Let My loving arms support you. Let Me, My children, be your loving God. My love is beyond measure, but so few accept it. My love pours forth in abundant measure to those who let Me be their God.

Holy people of God, you accept My love, you live My love, you prove My love. You are My holy ones. Your holiness reflects My holiness. You shine forth like the brightest star of heaven. Oh holy people of God, you are My beloved children. You are My gift to the world. Let your light be a beacon to those in the darkness. You light the way for those who are lost. You, My children, bring great joy to My heart. Speak out in loud voices and proclaim the goodness of your God. Proclaim His mighty power; proclaim His everlasting love; proclaim His mercy and justice. Leave out nothing. Proclaim My whole truth. The Almighty God has spoken. Go in My peace and be fearless shepherds of My flock. Thus says the Lord your God. That is all.

It is I speaking. Now say in the name of the Lord your God: Speak in My name. Say: I love you My people. Let My peace fill your hearts. Let nothing cause you anxiety. Let My holy consolation come upon you. My Holy Mother enfolds you in the mantle of her protection. Trust that I am with you always. That is all.

Now say: *I am the Living God! I am the Creator, The Redeemer, and the Truth!* I tell you who I am. There is no other God but Me. *I Am Who Am!, the One, the only God.* Mine is the power and the glory. I am the All! I am the supreme God of the universe, of the heavens, of all creation. All creation moves and lives according to My laws. My laws govern all My creation, seen and unseen. When you change My laws, My creation turns to chaos. There is no order, there is no harmony. Human beings are stewards of My creation. When they attempt to manipulate My laws, they create havoc. They think of themselves as gods who can control *My Creation!* They do not create their world; they do not create themselves. I created all that exists in time and out of time. You prideful creatures who usurp My authority — *I am the Living God and nothing lives without My consent!* You are not god — only I Am Who Am am God. All your works, all your designs, all your self-glorification will be brought to nothing and you shall know that I am the one God of all. All knees shall bend and all heads will bow in humble adoration to the Almighty God of heaven and earth now and forever. You lowly ones who raise yourselves to what you cannot be shall know the power of the one God, I will destroy the false idols who inhabit the earth. My judgment shall descend upon them, and not one of them will remain to pollute the earth with their blaspheMy. Hear these words oh people of earth, and know they are My truth. Thus says the Lord, your God. That is all.

Write this down . . . Now say in the name of the Lord your God: Oh miserable children of Eve, you can find no peace until you return to Me. Your loving God calls you back. My holy Mother shows you the way back. She is a gentle Mother; she is a loving Mother. She is the radiant Mother of My creation. I created her. She is My Mother created to be the Mother of My creation. She is the Mother of the Almighty God; she is the Mother of humanity. She restores to you the graces lost to you by the first Eve. Her graces, given to her to bestow on mankind, return you to the salvation won for you by her holy and divine Son, Jesus Christ. She brings you to My sacraments; she brings you to Me. Come to Me through My resplendent Eve, and what had been lost will be restored to you. My glorious Mother is the perfect Eve. Love her as I love her. She is your true Mother, the Mother of all that is holy. She is the Mother of all My creation. Sing her praises throughout the earth. My holy Mother brings honor and glory to the God who created her. She is the Song of Songs, the purest of the lilies and the perfumed rose. She is the garden of perfection. She is the Eden in its pristine perfection. She is perfection itself. All who sing her praises bring joy to My heart. My Mother is the joy of My heart. My joy is returned to you to fill your hearts with peace and joy.

Hear then the words of the Lord your God. I desire that you honor My most beloved Mother. Sing her praises. Be joyous people because she brings joy. Be loving people because she brings love. Follow her messages because she brings you to Me. Listen to the loving lessons of your Mother. You will be brought to love, peace, and joy. Thus says the Lord your God. That is all.

COME TO THE BREAD OF LIFE

Say in the name of the Lord your God: Sing to Me a song of joyous jubilation. Sing songs of thanksgiving from hearts overflowing with the abundance of My graces. Let your song repeat the great Alleluia — Jesus Christ is risen, Alleluia. All heaven and earth proclaim His majesty. All the elements in My creation acknowledge their triumphant God. He has won for you your salvation. The beauty of His sacrifice proclaims the nobility of each soul resplendent in the holy sacrifice of the Eucharist. His glory pours forth from sacred bread and wine. His wounds receive the salve of your reception of His suffering body in pure hearts. Gently heal the wounds. Lovingly enfold His broken body in the silence of your soul. Let it rest in the peaceful contemplation of its supreme sacrifice. Let your communion with body broken for you prepare you for your glorious resurrection of the body, the body healed in the healed body of your Lord and Saviour. The healed body of the triumphant Church shall rise and renew the face of the earth. The silence of the resting place will be filled with the joyous sounds of voices raised in praise and Hosannas to the everlasting glorification of our triumphant God. Thus says the Lord your God, glorified and eternal.

Now say: Your loving prayers and respect for My Holy Body and Blood are the ointments of healing. You are healed in My healing power. Come to Me in the Eucharist. Come and find the sweet balm for your broken spirits. I will heal your wounded hearts, your suffering souls. I will restore you to the life that gives life. Partake, My children, of the cure of all your ills. Come, My children, come to Me the Bread of Life. That is all . . . Thus, says the Lord your God.

10-27-90   WHAT IS TO COME IS THE ABOMINATION OF DESOLATION

Now say in the name of the Lord your God: My time is upon you. These messages are given for My chosen ones. They shall endure the persecution of the second holocaust. All who read these words will find My comfort in their suffering. All who hear My voice will find peace. Those who close their hearts and their minds will find no comfort anywhere. Empty shells shall remain empty. But those who hear My voice and heed My words will have no fear of what is to come. Satan has no power over My own. My own are specially protected against the forces that would destroy My Holy Temple. Evil will be throughout the earth. My prophets have spoken for all ages. I warn My creatures through My prophets. My mercy rests on those who heed their warnings. **Repent!** Turn away from your evil ways. You bring upon yourselves terrible destruction. Your cities will be destroyed, your countryside laid waste. No fowls of the air nor creatures of the land and sea will find a safe refuge. *Only those marked with My seal and protected within the Immaculate Heart of My Holy Mother will dwell in safety.* What is to come is the abomination of desolation. The world will be desolate, the earth barren. Vapors shall rise up to cover the carnage of man's bestiality. No stone shall be left unturned. The waters shall be riled up from their depths. All shall be in upheaval. The earth shall be torn asunder. That which has life shall perish. Thus says the Lord your God on high. Be at peace. That is all.

10-28-90 **BLESSED ARE THEY WHO MOVE WITH THE SPIRIT**

Now say in the name of the Lord your God: Salvation is won. The fruits of redemption are yours. Announce to the world that Jesus Christ is risen in splendor and glory. He reigns, the triumphant King. His Spirit comes to enlighten the hearts of His chosen ones. His Spirit inflames them with zeal. They proclaim the wisdom of the ages. Their hearts burn with the fire of superhuman understanding. They know the Mysteries hidden in the mind of their Almighty God. They are brought to communion with holy revelation. They are inspired with wisdom from on high. They have the power of the knowledge of God. He opens their minds and their hearts to receive the revealed word of the Lord.

Say in the name of the Lord your God: All holy is the Almighty God. Many are the blessings He grants to those who walk in His ways. His ways are made known through the power of His Spirit. Blessed are they who move with the Spirit. Their days are filled with wonder at the infinite depth and breadth of the all-knowing God. His knowledge is of all that is known and unknown. Man cannot conceive of what is in the mind of the Almighty God. How glorious is the mind of God; how wondrous are the works of His mind. In His mind all Is known in the present. There is no past or future. All is now. That which was in the past, and all that will occur in the future in time is in the present of the all encompassing infinity of the eternal Word of God. All who have My Word have My knowledge. My knowledge brings wisdom. Wisdom is the fruit of My Spirit. Thus says the Lord your God . . . That is all. Go in peace.

10-29-90 I COME TO BRING YOU PEACE

Say in the name of the Lord your God: I come to bring you peace, but the world does not want **My** peace. *Peace will not come to the world until men convert their lives.* Mankind must turn away from evil. It must turn to love, the love that is Almighty God. Mankind must turn away from evil. Mankind lives in the desert of spiritual destitution. They deny evil and sin. They deny the existence of the source of life. They find no solace for their emptiness. They look to material comfort and the pleasures of the flesh for happiness. *Without Me all their efforts are futile.* They find no peace, or solace, or satisfaction.

Now say: Let your emptiness be filled with the never-ending source of life. Fill your souls with the goodness of the Lord your God. You will be filled to overflowing with the presence of the Lord. His presence cannot be contained. It pours out and fills the world with endless gifts of love. Become once again the vessels from which the tender mercies of

God bring solace and comfort to the emptiness within mankind. Reach out and touch the empty hearts of your brothers and sisters with God's love. Let His love spill from your hearts in a torrent of life-giving mercy. I am a merciful God; be My merciful children. That is all. Thus says the Lord your God.

10-30-90 MAN IS MADE IN MY IMAGE

Now say in the name of the Lord your God: Holy is the name of the Almighty God. In the name of the Lord God speak to My people and say: *All Mankind Sins*. Their sins pollute My creation with every kind of abomination. Man was created to reflect My purity and My goodness. Man is made in My image. Man without God is not My image. Man without God is an aberration, an unnatural being, a being who rejects his very nature. Without God man is merely a creature of instincts and passions which hold sway over all his actions. Man is unnatural when He becomes an unthinking creature who acts without the love of God, without the desire for God's goodness. He is no longer My human creature. He is a creature without a soul. Without his soul there is no image of the God who created him. He is his own image. He acts not with love but only with self-gratification. He thinks not of anyone but himself. People with dead souls have nothing to see but themselves. They see nothing in their fellow men, nothing but an image of themselves.

Now say: I, your God, am what makes you truly human. I am the goodness and the love that makes you humans in My image. If I am rejected, you cannot come to know what is good and what is truth. You are false images of what you were created to be. Without Me you are distorted images. You act as distorted creatures. Thus, all that you do is unfocused, it has no meaning. My likeness is clear. I am the truth. The truth is clear. Come to My truth. My truth will free you from your self. It will return you to your rightful position as a child of God, in His

24

image and likeness, as the clear picture of peace, harmony and order. Hear your God, My people. Become once again My noble creatures; My people of dignity and worth. You are noble creatures. You are intended to bring your glory to your Almighty Maker. Return in glory as you were created. Open your hearts and let My Spirit restore you — body and soul, goodness and light, the union of the soul to its Almighty God that will restore you to what you are as a creature of nature and spirit. That is how you are created; that is how you must remain to be true human creatures of the Almighty God. Thus says the Lord your God. That is all.

11-1-90 HE HAS PROCLAIMED THE HOLINESS OF HIS HANDMAID

Say in the name of the Lord your God: All tongues shall proclaim the goodness of the Lord. He has performed His wonders throughout the earth. No eye that sees or ear that hears will be left unaided.

(Mother Mary speaks) - He has proclaimed the holiness of His Handmaid. I reign in splendor because of the greatness of the Lord. I shine forth from the light of His glory. My soul magnifies the Lord. His greatness becomes My greatness. He performs great works through Me. His greatness enlarges My being. His humble servant He raises up. He has done great things for Me.

(Jesus speaks) - Now say: I call you, My children, to recognize the greatness of My Holy Mother. Her pure soul receives My greatness. She is the perfect vessel of My Spirit. She is the golden cup of My eternal gift. All that I have she has. She is perfection. She is the Woman clothed in the sun. She is perfect love. She lights your dwelling place with love. She is glorified in heaven in the presence of the one God, Three-in-One. No tongue can sing her praises enough. Open your hearts to My Immaculate Mother. Let her fill you with My love. Sing her praises to the highest heavens. Wrap yourselves in the mantle of her loving presence.

She is always with you. Call on her, speak to her, reach for your loving Mother. She will embrace you in her welcoming arms. She will bring you to your holy God. Receive the gift of My Mother; I give her to you. She will bring you consolation and peace. She will give you the gift of her Son. We love you with a love beyond human understanding. Accept our love and live in the perfect love. Come, children, come to love. Thus says the Lord your God. That is all.

11-4-90   **NO OTHER IDOLS, NO OTHER IMAGES WILL I PERMIT**

. . . Now say in the name of the Lord your God: Live each day as though it were your last. My time is upon the earth. Be prepared, for My justice will be swift. No one knows the time of My coming. The time is near; My message is clear. In this place where evil abounds (a city in the United States) I will bring down My wrath. The monuments to man's decadence I will destroy. These temples of sin are an abomination. They are temples of excess, of gluttony, of vice, of self-indulgence.

Now say in the name of the Lord your God: The temple of God is raised for the honor and glory of God. Man's temples are idols in the image of sensual pleasure. Here men worship themselves. There is no thought for their God. What man has raised, I will destroy. Only My holy temple will stand as a witness to the majesty of God. No other idols, no other images will I permit. Know that I am the one, the only God of heaven and earth. There is no other. All else is idolatry. The Lord your God has spoken. That is all.

11-6-90   **I AM PEACE . . . I AM THE CALM REFUGE**

. . . Now say in My name: Holy God Almighty, how glorious are your works. Your holy presence lives in the hearts of men.

Where I am there is peace. Come to My peace, My children. Open your hearts to My peace. Be instruments of My peace. Live My peace. I am peace. There is no peace in souls because they do not know My peace. The things of the world are fleeting. Only I am constant. I am the unchanging God of love and peace. All else vanishes; all else is grasping at the wind that scatters all before it. Do not become subject to the wind but stand firm in faith and the love of your God. The changing forces of man and nature will have no power to disturb your peace. Let those who reject My Word be helpless in the changing patterns of the wind, but you, My children, come to My shelter from the storm. I am the calm refuge. In Me you have a safe harbor. Come to My safety. I protect you in turmoil; I bring you safely through the turbulent storms of life. I am the safe path to follow. All who know Me and hear Me know the path. There is no fear on this path. There is the peaceful knowledge of certainty, of truth, of love, of the one God of all. Know Me, My children, and you will know peace. Hear My Word; My Word is truth. My truth is the safe path. I am the Truth — follow Me and I will bring you safely into My kingdom. Thus says the Lord your God. That is all.

11-7-90 SOON THE EVIL ONE WILL APPEAR

Say in the name of the Lord your God: Oh holy people of God, the day is at hand for your deliverance. The forces of evil grow stronger. **Soon the Evil One will appear. He will persecute My chosen people with vengeance. He will destroy the works of My hand. His atrocities are unspeakable. The venom of His hate will bring death and destruction to every area of the earth.** No one will escape his terror. Not a piece of ground, body of water, or the air in the heavens will be left untouched by his colossal magnitude of viciousness. He shall spit out of his mouth obscene blasphemies. He shall bring degradation and corruption, death and destruction. Bodies shall lie on bodies. The whole earth shall be covered with bodies. For as far as the eye can see there will be nothing but carnage. Woe to the earth,

27

woe to living creatures. There will be no mercy.

I, the Lord your God, speak in final warning. No longer will My people be left orphans. *I, the all powerful, living God will rescue My faithful ones. Their groans will bring down My judgement upon those who look like men but act like beasts.* I will act, and they shall never cease to suffer terror and pain, and unendurable anguish for all eternity. They shall not mock their God. I have spoken. Thus says the Lord your God. That is all.

11-8-90 PRAY!

Say in the name of the Lord your God: Have complete faith in Me, My children. Remember I am always with you. I protect My flock. All who trust in My mercy will be saved. Be strong in your faith. Do not waver but remain firm. Neither be afraid; fear will be all about you. Pray! I will hear your prayers. Your God will not leave you abandoned. The time is grave. What is to come, will come. But you, My holy people, will triumph. The Lord your God has spoken. That is all.

"On the banks of the river shall the mighty battle rage. Sound the trumpets of the Lord; the battle begins. The decisive moments are at hand. The royal command is given. Commence! So shall it be."

Go and speak in My name. Thus says the Lord your God. That is all.

11-9-90 NO PRAYER GOES UNANSWERED

Now say in the name of the Lord your God: Holy is the name of the Lord, your God. Hear, oh Lord, the cries of your people. Hear the voices raised in petition, in supplication, in hope that what they ask for will be granted.

Now say: No prayer goes unanswered. I hear the cries of My people. Mine is the power to grant or withhold according to the will of the Father. That which is granted or that which is withheld is the providence of the all-knowing God. He acts always for your welfare. The Almighty God knows your needs. Have faith; your prayers are not in vain. You are given what you need for your salvation. Trust that I, your God, will provide for your needs. Each is answered according to his need. It is good that you seek My help. Come to Me with simple faith. Come to Me with love. Believe that I respond to all your prayers. Happy is He who trusts in My providence.

Your prayer is a sweet sound in My ears. Its melody flows through the chambers of the eternal dwelling place of the Lord your God. It resounds in the holy sanctuary of the most Sacred Heart of My beloved Son. It is welcomed in the encompassing love of My Holy Spirit. Your prayers are the songs that fill My heavens like a beautiful melody. Let Me hear your songs, My beloved ones. Raise your voices in joyous praise for the goodness of your Lord. Raise your voices in patient supplication. Raise your voices in thanksgiving, for the Lord your God is a generous God. Pray, My children. Let Me hear your voices. Speak with Me, My children. Do not leave your God in silence. Thus says the Lord your God. That is all.

11-12-90 I CALL YOU TO CONVERSION AND REPENTANCE

Say in the name of the Lord your God: . . . Hear My voice for the time is short. I call you to conversion and repentance. My voice rings loud and clear. Convert your hearts; confess your sins. Receive My Sacred Body and Blood. Love one another. My truth is simple: Open your hearts to the Lord your God. Become holy people. Live My commandments. Be My disciples. Love Me. Love My Mother. You have been given all that you need for your salvation. Choose for your God; your reward awaits you. Your happiness is with God. Bring joy to the heart of your loving God. Be My faithful children. Praise Me and love Me for I have done great things for you. Proclaim His mighty name. Speak no evil. Show compassion to

29

your brothers and sisters. Look to your neighbor's needs. To all give mercy and understanding. Follow My example in all things. Keep Me always in your heart. Let nothing disturb your peace, My peace which I give you. *Trust in your God; I provide for your every need. Call on your God and I will hear you. In everything that you do, or say, or think, give glory to Almighty God . . .*

Now say, the Lord God Almighty stands in His heavens and surveys all of His creation. He sees all, hears all, knows all. Nothing is hidden from the Lord. His day is at hand when He shall read each heart. Be prepared, for the day of reckoning is at hand. Come to your God with pure hearts. Thus says the Lord your God. That is all.

11-13-90 YOUR SINS DESTROY YOU

In the name of the Lord God say: Oh helpless people, your sins destroy you. You fester like a putrid disease that eats away your life. Your rankness pollutes the earth. Your stench reaches the highest heavens and fills the nostrils of your Almighty God. *What have you done to My creation?* You have turned goodness into corruption. You have turned perfection into distortion. You parody My Word and make it blasphemy. The innocent you persecute; the humble you oppress. There is no love in the hearts of men. You desecrate My Holy Temple; you dishonor Me in My own Church. You make yourselves gods. Oh foolish people! Your pride brings you to the brink of damnation. Do not insult your God with your arrogance. The mighty shall be brought low and the lowly shall be exalted in the kingdom of the Father. The Lord your God brings His justice against those who defy His commands. You hollow people will crumble before the power of Almighty God. You will be turned to ashes. You lowly ones will be nourished and sustained, and My mighty arm will raise you up. The Lord your God is a mighty God. By His might He will destroy the enemies of His faithful ones and

30

sustain His chosen ones. I choose those who choose Me. I accept all who come to My merciful love. Those who reject Me I spit out like the vomit from the diseased body. They shall know the wrath of their God. They shall not escape the eternal flames. Woe to those who deny their God; He shall deny them. Your God is a just God. His mercy is for those who ask for it. The rest will forever be denied the eternal presence. They shall never know the glory and the majesty of the sanctified life in the presence of the loving God. Thus says the Lord your God . . . That is all.

11-15-90 TO PRIESTS — MY CHURCH IS IN DISARRAY

Now say in the name of the Lord your God: . . . Now say, My Church is in disarray. Even My shepherds can no longer recognize My truth. They do not listen to My voice; they listen to the voice of the world. Satan's presence is real in My Church. He brings confusion, delusion, conflict, distrust of My faithful servants. There is no peace in My Church because those who should lead no longer understand My commands. I say to them: Behold your God crucified on the cross of your apostasy. My Church is for all time, but you seek to destroy what I established. Do I not know the needs of My creation? Where is your faith; where is your trust in My wisdom and knowledge? Do I not sustain My creation? *Do not challenge your God!* You are My apostles. I chose you to lead My people along My path. Instead you lead them on your path, which is not mine. You lead them to eternal damnation. Your responsibility is great; the eternity for souls is in your hands. Your Almighty God denounces you for your heresy.

(Speak, My daughter, to My priests. Tell them of the danger for their souls. Tell them they shall face My wrath for the souls they have led to damnation. They shall not escape My fury. They have brought dishonor to the royal priesthood. They bring shame where they should bring glory and honor to the Father. They are

31

abominable in My sight. Their betrayal demands justice; My justice shall be severe. They shall join the Evil One for they spread evil throughout My Church.)

Say: Repent My brothers. The Almighty God is a just God. Do not ignore My warnings. Say in the name of the Lord your God: I banish you from My kingdom you unfaithful servants. Your places will be given to those who have served Me faithfully. They shall rest in My glory; they shall know My love. But you, oh traitorous followers of the Evil One, shall have the reward you have chosen. Depart from My sight! He who rejects Me is rejected. Receive your just reward! That is all. Thus says the Lord God Almighty, King of heaven and earth.

11-16-90 THERE MUST BE NO COMPROMISE WITH THE EVIL ONE

Say in the name of the Lord your God: Oh holy people of God, respond to your God with hearts of love and joy. The glory of God surrounds you . . . Great events are about to occur. Nations shall rise against nation. The mighty shall fall. There shall be great suffering . . . Now say, My people must be courageous. They must not despair. They must pray with their whole hearts. There must be no compromise with the Evil One! . . . Thus says the Lord your God. That is all.

11-18-90 THE HOUR IS AT HAND FOR YOUR DELIVERANCE

Say in the name of the Lord your God . . . Now say, to all My people say: *The hour is at hand for your deliverance. Almighty God acts against His enemies. His judgment descends like a thunderbolt from the heavens. Men will perish in an instant. My justice will come without warning to those who have rejected My Word.* Others of My children will suffer martyrdom for the glory of their Almighty God. There will be wailing and suffering from one end of the earth to the other. My faithful ones, comfort each other. Stand one with the other

32

united in the love of God and each other. Care for each other. The trial will be severe. You must not falter. You must not deny your God. You must live in the brotherhood of God's anointed ones. Believe in the power of the Holy Spirit; His power will renew the face of the earth. His power generates the force of regeneration. *My Church will rise triumphant from the ashes of destruction.* Its splendor shall radiate from the majestic countenance (being) of Almighty God. *It shall not perish from the onslaught of the Evil One!* It shall come forth in shining splendor. No stain of the Evil One shall remain. My Church shall reflect the purity of its God. My people shall live in peace and prosperity. My judgment is ended. Thus says the Lord your God. That is all.

11-20-90 THE TRIUMPH OF OUR HOLY MOTHER IS AT HAND

Say in the name of the Lord your God . . . Now say, thank you for the honor and devotion you give to My most Holy Mother. Mary, the glorious queen, reigns supreme in heaven and on earth. Let My Spirit flood your hearts with love for her. When you love her, your love fills the heavens. She is joy without measure. *When you honor her, you honor Me. My Mother is My gift to you. Receive My gift. She is your loving Mother. My loving Mother intercedes for you. Whatever you ask through her I grant.* You are faithful people. Your response to our most Holy Mother pleases Me. Continue to love and honor her. My blessings fall abundantly where there is devotion to her. My blessings are upon you.

Now say: Rejoice My people, for the triumph of our Holy Mother is at hand. All heavens sing her praises. Raise your voices in joyous song and join the heavenly chorus in proclaiming the glory of our Immaculate Mother. Bring her songs of praise and thanksgiving, for the humble servant of the Almighty God has accomplished the will of the Father. Her role in My plan for your salvation is at an end. She has brought My people to the safety of My Sacred Heart. She

33

enfolds you within her motherly embrace. You are under her special protection. **Rejoice!** Let your whole being rejoice! Hear these words of the Lord your God. That is all.

11-22-90 IT BEGINS

Say in the name of the Lord your God: It begins. My time of mercy is at an end. The harvest is completed. My chosen are safe in the protection of their Almighty God. The fruit of the harvest is separated from the weeds. From this abundance shall come the renewal of the kingdom of God upon the earth. They shall bring forth the glorification of the Almighty and Omnipotent God. The earth shall return to the perfection of its creation. My creatures shall dwell in peace and harmony in the light of their loving God. A new earth, resplendent in its new raiment, flowers in the fullness of the new time. God's time is not your time. In His time He shall bring to fruition all that has been foretold for this generation. His time is upon you. *The wickedness of this world will be destroyed. The time is at hand for the restoration of the kingdom on earth. All hearts shall be open to the power of the Spirit. The Spirit will bring forth a new order.* The action of the Spirit on the hearts of men shall burst forth and fill the universe with songs of praise and thanksgiving to the Almighty God who is, was, and ever shall be through time without end. Amen. Thus says the Lord your God.

Behold what is planned for your faithful service to your Almighty God. You shall live forever in the light of the heavenly presence. Receive your reward, faithful servant. The magnificence of your sacrifice is accepted by the Almighty Father. All is accomplished according to His holy will. Enter into the place He has prepared for you. Your journey is ended. Come now to My presence and behold the glory that is your God. His light shines upon you and fills you with radiant light. You shine with the brilliance of God's own luminous incandescence. Your soul is adorned with the precious pearls of God's bounteous blessings. Oh glorious soul of God's creation, come in all your splendor to your everlasting reward. Thus says the Lord your God. That is all.

11-23-90 SO HUMBLE A SERVANT, SO POWERFUL A MOTHER

Say in the name of the Lord your God: Behold the Handmaid of the Lord, your Mother. Receive her into your heart. In her is infinite wisdom. She is the wisdom of the ages. Wisdom lies in the simplicity of faith. In the light of her eternal glory she brings you My wisdom. I infuse her with My knowledge. I give her My power to bring you My knowledge. She tells you to study My scripture; do as she tells you. She asks you to pray to My Spirit; My Spirit will enlighten you. She tells you to receive My sacraments; they will strengthen you. My Mother leads you to wisdom and knowledge. I am wisdom and knowledge. I am the source from which all blessings and graces come. My Mother is perfect grace. She is always filled with My grace. My grace flows through her in a never ending stream. My graces come to you through My Mother. My graces light her soul in brilliant purity. She is the radiance of the universe. She is the beauty in the heavens and on the earth. I, her Father, Son, and Spouse, have bestowed upon her the Queenship of My creation seen and unseen. She is magnificence in whom the glory of Almighty God is manifested. Rejoice, oh holy people of God; My Mother reigns resplendent. She is our Mother. *Accept her — she is the gift of the merciful God sent to restore you to the loving embrace of your Almighty God. I have spoken.*

Now say, pray to My Mother. Honor her with songs of praise and devotion. Open your hearts to receive her love. Be people of God through Mary, My Mother. So humble a servant, so powerful a Mother. Call on her in your needs. Your God hears the voice of His Mother. Thus says the Lord your God. That is all. Go in peace.

35

. . . Say in the name of the Lord your God: Dear Servant of Almighty God: In the name of all that is holy remember that you are the shepherd of the flock of our Savior, Jesus Christ. Jesus proclaimed His truth to His Church. As His priest, chosen by Him to follow in His priestly footsteps, you are called to teach His gospel to His flock whose shepherd you are. Compassion for God's children must not overshadow the truth of God's law, the truth that Jesus proclaimed to the world for all time through the Church that He founded on earth.

It is the moral duty and obligation of all God's shepherds to uphold that truth and stand fearlessly before your people and proclaim it forcefully and clearly so that there is no confusion, no doubt about what God demands of His children. It is the voice of Almighty God which must be heard and listened to. His voice is loud and clear in scripture. When all people hear that voice, the truth that comes from that voice, and respond to that truth, then the solutions you seek for the ills of the world will be found. *The solutions are in the Word of God. Men must convert their lives. They must turn away from sin and evil and seek forgiveness in God's mercy. There will be no solutions to the evil that confronts us until people return to the truth of the Lord our God. It is you priests and bishops who must lead your flock on the path that Christ showed us, not the path of heresy and apostasy.*

Think carefully of the day you stand before our God. Will you be His faithful servant or another Judas who betrayed your sacred vows. You have a tremendous responsibility, for the eternity of the souls entrusted to your care is in your hands. Our God is a merciful God, but He is also a just God. His justice shall descend upon those who make a mockery of His Church.

Dear priests of God, be holy priests, be faithful priests, be priests strong in the faith of Jesus Christ. Bring the glory that is God to your people. Give him praise and honor and thanksgiving for the royal priesthood, the gift of your vocation . . .

11-26-90 WHAT MEN HAVE REAPED ON EARTH, SO SHALL THEY REAP FOR ALL ETERNITY

Say in the name of the Lord your God: The day of destruction is at hand . . . The Pope (John Paul II) will die. His death will signal the reign of Anti-Christ . . . In three year's time will begin the reign of terror. Blood will flow like rivers across the landscape of the earth. Your sins bring down upon you the thunderbolt of divine retribution. My hand, which created the universe, will move over the face of the earth and wipe away every blemish that dares to destroy the work of the hand of your Almighty God. Every creature — man, woman, and child-who follows in the footsteps of the great deceiver will forever be condemned to the fires of eternal damnation. They shall cry out in agony without end, and the justice of God will grant no mercy to those who did not give mercy. The fires of hell burn in unceasing fury and engulf the souls of the damned in searing recompense for their blasphemies and their prideful arrogance in their persecution against the body of their Lord, Jesus Christ. My judgment is final. What men have reaped on earth, so shall they reap for all eternity. I have spoken. Thus says the Lord your God.

Now say: The fury of My justice will fall against those who deliberately seek to lead My people from the true faith of their salvation.

† **It shall come** against those who deny the very existence of the God who formed them.
† **It will come** against those who persist in breaking the commandments I gave for your salvation.

37

- † **It will come** against those who spread heresy and lead My Church into apostasy.
- † **It shall come** against those who profane the name of the Lord their God.
- † **It shall come** against those who persecute My chosen ones.
- † **It shall come** against those who have turned My Church into a disgusting monument to men's infidelity and betrayal of the truth and the sacrifice of their suffering Christ.
- † **It shall come** against those who insult My beloved Mother and scorn her role in My plan for the salvation of mankind.
- † **It shall come** against any and all who sin without remorse.

I, the Lord your God, will not permit the desecration of My Holy Temple. I, the Lord your God have spoken. Go in peace. That is all.

11-27-90 LET MY LOVE MELT THE COLDNESS OF YOUR HEARTS

Speak in My name. Say, I love you. Oh My people, if you only knew the depth and breadth of My love for you. It is a love that knows no bounds. It flows like the sea into the deep recesses of each heart. It is not confined within the limits of the flesh, but flows from the soul. The soul possesses an infinite capacity to receive the love of its Creator. The soul transcends all matter until it unites itself to perfect love. In love the creature and the Creator join their spirits in perfect communion — one with the other. The Spirit transforms the soul which responds with overwhelming gratitude in songs of praise and thanksgiving to the divine benefactor of eternal redemption. I love you. My heart bleeds in sorrow for those so far from My love. My poor lost sheep, how My heart yearns to fill you with the warmth of My loving presence. Let My love melt the coldness of your hearts. Let them blossom in the warmth of the sun. Receive the refreshing dew that falls upon the closed petals of your heart at the dawn of your flowering in the love of the eternal God. Let My love fill your souls; let it rain upon the parched souls who wander in the barren desert of sin and confusion. Love these lost brothers and sisters. Give them from the abundance I give you. Whatever you give to My poor children will be returned to you a hundred-fold. Do not let these children wander in ignorance of the love and the mercy of the God who created them. Thus says the Lord your God. That is all.

11-29-90 I AM THE ONE GOD OF HEAVEN AND EARTH

I command you to speak. This is what you must say in the name of the Lord your God. *I am the One God of Heaven and Earth.* There is no other God. I am the supreme, eternal God. All is subject to the God of power and majesty. My commands go forth to all My creation.

† **I give you** My command to love.
† **I give you** My command to live according to My Word.
† **I give you** My command to live according to the will of your Almighty Father, Son and Spirit, Three-in-One.
† **I command you** to love and honor the God who sustains you.
† **I command you** to know and revere our Holy Mother.
† **I command you** to live according to My holy law given for your salvation.

These are My commands. My chosen ones live My commands. They will be saved.

My commands I give to those who do not live according to My Word. I, your God, give you these commands to bring you to your salvation. You must follow My commands if you are to save your souls. My commands are for all people for all time. Your time is short. I stand as your God and tell you many will be cast into the fires of eternal hell. Do not be among that number. The time of the harvest is at an end.

39

The sickle in the hand of My obedient servant has the power to reap the harvest of the lost. They shall remain lost in the eternity of the Evil One. The sickle is wielded against those who follow along the path of sin and evil. They do not know the path of love and goodness because they choose Satan over the God of creation and redemption. I your God say: Begone from Me you faithless corrupters of My holy creation. Your God rejects you from His holy Temple. Your God has no ear to hear your pleas and cries for His mercy. Mercy was offered for your salvation, but you rejected it. Love surrounded you, but you chose hate. Truth was given in My Word, but you chose blasphemy and heresy and lies. I offered you My life, and you spit in My face. I offered you My Mother, and you denied My gift. I brought you salvation, and you chose damnation. Damnation is yours. Out of My kingdom you abomination, you vile rottenness, you unholy, stinking, diseased corruption. You shall no longer fester like an infected sore upon the soul of My creation. Herewith forever rot in the abyss of darkness. No more shall you be seen in the light of My kingdom. Thus says the Lord God Almighty, Lord of power and might, Lord of heaven and earth. So be it. That is all.

12-1-90 **THE POWER OF THE ROSARY SURPASSES THE POWER OF THE EVIL ONE**

Say in the name of the Lord your God: You have brought honor to My most holy Mother. Your love for her is a sign of predestination. You are destined to be soldiers in her mighty army against the forces of evil. *You who love her, accept with joyous acclamation her call to battle. Give her the weapons she needs to defeat Satan. You are her weapons. Give her yourself. Commit yourselves to the battle for men's souls. The forces of evil blind men to the reality that is your God. You must combat this blindness with your prayers and sacrifices. Say the rosary. The power of the rosary surpasses the power of the Evil One.* Gird yourselves in the power

40

of the rosary. No weapon invented by man has the power of the rosary. Mankind can renew itself through the power of the rosary. The rosary is your weapon offered to your most holy Mother in humble generosity that arms her for the final battle with Satan. Let your rosary become her armor as she approaches the culmination of her role in the will of the Father foretold at the beginning of time. You are a royal people called in the fullness of time to array your most holy Mother in the garments of victory. I have chosen you before you were formed to be the valiant army of the victorious Queen of heaven and earth. Be fearless soldiers for Mary, your Mother. Accept her call with total consecration to her cause. Her cause is your cause. Be vigilant, My people, and recognize the signs of your time. Soon, all will be accomplished according to My will. Your Mother calls you. The hour is at hand for her triumphant victory. Oh chosen people of your Almighty God, know that My time is upon you. Thus says the Lord your God. That is all . . .

12-1-90 MY TIME OF MERCY ENDS

Now say in the name of the Lord your God: My time of mercy ends. My Mother is recalled to the heavenly realm. The choirs of heaven resound the joyful triumphant anthem of the victorious Queen. All in heaven bow in homage to she who is the sovereign majesty in the glory and the power of the God of power and might. She is clothed in the garments of royal splendor. She sits at the right hand of the Son to reign forever as Co-redemptrix of mankind. She is woman supreme. My Mother reigns co-equally with Me in the kingdom prepared for the select of My flock. Her victory is great; her reward is great. I have placed My Mother at My right hand, and she will reign forever in the presence of the royal Godhead — Father, Son, and Spirit forever and ever, Amen. Thus says the Lord your God. Go in peace. That is all.

12-2-90 POPE JOHN PAUL II

Say in the name of the Lord your God: The wind howls its fury at the death of the loyal servant of God. The forces of evil conspire to bring about the total annihilation of My Church. My faithful servant, Pope John Paul II, has valiantly stood as a bulwark against the enemies who would destroy My Church. He shall be martyred in defense of the one true faith. Pray for My holy son and faithful servant. He shall be spared what is to be unleashed upon the earth. Pray to him. He is granted the odor of sanctity. His intercession on your behalf will be heard and answered. Follow the example of My holy priest-son. Be a loyal defender of the truth of the Lord God, Jesus Christ. He has worked tirelessly under the direction of the Woman Clothed with the Sun in total obedience and love. The reward for those who so honor My Mother is great in heaven. The suffering of this, My holy priest, is at an end. Pray for his swift release to the realm of eternal splendor. Thus says the Lord your God. That is all . . .*

* see Editorial note p. VI #2.

12-3-90 DRINK OF THE CUP

Say in the name of the Lord your God:

(Jesus speaks) - The sacrifice of My life for the salvation of mankind was ordained by the Father from the beginning of time. My sacrifice is freely given for sinful man in obedience to the will of the Father. Partake, O holy people of God, of salvation. Receive My Body and Blood, My life poured out for you in agony upon the wood of the cross. Take the cross of My humiliation and drink of the life-giving stream that flows into the cup of salvation. Drink of the cup. Accept the cross as I accepted mine. Suffering saved mankind for eternity. Suffering for the love of your eternal God brings redemption. Accept the suffering that is your lot as a gift given as a grace that brings recompense to Almighty God for the sins of the world.

Suffering is a mighty tool of restitution given for those lost in the vacuum of their godless condition. **(God the Father speaks)** - My Son's sacrifice must not be in vain. Offer your suffering with His for the salvation of souls. Join your cross to His in obedience to the will of the Father. Find peace in your humble acquiescence to what your Father has deemed necessary for your salvation. Be patient in your suffering as Jesus was patient. Follow in the footsteps of your brother and He will lead you to the kingdom of the Father, purified and resplendent. Let My will guide you in all things. Look always to My will for you, and you shall know My peace. I give you My peace. You shall never be tested beyond your endurance. Have faith in the Lord your God. I will give you the strength to overcome all adversity. Your God is always with you. Thus says the Lord your God. That is all.

12-5-90   **YOU ARE CHOSEN PEOPLE OF THE SPIRIT**

I call you, My child. I wish to speak to you. Now say in the name of the Lord your God: Hearken to My voice, My people. Know that your God cares for you. My presence is among you. I dwell in the hearts of those whose hearts are pure, in hearts on fire with love for the eternal love. My Spirit fills their souls with yearning for the presence of the Lord God. I come to those who seek for My goodness. They know that I love them. They come to Me in love. They long to see the face of the Almighty God who molds them in His image. They are formed in love. Their souls reach out to encompass the full measure of the all-encompassing love of their God of love. My Spirit enfolds them and fills them to overflowing from the storehouse of everlasting fountains of flaming desire to possess in their hearts He who is their Lord and God. My presence fills them with boundless joy. They possess My friendship, My constant faithfulness, My unending love, and My graces beyond measure. I fill them with Myself. I make them holy people. I lead them on paths of rest and repose. They know no anxiety. They trust in Me to provide for their needs. There is nothing they want or need but Me. When you possess Me you have all that you need.

I am Alpha and Omega. From beginning to end I am He who sustains your very being. I am He who brings you all good things. I am He who carries you upon the breath of My immortal power and might. I who Am come in the glory of My Spirit to claim you as My own. I have spoken. Thus says the Lord your God.

Let My Spirit awaken you and inflame you with the fire that purifies you and melds you into the crucible of God's holy temple. Receive My presence. You are chosen people of the Spirit. I give you My gift of peace. Go and be peaceful children of God. Live peace! That is all. Thus says the Lord your God . . .

12-6-90 THE TIME OF TRIAL IS AT HAND

. . . Now say in the name of the Lord your God: Accept My peace, holy people of God, the time of trial is at hand. I send My angels before Me. They announce the coming of the Lord. They wield the sword of My power among the people of the earth. They bring war and plagues. They bring disease and disharmony. If My people heed not their God, they bring upon themselves pestilence and disorder. My holy messengers reap the harvest of what man has sown. Fear not, people of God, your harvest flows from the seed of the Word of God. You have sown the seeds of holiness and faith. The seeds you have planted reap in abundance the fruits of the Spirit. I gather you into the storehouse of My Sacred Heart. I present you to the Father in the fullness of My time for you. Have faith My children; you are safe in My loving heart. You are gathered safely in the kingdom of the Lord your God. I am your God who completes what was foretold by the prophets of old. Thus says the Lord your God. That is all.

12-7-90 MY ENEMIES ARE POWERFUL

Say in the name of the Lord your God: My heart is in anguish at the death of My beloved son (Pope John

Paul II). He has suffered martyrdom at the hands of those who denounce My Word. I welcome My sainted son and place him in the army of those who shall ride forth at My command with My triumphant Son (Jesus) to claim My creation. It is not for you to know how His death was accomplished . . . Pray that enlightenment comes upon you. Go in peace. That is all.

12-9-90 ALLOW MY LOVE TO TRANSFORM YOUR HEARTS

Now say in the name of the Lord your God: Speak, My child, to My people. Tell them I love them. The Lord their God offers solace to the weary wanderers of the earth. In all things trust that the Lord your God knows what is necessary for your salvation. Respond to My care for you. Open your hearts to My care. Allow My love to transform your hearts. Become images of love. Love as I love. A holy love formed in the recesses of a heart united to the love of its Creator becomes a beautiful portrait of the artist. I am the self-portrait of love. The brushstrokes of the artist create works of beauty. The brushstrokes of My creation are My people whose beauty is revealed in their hearts of love. See how beautiful you are. Recognize the hand of God as the artist who formed you, the Spirit of God who arrays you in virtues of brilliant colors, the Son of God who brings you to perfection as the magnificent masterpiece in the plan of redemption. You are priceless treasures to the God who created you. You are irreplaceable children in the masterpiece of My creation. All that is created comes from the hand of God. All that exists, exists because I am the supreme artist. When you look at My creation, see in it the work of My hands. Mine is the power to create and destroy. Thus says the lord your God. That is all.

12-10-90 BE LIVING WITNESSES OF MY TRUTH

Now say in the name of the Lord your God . . . Rise, My people, in the service of your one God. Be living witnesses of My truth. Love one another in My love. Stand forth and affirm the faith of the Lord God, Jesus

Christ. You have been called to be witnesses for Christ. My beloved Mother has formed you in silent preparation for the coming of the Lord, Jesus Christ. You are called to the final battle against Satan. Follow the one whom I have chosen to lead you. I give her My truth. She is My chosen one. Perilous times are upon you. The great deceiver has taken his place. Many will follow him. You must not follow him. Walk only upon the path I have revealed to you. Thus says the Lord your God. That is all.

12-11-90 MAN WILL DESTROY HIMSELF

Say in the name of the Lord your God . . . Write: In all things obey the Lord your God. Now say: I, the Lord your God, have loosed the Angel of Death to wield My judgment against the infidels. He brings upon the earth just retribution. The unjust shall suffer My wrath. Their corpses lie upon the earth as witness to man's own folly. ***This is what man will achieve for himself: It is his own destruction. Man will destroy himself. That is My judgment.***

Your God makes this final pronouncement. It shall be as I say. The power of the most high God overshadows the earth. There is darkness and destruction. All is laid waste. Desolation is upon the face of the earth. My angel cuts down those who cringe in terror before the power of the one God that is brought against them. They shall howl like demented creatures. They will find no relief. They die in unutterable pain and anguish. They die in the hell they have prepared for themselves. I will not remove this judgment against them. Thus says the Lord your God.

Now say: This judgement is upon you. The forces are aligned. The power of evil is unleashed in all its fury. Fire rains from the sky. Oh My creatures, this is what you have wrought. It is so. Thus says the Lord your God. That is all.

Now say: (A named country) will be destroyed. No

46

trace will remain. Not one stone will be found to give proof of its existence. I, the Lord your God have so decreed. And still man will not take heed of the Word of God.

12-13-90 WHY DO YOU DENY ME?

I, the Lord your God say: Foolish man who denies your God. Say: I love you. Why do you deny Me? Have I not given you all that is good? Have I not sustained you in the midst of trials and tribulations? Has not My hand wiped away your tears and raised you up in dignity? Have I not provided for your daily sustenance? Do I not bring joy and gladness in the midst of sorrow and grief? I command every moment in time. Do you not know that each moment that you have life is My gift to you? Why do you deny My gift? I it is who have determined the number of your days. If I give you your days, do I not also provide for the needs of your days?

Do not be hard-hearted people. Open your hearts to My presence. I tell you, *I Am Who Am.* I exist in all eternity. I live in your midst. I wish to give you My peace. Open your heart and receive your God. I, the Lord your God, have spoken . . .

12-14-90 REPENT!

Now say in the name of the Lord your God: In all things be obedient to the Word of the Lord your God. I have spoken through My prophets. I speak through souls who have responded to My call. Many have spoken in time through the ages. They call My people to repentance. Their voices cry out to all sinful creatures — *Repent! Come back to the Lord God of Hosts!* They bring warnings of My judgment in ages of sin and evil. *YOUR TIME IS EVIL; MY CREATURES SIN.* They deny their Almighty God; they destroy the holy temple of God. I send My chosen ones among the sinners. They cry out in loud voices and proclaim the coming of the Lord Jesus Christ in all power and glory. His coming is at hand. *The power of God shall*

47

descend from the heavens. It shall clean the earth and make it ready to receive its King and Redeemer. The helpless babe returns in power and glory as the Risen King of Creation. Hosanna to the Almighty King!

Prepare yourselves for His coming. Turn aside from sin and evil. Repent of your sins. Perform acts of penance and reparation. Sing songs of praise and thanksgiving for the mercy of God. He warns you, in the depth of His love for you, of your danger if you do not reform your lives. Hear then, oh people of the earth, the warning of the Lord your God in the words of His prophets. Hear the words of His chosen ones. Take heed, for the time of redemption is at hand. The Lord God comes to gather His own out of the desolation of the earth. I COME!

Now say, I come for you My holy people. The Lord God gathers you to His bosom and embraces you with loving arms. Your faithfulness is rewarded. Thus says the Lord your God. That is all.

12-18-90 I RESTORE WHAT HAS BEEN LOST IN SIN AND EVIL

Now say in the name of the Lord your God: All heaven and earth prepare for the coming of the Lord Jesus Christ. I, the God of power and might, stand upon the firmament and raise My voice in lament because of the desecration you have brought to My creation. I, the Lord God, tremble in rage at what mankind has wrought. I, the Lord God, will no longer restrain My wrath against the corrupters of what I created as good. The defilers of My goodness will come to know the power of My mighty arm raised against them. *My power is immense. I shall use it to cleanse the filth of their abominable deeds from every corner of My creation. I shall restore it to its pristine beauty and purity. It shall shine in splendor and light the universe with its radiance. There shall be no darkness. Peace will reign among the remnant.* My graces will fill their souls and they shall

48

rejoice in the company of the Lord, their God.

I give you peace, the same peace that they will be given in abundance. They shall know no evil; the powers of evil shall no longer dwell upon the earth. I restore what has been lost in sin and evil. The sacrifice of My Son is not in vain. His blood washes you clean. His Spirit clothes you in the garments of salvation. I receive the holy sacrifice given in perfect obedience to My will. I will the redemption of fallen mankind. Your redemption is accomplished in the sacrifice poured out for you on the cross of the eternal Son. He has ransomed My people out of the tyranny of the Evil One. The triumph of the cross overcomes the frailty of the human spirit. It defeats the power of evil; it restores the kingdom to the righteous and faithful servants of the Lord God of hosts. I shall not forsake the agony of My Son. What He has given for your salvation is the triumphant exaltation of the God of power and might in His conquest over the forces of evil. Thus says the Lord your God. That is all.

12-19-90 I CALL YOU TO HOLINESS

Now say in the name of the Lord your God: I call you to holiness. Be holy as My Mother is holy. Look to My Mother and she will lead you on paths of holiness. Holiness comes to you when you open your hearts to the will of the Father. *His will for you is holiness marked with a Spirit of joy and thanksgiving. Holy people are joyful people. In the midst of the trials they endure, they sing songs of praise and thanksgiving to their Creator. Their burdens become crosses of joy, for in the cross is their salvation.*

12-28-90 THE THREE-IN-ONE BECKON YOU TO COME TO THEIR SAVING GRACE

Say in the name of the Lord your God: All hail the Almighty God. Give praise and thanksgiving to the God of power and might. Our God comes in glory and majesty.

The supreme Godhead brings salvation. The power of the spirit overshadows the penitent soul and enlightens the dark recesses of the heart. My Spirit renews the soul with gifts of peace and joy. *Pray for the gifts of My Spirit.* He leads you to springs of life-giving water. He inflames your hearts with zeal for the Word of Almighty God. The Word speaks to the soul. The Word leads you to redemption. The Word of the Lord God is given for the salvation of souls. The Word is My Son in the flesh of Jesus the Christ. He who follows My Word will be saved. The Word is given for your salvation through the power of the Father who knows all that is needed to restore fallen humanity to the perfection of its original creation. No one comes to the Father, except through the Son. The sacrifice of the Son poured out for you on the cross, offered in perfect love and obedience, is acceptable to God the Father in reparation for the first sin. Make reparation for your sins, My children. Come to the victory inspired by the Spirit and won for you by the Son. The Three-in-One beckon you to come to their saving grace. Eat of the fruits of their action; you will be saved. Thus says the Lord your God, Redeemer and Savior. That is all.

12-29-90 DO NOT BE BLIND TO THE SIGNS I PLACE BEFORE YOU

Now say: I, the Lord God, the God of power and majesty, send out the command to commence the beginning of the end. *Do not be blind to the signs I place before you. The signs for your time were foretold by Me in Scripture. Take heed.*

My child, in My wisdom say: The mighty of the earth speak in loud voices with words of doom and destruction. They speak of peace with forked tongues. They do not speak of the peace that comes only from the God of creation. There will be no peace until mankind brings itself to the brink of self-annihilation. In their pride they deny their God who is peace. They fill their hearts with hatred, vengeance, and revenge. There is no room for peace. There is no room for their God. They assign to themselves the power that is

50

God's alone; they usurp the place of Almighty God in His creation. They have deluded themselves. They follow in the footsteps of their first parents. I bring this corrupted Eden to an end. I restore the kingdom to those who follow in the footsteps of My perfection.

I, the Lord God, announce My judgment. I, the Lord God, announce the restoration of My kingdom. I, the Lord God, speak! Thus says the Lord your God. Amen and Alleluia! So be it. That is all . . .

12-30-90 GUARD AGAINST THE ABOMINATION OF ABOMINATIONS

Now say in the name of the Lord your God: My patience is at an end. I loose upon the world the one who seeks to revenge his fall from My grace upon My faithful ones. His anger drives him to fury. His jealousy drives him to madness. His pride underlies all his actions. It is the force that drives him in his diabolical evil. He would make himself god above God. This cannot be, for I alone am God. This fallen creature of mine rages at his impotence before My power. He seeks to destroy My kingdom by perverting My weak and imperfect children. He seduces you in falsehood. He is subtle in his deceptions. He leads My people astray. They follow him like sheep to the slaughter. He controls their minds and their hearts. He introduces them into perversity and degradation. He fills them with pride and arrogance. He fills them with flattery and falsehood. He closes their ears to the voice of truth.

Guard against this abomination of abominations. Be vigilant that you too are not seduced by the liar of liars. He attacks ferociously the heart of My Church— My faithful and loyal followers. Be strong in the strength I give you. Come to My presence. Your strength comes from the God of power and might. Ask and it shall be given to you. You must be strong for the time of trial which is upon you. Many will try to lure you away from My one truth and faith. Do not follow them; they are agents of the Evil One. I alone am the Lord God. Those who speak falsehood in My

51

name speak heresy. They blaspheme all that is holy. They are vile vermin who bring death and disease to My Church. Be on guard against these apostate creatures. They bring scandal to My Church and confusion to the faithful. These are they who, in the fullness of time, denounce the truth and follow the lie. Against these I will not spare My justice. The tormentors of My faithful church will themselves be tormented by the plagues of My judgment. I, the Lord God, have spoken. Go in peace, My child, to serve your God. Thus says the Lord God. That is all.

Tribulations and Triumph
Revelations on the Coming of
THE GLORY OF GOD
1991

"DO NOT DELAY YOUR PREPARATION"

"Be penitent, therefore, and be converted, that your sins may be blotted out. That when the times of refreshment shall come from the presence of the Lord, and He shall send Him who hath been preached unto you, Jesus Christ . . ."

(Acts 3:19-20)

1-4-91   THE PEOPLE OF EARTH MUST CONVERT THEIR LIVES

. . . I speak now to bring hope to My faithful ones. Do not be deceived by talks of peace. The people of the earth must convert their lives. They must turn away from the evil which they plan. They must return to My commands of love. I hear the prayers of My people. Peace shall be theirs. In the midst of the groans of the faithless they shall be consoled. Do not despair, My people. Turn to your God with firm faith. When the exalted fall the lowly shall rise. They shall be exalted in the kingdom of the Lord. The least among you will find their place among the elect. Their suffering is joined to the suffering of My Son for the redemption of souls. They shall rise in glorious triumph to join their brother in the life of eternal light. Believe the words of the Lord, your God. Mine is not an empty promise. Mine is the certainty of eternity for those who hear the voice of the Lord their God. I sustain My faithful; I preserve them from the evil one. Hear Me, oh people, and trust in the faithfulness of your God. I bring you to your eternal

home. I know My own and they know Me. Your hope
is in Me. Those who belong to the world will stay in
the world. Those who belong to Me will walk in peace
and joy to the kingdom. My words are truth. It shall
be so. Thus says the Lord your God . . .

I WILL NO LONGER PERMIT THE SUFFERING OF MY MOTHER

Say in the name of the Lord your God. Speak in My
name. Say: The tears of My Holy Mother bring sorrow
to My heart. I can no longer allow her suffering to
continue. She endures supernatural pain for the sins
of her children. She knows the day and the hour
when I will close My ears to her intercession for My
fallen creatures. Those whom she has gathered under
her mantle bring joy to her heart. Her tears fall for
those who will never know the love offered to but
rejected by so many of My created ones. The harvest
of the Evil One is great. The Mother sees those
created for glory in the kingdom of the Father follow
the path of darkness to final damnation, and her heart
breaks. The sword pierces it for each child lost. The
blood that flows from her pierced heart can no longer
be contained in the cup of her grief. The blood of the
Son was poured out for the redemption of sinners.
The blood of the Mother is poured out upon a flock
which does not hear the voice of the Shepherd. That
is all.

Now say: I will no longer permit the suffering of My
Mother for ungrateful creatures. I will bring to an end
the evil that shatters her heart into fragments of infinite pain for her lost children. They have forsaken
their Mother. **I have commanded you to honor your
mother and your father. Do you think that
command applies to only your earthly parents?
Mary, Queen of heaven and earth, is your Mother
in heaven as well as on earth. Sinful man
dishonors its Mother. It brings her pain and
anguish.** Those who dishonor their parents bring
upon themselves alienation. You have dishonored

54

your heavenly Mother. She is removed from your vile evil ways that wound her and bring her great suffering. When you fail to love love, and Mary is total love, you separate yourself from your true home. I bring My Mother to My true home. You are left in isolation to walk in darkness all the days of your life. Thus says the Lord God. That is all.

1-10-91 I SPEAK OUT IN JUST ANGER

Now say: I speak out in just anger at those who plot against the foundations of My church. I am the Lord God, Creator of all that is seen and unseen. I am the power and the glory. I raise My voice and cry out against those who would destroy what I have established for the salvation of mankind. *They shall not triumph for I, the Lord God Almighty, shall prevail over the agents of evil and destruction.* My wrath reverberates throughout the universe. These hypocrites who call themselves My loyal servants but pervert My truth, will quake in fear before the judgment of their God.

Be consoled My faithful followers. The earth wallows in the darkness of its apostasy, but your way is lighted through the darkness. I am the light that lights your way. I lead you on paths of truth and righteousness. When none can be found who proclaim My truth, recall the truth of the Father in heaven given to the world in the words of the Son and inspired by the Spirit. Do not respond to the voices of the false teachers. Do not be seduced by lying tongues. Do not deviate from what I have commanded you from the beginning of time. You shall know the Lord your God in the words of the Savior. In them is My truth. Thus says the Lord God, Infinite wisdom. That is all.

1-14-91   REPENT ALL YOU PEOPLES OF THE EARTH

I wish to speak. Say in the name of the Lord God most high: I deliver My people from the bondage of sin. I speak in a loud voice and call out — **repent all you peoples of the earth!** Your sins foul My creation. Turn aside from your evil intentions. Can you not understand the power of the Lord God in His wrath against the doers of evil? Why do you persist in your stubbornness? **I call you to repentance!** Heed My call! Thus says the Lord God Almighty.

Now say: Be strong My people. Confess your sins. I desire reparation for the sins of the world. Turn to My Mother and she will bring your gifts of reparation to her beloved Son. Many, many will die without My forgiveness. Pray without ceasing in this time of your great trial. Look only to the goodness of the Lord. Praise His name among the nations. Praise God, Alleluia. Let His name be on your tongues and in your hearts forever and ever. Amen. Thus says the Lord God Almighty, Savior and Redeemer. That is all.

1-15-91   THERE CAN BE NO PEACE UNTIL THERE IS PEACE IN EACH HEART

Say in the name of the Lord God Almighty: How wondrous are your works throughout the earth. Oh Spirit of God renew the face of the earth. Bring refreshment to humanity suffering in the desert.

Now say: There can be no peace until there is peace in each heart. Pray that each man, woman, and child upon the face of the earth will open their hearts to peace. My faithful followers are people of peace. Your voices cry out to Me with prayers for peace. When you live My peace, the peace I give, then peace will flow out and fill the desert of the earth. I grant peace to those who ask for it. Many do not ask for peace. There shall be no peace until all hearts receive My peace. So many hearts have turned to stone. So many stones will be crushed into tiny particles by the forces of evil. They have refused the graces that flow to them through the prayers offered on their behalf. Nothing is left for them but death and destruction. I have heard your prayers, My people, but My creatures do not hear the voice of their God. They have closed themselves to the gentleness of My love and mercy. Now they shall feel the power of My wrath. I, the Lord God, God of power and majesty, commence the judgment upon the earth of My creation. Thus, it begins in all its fury. So proclaims the Lord God Almighty. The time of mercy is ended. Suffer now what you have brought upon yourselves. I, the Lord God, permit your destruction. You have freely chosen what is to come upon you. There is no turning back.

Commence the judgment! All power and glory be to Almighty God. Thus says the Lord God, supreme God of heaven and earth, the God Almighty who fulfills the words spoken through the prophets. It is accomplished as I have ordained. The mystery of redemption is completed. Thus have I spoken; so shall it be.

1-20-91 Prepare now for the coming of Anti-Christ.

1-22-91 MY COMMAND IS THE LAW OF THE UNIVERSE

Say in the name of the Lord God Almighty: I, the Lord God, have dominion in all of My creation. My command is the law of the universe. I have established My order upon the face of the earth. The earth and all that it contains is subject to My command. In time and in eternity mine is the power and the glory. I place My mark upon My creation. It shall not be delivered into the hands of My adversary. I claim My own. When all appears to be lost, My glory will shine forth. I will come like the flash of the lightning in the darkness of the storm. Be prepared, for the coming of the Lord is at hand. In loud voices cry out: ***Come, Lord Jesus, Come!*** Save us, oh Lord God, from the works of the evil one. Have pity on us, Oh Lord.

In the recesses of your hearts prepare a place for the

King of Glory. Be wise, My people, and know that My time is upon you. My coming will not be delayed. Hear the words of the Lord God.

Now say: The days granted to My adversary are numbered. In the days remaining He will strike with vengeance against My faithful ones. Many will submit to His wiles. They submit themselves to unspeakable atrocities. They will condemn themselves to the eternal fire. Be vigilant, My people. Know that My hour is upon you when I will deliver you out of the abyss of sin and evil. Prepare for the glorious return of your triumphant God. Behold, the hour is at hand when the Son of God shall appear with the heavenly host in the splendor and glory of the living God . . .

1-23-91 I AM A JUST GOD

. . . Repent of your sins. Do not wait, for My judgment is upon you. Be prepared for the coming of the Lord. The time is urgent. The onslaught of the Evil One is vicious. My enemies are everywhere about you. They work tirelessly for the ruin of souls. They hear not the voice of their God. They follow in blind adoration the one who blinds them to salvation in their God. They cannot see what is before their eyes. I am before them, but they cannot see Me. I speak, but they do not hear. My presence is among you, but they do not recognize it. I have poured out My mercy to all mankind; only a few have accepted it. My adversary leads people on paths of destruction. They hear no voice but His. They close themselves away from the life-giving power of their God. They have relinquished their souls into the keeping of the power of hell. My judgment is upon them, and still they remain blind and deaf. They can do nothing; they are lost. Weep not for these lost children. My judgment against them is just. I am a just God!

Now say: Tell My people that they must turn away from sin. ***They must not continue to ignore My commands!*** They must stop committing evil acts.

58

They must not defy their God. Who will hear My voice, they shall be saved. Hear, My people, what I tell you. You cannot begin to understand the enormity of My judgment if you do not repent of your sins and sin no more. The Lord God calls you by name. Harden not your hearts to His call. Thus says the Lord God of power and might: I call out to you — **Come to My mercy; come to My love!** I am here. Look, and you will see Me; listen, and you will hear Me. Do not persist in your waywardness, but come to Me and I will set you free. I love you. Let My love free you from the bondage of the Evil One. He cannot give you love; he cannot give you peace. He can do nothing but lead you to eternal damnation. I am truth; he is lies. The struggle for men's souls lies in truth or falsehood. Come to truth. Hear the call of the Lord God, and you shall know truth. You shall know salvation. Thus says the Lord God. Hear and be saved. That is all.

1-24-91 THIS IS MY LAST WARNING TO SINFUL MAN

Say in the name of Almighty God: Your transgressions against My Holy Word bring down upon you calamity upon calamity. There is no end to the destructive forces of the Evil One. He goads men into irreversible catastrophes. His instruments bring ruin upon the face of the earth. My innocent children suffer unspeakable atrocities. They wail in anguish, and there is no relief for their suffering. My poor hapless children, what you have wrought from your pride and self-righteousness! Can you not see the afflictions you have brought upon yourselves in your apostasy? Can you still not see that your salvation comes only from the Lord God whom you have rejected and blasphemed? I tell you, all shall now be accomplished as I have ordained against this sinful and faithless world. You shall not escape the judgment you have incurred upon yourselves. Oh sinful man, My warning is upon you — **Repent and sin no more!** The Lord God calls out in a loud voice — **This is My last warning to sinful man!** Do not offend your God any longer. My hand is raised against you. It shall move to smite you; it shall descend upon you with a mighty blow. My power is absolute. My judgment is not revoked. *I am the Lord God! I Am Who Am!* There is no other but Me! I have spoken. I, the Lord God, am supreme in heaven and on earth. You shall not be spared from the consequences of My anger. These are the words of the Lord God Almighty. Thus says the Lord God. I will act in the fullness of My power, and you will know that I am the Lord God. Thus says the Lord your God. Hear and be warned.

1-26-91 MOTHER MARY SPEAKS — about 4 p.m.

My dear children, I speak to you in the name of the Lord, My Son, through His instrument. I say to you that My time on earth is ended. I am recalled to the kingdom of the Father. Your Mother loves you. Thank you for having responded to My call. I have formed you into a holy people. Continue to respond to the messages I have been giving you. You are in My heart. Have no fear but rejoice in the triumph of your Mother. My triumph over My adversary is accomplished. His power cannot harm those under My special protection. Your faithfulness to the word of My Son is rewarded in the safety of My Immaculate Heart. I go now from your midst. Your loving Mother leaves you. Rejoice and be glad for the Lord God has accomplished great things through His humble servant. I am with you in the words I have given you. Thank you, My children, for having answered the call of your Mother. That is all.

Second message given at midnight.

This is the Mother speaking to her children. I can no longer remain with you, My children. Be brave. The power of evil shall not prevail over you. Your Mother is protecting you. Go in the peace of the Lord God to be holy people in His name. Your Mother leaves you to await your coming into the kingdom of the Father. Thank you, My children, for answering the call of your Mother. That is all.

1-29-91 TRUST IN MY MERCY, TRUST IN MY LOVE

I, the Lord God, speak. Thus says the Lord God: My mercy flows like a mighty river into the parched land. Where there is faith in the hearts of men the Lord God showers upon you a torrent of purifying love. I wish to say, My love cleanses you of your sins. My love washes over you, and you are made clean. My love engulfs you in the depths of My mercy. Your God loves you. Come to Me and refresh your souls at the fountain of renewal. Trust in My mercy, trust in My love. Trust that you are made clean. All who come to Me find refreshment and peace. The waters of mercy run deep. Immerse yourselves in My mercy. Partake of My gift to you. Wash yourselves in My blood poured out for you. I, the Lord God, call you to repentance. Rid yourselves of your sins. Make yourselves white in the sacrament of peace. Reconcile yourselves to your God and your brothers and sisters. Bring your purified souls as a gift to the King of Peace.

Now say: My peace is with you. In your hearts welcome your God who is peace. Prepare for the coming of the Lord God. Let no stain of sin blemish the chambers of His dwelling place. Make holy the temple of the Lord. Purify your souls, oh My children, so that I, the Lord, My find a fit receptacle for My holy presence. Thus says the Lord your God. That is all.

2-1-91 FOLLOW IN MY FOOTSTEPS

Now say: I, the Lord God, speak. I say unto you prepare the way of the Lord who comes with power and might. Make straight the path to My kingdom. The road is long and narrow. All who travel My road see the light of the Father beckoning them onward. Those who choose the twisted path cannot find the beacon of their salvation. They wander in the wilderness. They do now know the way. They wander aimlessly and know not where they go. There is only one path to salvation. I am the Way. I am the Path.

All who walk with Me walk with certainty to the Father. I am His light that lights the way before you. Follow Me, My children, and you will not lose the way. I am the truth and the light. Follow in My footsteps. I have prepared the way for you. I walk with you each step of your journey. I am beside you and before you. Look about you and you shall see that I am always with you. Take heart My people. Come to recognize My presence. I traveled the same road you travel. I faltered and I fell. So must you. I rose in triumph; so shall you. The promise of the Father is for all generations until the end of time. Hear then, My people, the promise of your God. It stands inviolate through all time and in all eternity — I am your God. I show you the way and lead you upon the path. I am always with you. I do not abandon you. Trust that this is truth. Come then and follow Me, and I will bring you home. I, the Lord God, have spoken. That is all.

Now, My child, say: Travel on My path with joy in your hearts and songs of praise in your mouths. Give praise to the Holy God who brings you out of the dominion of the world and into the light of eternity. Praise your God for the wondrous deeds He has performed for you. Praise Him with your hearts and voices. Let a mighty anthem sing His praises. Let your Alleluias resound in the highest heavens. Pour forth the wonder and the glory of God in glorious words and songs. The mighty God of all watches over you and protects you. How wondrous are His works throughout the earth. Loose your tongues with songs of love. Praise the Almighty God. Thanks be to God, for He is worthy of praise and thanksgiving. Thus says the Lord God, Almighty King, Almighty God of power and majesty. That is all.

. . . In the name of the Lord God Almighty say: Be prepared, My children, for the coming of the Lord God. The time is near when I shall proclaim My dominion over all the earth. All shall know that I am the Lord God. Be alert, My people. I, who am the God of all, announce to you that I come in power and glory. My holy Mother has formed you into a holy people. I claim you as My own. I am coming soon. Be prepared for My coming. The Lord your God has spoken. That is all.

"The promise . . . The promise of My coming is about to be accomplished. Be prepared. I am coming, My child. I am coming."

2-3-91 ## A NEW HEAVEN AND A NEW EARTH SHALL I CREATE

I, the Lord God, speak. Say in My name: **When the power of Almighty God descends upon the earth the foundation of the universe will be shaken to its core. I bring My mighty power to re-form My creation. A new heaven and a new earth shall I create.** I shall form them in the image of My love. In My Spirit I scatter My fruits among the elect. They work prodigies in My name. In My name they heal the suffering. In My name they proclaim My truth. In My name they renew My Church. All shall be restored as I intended from the beginning. The sin of the original ones is expiated. The power of the most high is upon the face of the earth. The forces of the universe move at My command. What was destroyed will be restored. Peace shall reign supreme and all creation will exist in harmony with its Creator. I come upon the depths of the deep; I soar through the highest heavens; I bring My healing grace upon the firmament. In My heavens the bodies that give light will be no more. All that exists will live in the light of My presence. There will be no darkness; in My light will they have their being. What man has destroyed I will make new.

Now say: The power of the Almighty God will move and the new earth will be formed out of the old. Springs of living water will flow through the land. New growth will spring forth out of the soil. All will flourish, and the face of God will look with favor upon what He has brought forth. I, the Lord God, have spoken. Go in peace. Thanks be to the Almighty Trinity from whom are we ransomed into new life. Bow down, oh holy people of God, to the saving power of the Three-In-One. Thus says the Lord God. That is all.

2-8-91   **TO PRIESTS**

. . . Now say: The coming of the Son from the right hand of the Father is ordained and proclaimed by the Father so that My people are forewarned. I tell you, the time for His coming is upon you. I call out to you and say: ***Repent of your sins***, for the hour of His coming you do not know. I am a loving God. I send My messengers before Me to prepare you for His coming. I warn you of the dangers that surround you. The power of Satan is manifest throughout the earth. His influence is felt even in the bowels of My Church. My holy sons rebuke not the perpetrators of abhorrent deeds. Few voices speak out in defense of My statutes. So many have forsaken their sacred vows. So many no longer respond to the voice of their conscience. So many refuse the mercy of the God to whom they have sworn allegiance. They have forgotten My love and replace it with the seductions presented before them by the hand of the liar from hell. They are so far from Me these sons of mine. They do not know Me. They fly from the face of their God and lead My people astray.

Be strong, My priest-sons, against the snares of Satan. I call you back to your solemn vows. I call you back to My mercy. I call you to hear My voice and answer your God. Open your ears to My voice. Come, My sons, take My hand. Reach for it, and I will grasp it in My own. I will hold you firmly and bring you back to truth and love. I open My heart to you; enter into your salvation. In Me you will find repose. In Me is your vocation. In Me only must you place your lives. In Me are you called to serve My people. Be My true sons in the service of the one God.

Holy God be praised. Hear Me My beloved ones. Find your strength and power in My truth. Free yourselves

64

of your bondage to the Evil One. Open your hearts and your ears to My Word, and I will set you free. Thanks be to the Almighty God who saves His people. Praise Him in the highest. Praise Him with hearts full of love. Praise Him! Praise Him! Love Him! Oh holy sons of God turn your faces toward Him who is all mighty and you will know the magnitude of My love for you. Thus says the Lord God Almighty . . . The Lord your God has spoken. That is all.

2-16-91 GOD THE HOLY SPIRIT

Now for today I wish to speak. Say in the name of the Lord God: My peace is with you. Come with humble hearts to receive My gifts given for your salvation. The Spirit emerges from the recesses of hearts open to love. I am love. My Spirit is set free by the power of My graces freely given in abundance to souls awakened to His presence. My Spirit brings repose to the soul. His gifts He distributes each according to the will of the Father. The indwelling of the Spirit manifests itself in the practice of the virtuous life. My holy people are virtuous people. They heed the voice of the Lord God. They increase in holiness. They come before their Lord arrayed in garments made clean by the noble adherence to the virtues. He who knows the Spirit knows the Father and the Son. He who calls on the Spirit is answered by the Three-In-One. He who accepts the action of the Spirit accepts also the salvation grace granted by the Father through the Son. The power of the Spirit flows from the Father through the Son, and the power is the same in each, yet one. In My Spirit is renewal. In My Spirit is the fire of love which burns away the darkness of the mind and the soul. In My Spirit is wisdom and truth. In My Spirit is love and peace. In My Spirit is understanding of hidden truths and acceptance of the mysteries which cannot yet be revealed to the human intellect. My Spirit is powerful. Call on His power and you will be restored and renewed. Thus says the Lord God. That is all. Go in peace to serve your God according to His will.

. . . I send My Spirit among you. To each is given the gifts necessary for His (or her) salvation. Pray to the Spirit. Accept what is offered. Respond to this request of your God. I have spoken. That is all.

2-18-91 ALL CREATION RIGHTLY GIVES ME PRAISE

I wish to speak. Say unto My people in the name of the Lord God most high: Almighty is the Lord God. From the bowels of the earth to the highest reaches of the heavens is the power of the most high manifest. Mine is the power in all creation that sustains its existence. Mine is the glory that permeates the goodness of My creation. All creation rightly gives Me praise, for mine is the hand that upholds the righteous and smites the unjust. I raise you up from the least among you to the most exalted. All which I created is the manifestation of My infinite love. Its (creation) grandeur speaks of the magnificence of My love. The sounds of nature repeat the sounds that emanate from the voice of the Almighty God. I speak in the softest murmurs to the loudest thunders of the heavens. I speak to the hearts of men and to the elements of nature. All hearken to the voice of its Creator except prideful man. He it is who brings disharmony to that whose harmony is ordered by the power in the hand of its Creator. Man is the discordant note in the melody of the universe. They clang with loud noises like bells cracked and broken. Their sounds are harsh and strident. They speak not with gentle sounds and words of love, but from throats filled with harsh rattles. They fill My world with destructive sounds of strife and violence.

Now say: The sounds of voices raised in prayer restore harmony and gentle sounds to the ears of the Creator. Speak from hearts filled with love. Love speaks kindly, it speaks quietly, it speaks with the voice of the Almighty. Sounds spoken with love bring solace, they bring peace, they bring union in the love

66

of the Almighty love. Use your voices to bring comfort and the soothing wisdom of My truth to those who cannot hear beyond the raucous sounds of their own cracked and broken selves. Let the melodious notes that flow from hearts filled with the praise and the love of their all-loving God restore the sound of the voice that speaks softly to quiet hearts. Let the voice of the Lord God be heard once again in the stillness of hearts which listen for the sounds that speak of the presence of their God in their midst. Still your noises and listen to the words of your God who speaks to bring you peace and salvation. I have spoken. Thus says the Lord God. Hear Me, My people. That is all.

2-19-91 PICK UP YOUR CROSSES

(Jesus Speaks): The Lord God cries out in a loud voice: The time of trial is upon you. Say in the name of the Lord God: Pick up your crosses and walk now the path of agony. Bear your suffering with fortitude and complete trust in your Savior. The cross is heavy, the path tortuous. I have carried the cross before you and walked the path which you now follow. The glory of the cross is your salvation. Bear it with dignity and patience. Stand firm against those influences that claim the cross is an unnecessary burden, that suffering has no value. Suffering redeemed mankind for the kingdom of glory — suffering has eternal value. Suffering washes away iniquity. The power of suffering can lead souls to conversion and redeems many from the power from hell.

(God the Father Speaks): Now say: Your cross is a mighty tool against Satan. You are mightily blest when you join the weight of your cross to the cross of your brother (Jesus). His suffering was no less than yours. Whatever you suffer He bears with you. Take comfort from the cross of My Son. He has borne all before you even to dying for you. His agony is no less than yours. When the Son of Man returns in the glory of His resurrection, you will be taken up to share in His glory. His glory is your glory.
I say to you: Accept your suffering with a glad heart,
67

for those who suffer are called in a special way to the triumph of Jesus the King. From the ashes of pain you too will rise resplendent in the brilliance of the Risen Christ.

(Jesus Speaks): I call you, My people, to pick up your cross and come, follow Me. We journey together on the path to Calvary. I, your suffering God, have spoken. Thus says the Lord God. That is all.

2-26-91 THIS SHORT TIME IS GRANTED FOR CONVERSION AND REPARATION

Say in the name of the Lord God: The mighty nations of the earth do battle at the command of the Evil One (refers to the Persian Gulf War). Men without souls battle men with no hearts. I will grant a short time of peace to the mighty warriors. *I hear the prayers of My people. Continue to pray, My people, and the time of My judgment will be shortened. Repent of your many sins.* Seek peace in your hearts and peace will come into the world. Pray for the conversion of sinners. Let no man hate His fellow man. Reach out each to the other in the love of God. Set aside your selfish pursuits and self-centered interests. Look beyond your self and look to the needs of your neighbor. Call upon the name of the Lord your God. Ask for His mercy; seek His forgiveness. Stop your evil deeds and act according to My commands. This short time is granted for conversion and reparation. Heed the words of the Lord God. The next warning will be even more terrible for those who refuse the goodness of the Lord God. I have spoken. Thus says the Lord God Almighty. I have said it; thus shall it be. That is all.

2-27-91 NOTE: President Bush announced a cease fire in the Persian Gulf beginning at midnight.

Now say in the name of the Lord Jesus Christ: Dominion is mine over all that exists in creation. I am the Lord of all. The Father has given into My hands all power to accomplish His will for the redemption of sinful man. My power triumphs over the darkness of sin; it raises up the dead into everlasting life. My power triumphs over the forces of evil. I come with power upon the throne of My royal priesthood. All eyes are raised in wonder at the sight of My coming upon the clouds of glory and majesty. I am the resplendent King enthroned upon the seat of judgment. I am the glorified Christ seated at the right hand of the Father from whom I was sent into the world. *I am the Lord God Jesus Christ, Son of the Father.* I it is who reclaims the kingdom of the lost for the Father. I it is who fulfills the promises of the prophets of old. I bring good tidings of My saving grace. I gather My people out of the harvest of the earth. I accomplish all that the Father commands. *I am the Lord God.* He who denies Me is denied by Me. I come in power and glory. *I am the Lord God.* Thus says the Lord God.

Now say: Rejoice My loyal ones, I come! The time of your loyal service will soon be rewarded. I take up My place among you. *I am the Lord God.* My peace is with you. Await with joyful anticipation the coming of the Lord, your God. I shall not delay My coming. Sing the praises and the glory of God with hearts filled with wonder, for the time of the Lord is at hand. Thus says the Lord God. That is all . . .

Say in the name of the Lord God: My mercy is granted, during this time of grace, upon those who repent of their evil deeds. This time for repentance is short. The Father calls to His errant children . . . *Reform your lives!!*

[My child, it is imperative that you speak of these messages. My children must be warned. They shall bring upon themselves My next warning if they persist in the path they have chosen. I, the Lord God, permit the consequences of man's evil (in order) to reveal the destructive power He brings upon himself].

Now say: Make reparation for your many sins. The power of the Almighty God is restrained. I grant My restraint as a sign of mercy. Come to My mercy. Return to Me in prayer and repentance. Soon the horrors of the Evil One will be made manifest. Once again mighty forces will do battle with each other. Death and desolation return to the earth. Pray with fervent hearts, My children, to open the heart of My mercy upon the victims of Satan's madness. Pray with hearts made clean in the power of My forgiveness. Be with Me, My children, in thought, and word, and deed. Immerse yourselves in My holy presence. Let My Spirit move you to open your hearts and your minds to the knowledge of your Almighty God. Open yourselves and permit your God to enter in. I am your God; be My holy people. Seek Me first above all else. I come to those who call My name. I hear the softest whisper. Come, poor children, come to the Father who loves you. Do not tarry, for the number of days granted for conversion are few. Have pity on the suffering of your holy Mother and your divine Brother. Bring gladness to their hearts by responding to My call. They have lived to bring to you salvation. Come to salvation. Thus says the Lord God. I have spoken. That is all.

SEEK FIRST THE KINGDOM OF GOD — TURN TO MY MOTHER

Now say in My name: The Lord God of power and might says to you, seek first the kingdom of God. *Resist the forces of evil whose power is becoming stronger as the time for their defeat draws closer. They attack with vengeance especially those devoted to My most holy Mother. Be aware, My people, of the seductions of the powers of hell. They seek to destroy your allegiance to the Mother of all who is protecting you from the onslaught.* The will of the Father accomplished through the humble obedience of Mary, our Mother, will triumph. The power of the Father given through the hands of holy Mary, releases you and returns you to your salvation. She frees you from the grip of Satan. She wipes away your tears, she consoles your wounded spirits. She places you before My merciful heart. She opens the door to the cleansing flow of My divine blood poured out for the salvation of all mankind. You are washed clean in the blood of your Savior. She keeps you safe in My Sacred Heart.

Turn to My Mother, My dear ones. In her presence you are safe from the Evil One. She triumphs over her nemesis. The Evil One has no power where she is. Dwell in the safety of your Mother's arms . . . That is all. The Lord, your God has spoken. Thus says the Lord God.

3-10-91 HOLY IS THE NAME OF THE LORD GOD ALMIGHTY

Now I say unto you, in the name of the Lord God say: Holy is the name of the Lord God Almighty.

Now say: When the power of the Almighty God comes upon the face of the earth, the infinite majesty of the Lord overshadows all of creation. There is no other God but Me. No creature in all of creation understands the grandeur of the living God.

My holy name is a hymn upon the tongues of those who praise the splendor that is your God. My name, spoken with love, is balm to the aching heart of your God suffering the insults from tongues which speak My name in vain. My name is spoken in anger and false swearing. It has become a word of derision. It is spoken without reverence and faith. My name has no meaning in a world which does not admit My existence. *I am Jesus the Christ!* My name was chosen by My heavenly Father. It was chosen in the fullness of time to being glory to the Father. I am the Son of the Father. When you speak My name, you affirm the authority of the Father and the submission of the Son in perfect obedience to the will of the Father. My name was given to bring comfort to those who call to Me with hope. My name brings mercy to those who ask it of Me. My name protects you from evil when you invoke it against the powers of evil. My name covers you like a mantle and shields you from the forces that seek your damnation. My name is a powerful weapon.

Speak My name with reverence. Let My name be in your hearts. Let it not cross your lips as a term of derision. Do not mock My name or blaspheme what was made holy by My suffering. Respect the name given by the Father to only He who brought redemption to fallen humanity, to He who came as God and man, to He who comes to judge the living and the dead. My name is the name of the Lord your God who has power over life and death, the living God of your salvation. *I am your God. I am Jesus.* Speak My name — *Jesus*. Pray My name, sing My name — *Jesus*, God of love, God of mercy, God of power and might, God of glory and majesty — *Jesus*.

Now say: People of God open your mouths and glorify the name of Jesus. Speak His name in hymns of praise, for the name of the Lord God is the name of love; it is the name of sacrifice; it is the name of salvation. I, the Lord God, Jesus Christ, have spoken. That is all.

Now say in the name of the Lord God Almighty: Peace to My people. I grant you this time of peace. I call you to myself. Restore your souls in the sacraments of My peace. Use this time to pray and draw closer to your heavenly peace. So many are still so far from Me. I call to you, My people. *In the name of the Lord God, pray for the conversion of sinners.* My holy ones, offer yourselves to My Sacred Heart. I accept all who come to Me. Your loving God waits with outstretched arms to receive your offering. I enfold you in My embrace. I wipe your tears. I raise you up and set you on the path which I make straight before you. I am your hope. I am the light that shines in your darkness. All who come to Me will find light and peace. All who call My name will be consoled.

Now say: Come close My children. Do not be afraid. Your God loves you with a gentle heart. Come as a child with trust that you are not forsaken. What parent who loves His children will not do all in His power to ensure the safety and the welfare of His offspring. So too, the Father, who loves His children with a limitless love, provides for your every need. *Trust that the Lord God will provide for you in the time of trial. Great events are about to occur in the world of men.* Do not be afraid. I am with you until the end. I, the Lord God of power and might, have spoken.

. . . Continue to pray with hearts open to My words. Let My words guide you through the coming turmoil. All that has been spoken through My prophets is soon to be accomplished. *My Holy Mother is protecting you from the powers of evil. The power of the rosary is your weapon against the Evil One.* Your faithfulness to the call of My Mother is pleasing to Me. Through My Mother I pour out My graces upon you. Do not waiver in your response; you are richly rewarded. Open your hearts and your minds to the promptings of My Spirit. My Spirit inspires you and strengthens you for the time of trial. Be prepared, My children, and rest peacefully in the knowledge that the Lord, your God, holds each of you safely in the palm of His hand. Thus says the Lord God.

Now say for those to whom you will speak: Hear the words of My daughter whom I have called to speak in My name. Through her I say to you: Prepare yourselves with humble hearts for the coming of the Lord God most high. I call you to make acts of reparation for the many offenses against your holy God. Mankind does not repent of its grievous sins. It closes its ears to My call for repentance and conversion. It continues to deny that I exist. It continues along the path to self destruction. I plead with you, My people — *do not delay your preparation*. Be reconciled to your God. My coming is imminent. Put aside worldly matters. Open your hearts to My Spirit. Pray with hearts open to My word. Confess your sins. Be reconciled to each other. Love My Mother as I love her. Hear the words I give to My servant. My words are truth. In all ways act for My greater honor and glory. Be shining examples of the transforming power of My love. I love you, My people, with an endless love. Come to My love. Thus says the Lord God. That is all.

4-6-91   THE TIME FOR YOUR CONVERSION IS SHORT

Now say in the name of the Lord God: I say to you, the time for your conversion is short. The powers of evil are even now planning their diabolical destruction of My creation. Mankind closes its eyes and its ears to the forces of evil which daily grow stronger. The earth has become a cesspool of sin and corruption. Its rottenness fills the heavens with its stench. I hear the cries of My suffering ones. The agony of their persecution brings My wrath against those who cause their suffering. Man has refused My hour of mercy. They choose to follow the path of evil. They have closed their ears to the voice of love and mercy. They wreak the vengeance of the Evil One on the helpless and the innocent. I, the Lord God of heaven and earth, see their deeds. I, the Lord God, will bring My justice against them. My wrath can no longer be restrained. I loose My hand against them. I smite them with a mighty blow. My holy Mother has warned you repeatedly of the power of Satan. *Heed her warnings!* I tell you, His forces prepare for His physical manifestation. The power of Satan is manifest in the deeds of humankind. Soon He will reveal himself. My people must prepare themselves with prayer and sacrifice, for the hour of His coming is upon you. The persecution He employs upon the earth is such as has not been since the beginning of time. Know that the hour of His vengeance has begun. All that He has wrought upon the earth in all time will He again employ in one last mighty effort to make himself master of My kingdom. *He will not succeed!* I, the Lord God, have dominion; My love and mercy endure forever. Whoever comes to Me will find salvation.

Now say: Prepare yourselves for the mighty confrontation. You do not know the hour. I say to you, My judgment is upon you. The hours granted for conversion and repentance are now but minutes. Put aside the cares of the world. Focus on that moment when you will stand before Me. For sinful man that moment is upon you. *Do not delay!* I, the Lord God, have spoken. Thus say I.

Now say in My name: I warn My people from a heart filled with love and compassion. *If sinful creatures do not change their evil ways, fearful suffering will be the fate which comes upon humanity. I call you to conversion!* Thus says the Lord God.

75

4-10-91 NOW IS THE TIME OF YOUR WITNESS

Now say in the same of the Lord your God: Now is the time of your witness as children of the Father and brothers and sisters of the Lord Jesus Christ. I call My children to be witnesses of My truth. I call you to bear witness to the faith as it was given to all mankind by the holy Son in obedience to the command of the Father. Stand forth as a loyal follower of Christ Jesus, the Lord. Accept the call; stand firm in your faith. Many will be the martyrs who refuse the mark of the demon from hell. I say to you — **stand firm**! Remember that I, the Lord God, deliver you into the hands of the Father in heaven. In the hour of travail call My name. I, the Lord Jesus Christ, bring comfort to the suffering. No one who calls My name is left unaided. Pray thus My children:

"Mighty God, eternal Father, Son, and Spirit, grant your children the comfort of your compassionate heart. Hear, oh Lord, our voices calling you. We plead to you to rescue us from our oppressors. Deliver us, oh Lord. Rescue us, oh Lord. We, your children, come humbly before you and beg your mercy. Hear us, oh Lord. Your people call your name. Amen."

Now say: When the power of the Evil One comes upon you, recall the words spoken through the prophets: He will deliver you out of the land of Egypt. He will wipe away your tears. I will be your God, and you will be My people. Ponder these words! I, your God, will deliver My people from the wrath of Satan. In My presence you will know repose and peace. My faithful ones are My chosen ones. I am your Sovereign God for all eternity. Thus says the Lord God.

4-12-91 YOU MUST NOT REMAIN SILENT!

Say in the name of the Lord God: In the days to come the power of the most high God will meet in mortal confrontation with the power from the bowels of hell. My mighty army, which My dearest Mother has gathered from the harvest of the earth, will engage in mortal combat to defeat the despoilers of My holy creation. She has gathered them from the elect. You are called to the mighty battle. Be valiant soldiers in the battle for men's souls. *You must not remain silent* (uncommitted)! Your voices lifted in prayer must fill the heavens. Your mouths must be opened to plead for justice for the innocent. Your tongues must proclaim your fidelity to the truth of the Lord Jesus Christ. Your throats must pour forth songs of praise and mighty Hosannahs. Do not be silent, My people.

4-22-91 I CALL EACH ONE

Let your hearts be filled with fervent desire to proclaim the mighty Word that is Jesus Christ — Jesus the Lord, Jesus the redeemer of sinful mankind. Jesus, My God and My Savior, have mercy on us. The mercy of the Lord God endures forever. Oh hearts opened to the Word, blossom with zeal and witness to the everlasting goodness of the Lord your God. I call each one. I hold out My hand to you. Will you not come to Me My beloved sons and daughters? Will you not respond to the call of your Father who loves you? Will you not open your hearts and let the Spirit of love inflame you with the fire of divine love? Do not let your hearts remain closed My beloved ones. How sweet is the fruit of My love for you. Taste of it. I wish for you to know the goodness of the Word made flesh. Taste of Him; His mercy endures forever. Partake of the feast of divine fruits. It is placed before you. Sup and be filled. I fill you with My goodness. All who

come to the banquet I have prepared for you will not
go away empty. They shall know the fullness of the
Lord God. They shall be filled with every grace and
blessing. They shall know the Lord God. Thus says
the Lord God.

Now say: Peace to My people. I am here with you.
Just reach out your hand, and I will take it. Just call
My name, and I will answer you. The Lord your God
sustains you in the trial. Be not afraid My people, for
the power of the Lord God protects you from evil. I
love you and you are mine. That is all. Thus says the
Lord God.

5-2-91   DO NOT BE DECEIVED BY FALSE PROPHETS

(Mother Mary speaks) — This is the Mother speaking.
In the name of the Lord Jesus Christ, I bring you
greetings. I wish to say to you through the instrument
of the Lord God, *do not be deceived by false
prophets*. Many are they who claim to speak for Me.
Only those chosen by the Father from those whom I
have selected are called to speak for Me. Satan is
working very powerfully to bring discord and false
witness in order to lead My children into confusion
and despair. I tell you this from a heart filled with
compassion for those who are so easily swayed from
the path of holiness. Warn My children that Jesus
only is Lord. Do not follow the false prophets. They
cannot bring you to salvation. Be warned, My
children! Your Mother warns you.

(Jesus speaks) - Now say, in the name of the Lord
Jesus Christ say to My people: Heed the warning of
our Mother. The forces of evil seek to cloud the minds
of the faithful with lies and deceptions. Open your
hearts to My Spirit. Heed the words of My select
souls. They are called to lead you in the truth. My
truth is but a tiny flicker in the darkness. Evil and
falsehood seek to extinguish My light from the world.
I am the truth — the power of evil has no power over
Me. Keep your eyes focused on the light of My truth.
I say to you, My light lives in the gospel of My Word.

(Mother Mary speaks) - My dearest Son has revealed to you what is necessary for your salvation. Follow His revealed Word. I, the Mother, have spoken. That is all.

(Jesus speaks) - You shall now say for My holy Mother: Reform your lives; convert your hearts. So many have not responded to My call. So many continue in the darkness of sin and evil. So many are lost because they will not respond to the call of love and conversion. Pray, My children. Pray that you also will not be seduced by those who speak falsehood. Do not stray from the protection of your Mother. Thus says the Lord God.

Now, in My name say to My faithful ones: These latter days grow darker and darker because mankind's sins grow more heinous and more vicious. The days of Satan and His followers are now but a few. The majority of mankind are under His spell. The majority of mankind will perish at this hand. Thank you, My loyal followers, for accepting the call to be My remnant in the transformed world. Your Almighty God thanks you and blesses you. Your suffering is not in vain. Thus says the Lord God, the God of power and might who comes to restore the kingdom.

5-4-91   STAND FIRM AGAINST THE EVIL ONE

I wish to speak. Say in My name, say to My people: I wish to warn you, dear children, of the impending disaster which will soon devastate a great portion of the earth. Thousands are already suffering and dying because the forces of evil run rampant among the peoples of the earth. Evil outweighs good. Soon there will be only a few left who will remain to follow the path I have prepared for you. The forces of nature will devastate the land. The earth will be rent and the fires that burn below will devour what is on the surface. Black clouds will envelope the face of the earth. Demons will roam freely in the darkness. The power of the most high God will be restrained until the number of days allotted for the torment by the Evil One are accomplished. I, the Lord God, have *numbered His days. His power will not prevail. He is granted this time as a test for My created ones. The trial will cause even the most stout-hearted souls to tremble under the ruthless persecution He will enforce upon all of mankind. The test will be severe.* My judgment is just. I, the Lord God, warn you and prepare you for what is soon to come upon you. You must not be unprepared. The secrets of the most high will bring justice to sinful souls and solace to their victims. I, the Lord God, have spoken. All shall be as I have said. The hour for mercy and conversion is withdrawn. The judgment is permitted to continue. The next will be worse than the first. The Lord God will no longer endure the sins committed against My kingdom. I say to you — *no one who sins against My kingdom will be spared.* These are My words. So shall it be. The Lord God has spoken.

Now say to those My faithful ones: Your suffering will be great. I do not forsake you. Endure with firm faith and perseverance. Call My name in the Spirit. He will uphold you; He will sustain you. Those who call My name will be granted the grace of perseverance. Look with hope to the coming of the Son. Rejoice at your deliverance. The power of the most high God will triumph. You will be set free. Thus says the Lord God.

Now say: My peace is with you. Stand firm against the Evil One. *You will be tempted to deny your God. Resist!* The reward for My faithful ones is everlasting life; the reward for those who deny Me is everlasting death. I have spoken. Thus says the Lord God.

ABORTION

I wish to speak. Say to My people in the name of the Lord God: Prepare the way of the Lord. As My disciples in the battle against the forces of evil, your voices must be heard proclaiming My truth. Pray for the guidance of My Spirit. Be open to His power.

In the name of the Lord God say to My people: Be holy people. Pray unceasingly in reparation for the sins of the world. Seek justice for the downtrodden. Pray for the innocent lives sacrificed daily in the godless centers of death. These My innocent ones must not be forsaken. *These innocent ones suffer immeasurably. Their suffering must be expiated. I call you, My people, to offer many sacrifices.* I call you to kneel before My image and beg the mercy of the Father for these, the most helpless of all My children. Come before the presence of your Almighty God and beg His justice to end the scourge that destroys humanity. *My call is urgent!* The innocent must be protected. The pitiful cries of these who suffer such agonizing deaths are louder than the loudest thunder. Their wails proclaim the abomination of the barbaric actions of prideful creatures. Do you not know that I, the giver of life, can cease to give life? Do you not know that your wombs will remain empty and the seed of life become as nothing but dust in the withered tomb? How long will you try My patience? I say to you: Now is about to come upon you the desolation of the silent graves (wombs) that were created for the sounds of life. I give life; you destroy life. Life will no longer be given for you to destroy. Sorrow will be in your hearts. Anguish will be throughout the earth. Thus says the Lord God Almighty.

81

5-22-91 THE GLORIOUS KING RULES VICTORIOUS IN HIS CREATION

Say in the name of the Lord God: My time is upon you. Pray with fervent hearts, for the hour is at hand when the Son of the Eternal Father acts in the fullness of time to reclaim the kingdom of the most high God. The majestic King comes in splendor and glory. All eyes will see the coming of the King of Glory. I come to rule the earth with justice. My reign endures forever. The bridegroom comes. Prepare the celebration of His coming. Make ready! The day quickly approaches when the forces of evil will bow to the mighty God whose power they cannot withstand. The glorious King rules victorious in His creation. Ye loyal followers of the royal priest, ye humble servants of the Lord God, know that your hour is at hand. You shall come into your inheritance in the kingdom I have prepared for you. Be ready for the joyous celebration. The heavenly host proclaims the return of the Lord God, Jesus Christ. All is in readiness. Do not delay your preparation. The power of the Most High lifts you and carries you into the eternal kingdom. Have no fear, My loyal ones. Fear is the handmaiden of Satan. Let joy fill your hearts, for I deliver you out of fear. I deliver you out of what is to befall the followers of evil. I deliver you into the kingdom where you shall reign in the glory of the Father. In the time of trial be faithful followers of the one true God, one God in three. Only those who have prepared well for the meeting with their mighty King will know the time of His coming. Prepare well, My people. Open your hearts to My Spirit. His voice is the instrument by which you will come to recognize the signs I have prepared for you. When you see these signs you will know that the triumph of the Lord God, Jesus Christ, is at hand. Come, royal children. I call you to make ready. Clothe yourselves in the royal garments of your King. In My kingdom you shall be royal people. Thus says the Lord God.

Now say: Cleanse your souls and live in purity. Seek My forgiveness for your transgressions against My law. Sustain your souls with the Bread of Life. Pray in earnest and with hearts open to the Spirit. Hearken to My Word. Follow the instructions I give you through My servant. Prepare your hearts to receive the words I give you in the Spirit of the one God. Prepare, I say, for catastrophic events are soon to fall upon the earth. I, the Lord God, have spoken.

Now say, go with joyful and peaceful hearts to make ready for My coming. I have spoken. That is all.

5-30-91 HAVE MERCY ON YOUR LOVING GOD

Say in My name, say to My people: My heart groans in agony and My voice cries out in loud lamentation. The sins of the world grow more numerous. I am weighed down under a cross made heavier and heavier by the terrible weight of man's increasing sins. My soul cries out in anguish for mercy — have mercy on your loving God. Relieve My suffering; sin no more. My tears fall in bitter sorrow, for I see the multitudes who reject My agony of salvation. My suffering is for naught; it is despised and rejected. It is meaningless in the hearts of those who refuse redemption. So many are they, so many. I grieve for My lost children. The pain of My grief for each child lost seers My heart with red hot flames of agony. My suffering is as deep as My love. Have pity on Me, My children. Holy is the Lord God. Hear Me crying for you, My lost children. Use My tears to wash away your iniquity. Come to My cross and witness the immensity of My suffering. Place your hands on My quivering body. Feel My life being poured out for you. Bring Me the comfort of your love for Me. I am alone and abandoned. Console your suffering God and return to His love. My torment is great. Help Me, My children, help ease My suffering. Come to Me. I wish your consoling presence. I wish to hear your gentle voices raised in prayers of thanksgiving and alleluias. Give praise to the Almighty God for what He has accomplished for your salvation. Rejoice and accept the call to salvation. Accept the glorious triumph. Accept the cross. I, the Lord God, have spoken. Thus says the Lord God.

Now say: Accept the infinite love poured out for you on the cross. Love as My suffering teaches you to love. Love unto death. Let love live in your hearts. Let love console your neighbor in need. Let all your actions flow from love, the love that is your God. Do not scorn My love, but pursue it through the power of the Spirit and the care of the Mother. I am love. I love you. The Lord your God has spoken. Thus says the Lord God.

6-8-91   **HONOR MY SACRED HEART**

I, the Lord God of power and might say, in My name say to My people: My heart beats in measured time the beginning of the end. Each beat of My heart counts the minutes now remaining until the coming of the Lord God in power and majesty. The risen God triumphant ascends to claim the throne of the kingdom. The risen, glorified, Jesus the Christ reigns upon the mighty seat of justice. The holy God immortal who is, was, and ever will be, restores the kingdom made desolate by fallen creatures. The power and the glory of the Almighty living God transforms the darkness of sin and evil and restores the grandeur of the light of truth. The beams of light that emanate from the beats of My heart dispel the darkness. Mercy flows out like rivers of water upon the parched land. The heart of your loving God sends forth fountains of purifying love. The rhythm of the universe is sustained by the rhythm of My beating heart. In My heart you will find your sustenance. In My heart will you find rest and repose. In My heart lies justice and mercy. My heart opens to receive its repentant creatures. My heart was pierced to set free the blood poured out for your salvation.

Now say: Honor My Sacred Heart with fervent devotion. When the hour is at hand for your deliverance, come to My Sacred Heart. I will wash you clean in the blood of My agony and set you free in the beam of My mercy. Thus says the Lord God.

Now say: The time of your deliverance is at hand. The time for the triumph of My merciful heart is upon you. The time for the coming of the Lord God Almighty is imminent. I am the Lord God Almighty. As I say, so shall it be. Thus says the Lord God.

6-18-91 I AM PREPARING YOU

. . . Now say to My people: I am preparing you for that which is soon to occur. Take heed of My instructions. Be reconciled with your God. You know not when or where the power of the Almighty God will come upon you. The signs that are soon to appear in the heavens and on the earth are given to warn you that I am about to act according to the promises I have given through the words of My resplendent Mother. When the time approaches for these yet unrevealed events, look to the heavens, for the Father will place His mark for you to see in the Eastern sky. Be forewarned that the Evil One will perform many prodigies in the heavens. Do not be deceived by these false wonders. The Spirit will open your eyes to My sign, and you will know that the hour is at hand when I shall restore My kingdom. Come to My Spirit. Only Those open to His gifts will know what is of Me. Be constantly on the alert so that you are not deceived by the Evil One. Do not be among the many who do not know the sign of their Almighty God. I tell you there will be many unusual wonders throughout the universe. They are not of Me. I have spoken. Thus says the Lord God.

Now say: Many are called to speak in My name. Heed the words I give them. I do not deceive My own as does the father of lies. I have spoken. Thus says the Lord God.

85

I wish to speak. Say in My name, thus says the Lord God of heaven and earth: *I pronounce My judgment.* I act upon those who defile what is holy. I, the Lord God, know what evil is planned in the minds of sinful creatures. All that is holy is attacked in the blasphemies that stream from the obscene tongues of those who revile the name of the Lord God. They act in utter contempt of all that brings honor and glory to the mighty Savior. They cannot now recognize the need of their Almighty God to act in justice because of what they have wrought by their slanderous tongues. They proclaim My death: I say to you, I exist. They deny My divinity: I say to you, I am divine and human. They say I have forgotten My creation: I say to you I do not abandon what I created. I act in My creation in time and in space to bring it to fulfillment in the promise of My kingdom. They say that what is evil is part of My nature: I say to you, no evil comes from Me. I created you in love; I sustain you in love, My love is your salvation. *Evil is the result of mankind's willful disobedience to My commands of love and faith in My saving grace. I say to you, you confuse evil with suffering. Evil is the abandonment of My commands by hearts closed to remorse or the voice of conscience. Suffering is the expiation of evil by hearts united in love to the sacrifice in suffering of the Lord God.* They say it was not I who died on the cross: I say to you, they are liars. The account of My death and rising was told by those who witnessed them. As they say, so it was. They say I am an imposter: I say to you, I am the promised of the Father, born of The Woman, He who comes in power and glory and majesty. *I Am Who Am.* Thus says the Lord God. That is all.

Now say in My name: Wherever I am there is peace. Say to My people, I call you to peace. In the depths of My heart is your peace. My heart enfolds you in flames of purifying love. Feel My love flow over you. Feel My love melt your frozen hearts. Let Me come to you like the warmth of the sun that heats the soil frozen in the harsh coldness of the winter. Open your hearts like the opening buds of spring. Burst forth in full bloom in the shower of graces that I let fall like the water that nourishes the earth. Reap the harvest of My love for you. Become the ripe fruits that fill the storehouses of the heavenly kingdom.

My dear children, grow in My love. Become as the flowers of the fields. Let the seeds of My love scatter in the wind. Be My seeds of love. Sow My love to all you encounter. Pray that they may take root in souls frozen in sin and ignorance. I wish to save all My creatures. Call on the giver of life to restore the life of the Spirit quiescent in so many hearts. Let My Spirit refresh your parched souls. From the seeds of My love for you bring forth the fruits of the Spirit. Let My peace reign in your hearts, and peace will flow throughout the earth like the water that brings forth new growth.

I call you all My children. There is not one who is not My child; not one who is not nourished and sustained by Me. Will you not come out of the desert where nothing flourishes, where there is no relief from the scorching sun and the winds that blow at will? Will you not come to the well and restore your arid souls? Come to Me! I am the life-giving water. I bring you the refreshing power of love. I open your hearts to peace. Will you not be the fruits of the vine? I am the vine. Let the harvest be abundant. Thus says the Lord your God . . . I have spoken. That is all.

Say to My people, say in My name: Hear, oh people, the voice of your God. I call you to repentance. Cleanse your souls in the fire of My Divine Love. Through the power of My Spirit approach the font of mercy. *Do not be afraid.* I, the Lord God say to you, your sins are grievous. You hear not the commands I have given to mankind. You hear not My command to love. You hear not the voice of the Mother warning you of the power of the Evil One. You hear not My call to conversion. You hear only the clamoring voices of power and greed, the voices of pride and self-love, the voices of strife and warfare. You cannot hear My call to salvation in the din of worldly affairs. I say to you:

✝ **Repent your many sins.** Make reparation to the God of love who grants you mercy and pardon.

✝ **Reform your lives.** Put aside your evil inclinations. Refuse to be subject to the temptations of the Evil One.

✝ **Confess your sins.** Let the light of My Spirit once again remove the darkness in your souls stained black by your evil deeds.

Come, My children, restore the purity of your souls washed clean in the sacrament of love and mercy. Do not fear to come to Me in the presence of My holy priests, for the time of mercy is soon to be withdrawn for those who refuse My call to repentance. Many are they who will refuse. They shall suffer eternal damnation. Come, My children, refuse not the mercy of the Lord your God. Make yourselves ready to greet the Lord God Almighty when He comes in power and majesty to restore the kingdom. Heed My call, My children. Your time is short. Thus says the Lord your God. That is all . . .

7-12-91   I SPEAK TO YOU THROUGH MY LITTLE CHILD

. . . I am the Lord God who speaks to you. I speak to you through the words I give My little child. She is to give you My words. Now she is called to spread My words to all My children. Many will reject My words, but those who trust in them will be brought safely out of the darkness and into the light of My kingdom. Support your sister in her trials; they will be many. Love each other as I love you. I have spoken. Thus says the Lord God. That is all.

7-23-91   I COME!

Now say in My name, say to My people: The hour of the coming of the Lord God is at hand. I say to you — I come! Many are they who scoff at what is imminent. Say to them: The Lord God does not delay His coming. Now is the time foretold in scripture, the time of the mighty battle between the Woman and the Serpent. Now is the time of reparation. The struggle intensifies. *The battle lines are drawn. On one side stand the forces of evil; on the other the mighty power of the living God given to those gathered under the protection of the Woman Clothed in the Sun. The power of these My faithful ones, armed with the beads of the rosary, form a mighty fortress against the wiles and the snares of the Evil One. Throughout the earth the light of the Woman shines forth to guide you in the battle, strengthen you before My enemies, and is the beacon that leads you safely through the chaos.* The light of the Woman is joined to the light of her Son. In both together, by the power of the Spirit, will you be brought forth in triumph from the abyss. I am flesh of her flesh; she is spirit of My Spirit. We are one in Spirit and flesh.

Now say: Those who reject the role of the Woman reject also the role of the Son. The one who honors her honors Me. Together, in obedience to the will of the Father, do we work to restore His creation to the kingdom. She brings you to My presence. Each and every one she brings before Me receives My mercy and is made clean in the blood of salvation. Each enters into My Sacred Heart. Each is carried to the Father and placed in His loving arms. She calls each and every soul to come to salvation. I tell you: Only a few remain who will respond to her call. When the last one has been restored will I then come in power and glory to bring My justice upon the world.

The time for My mercy is at an end. The work of the Woman is complete. *I come!* Thus says the Lord God. That is all.

7-25-91 THE TIME IS URGENT

I wish to speak. Say in My name: I warn you, My people, of the gravity of the impending warning which is about to be unleashed against unsuspecting mankind. The ferocity of the evil attack will be unmatched in all of history. A portion of the earth will perish. I say to you: *Heed My warning! Do not delay. Come to My mercy. The time is urgent.* This event will be a scourge in all the earth. No area will be spared. All you peoples of the earth, hear what I say to you. You have not heard Me calling you to come to My mercy. You refuse to see the signs I have placed before you. You close your minds to My truth of salvation. You refuse all that I have offered you in love and mercy. Now My justice descends upon you. Now will I permit the consequences which you choose.

Now say: Save yourself in My mercy. So many times have I called you; so many times have you refused to come. I, the Lord God, must act with justice in response to those who suffer the agonies inflicted upon them by the injustices of the Evil One. I say to you: *I act now to save My own. This time is urgent for My chosen ones.* Pray that you will not falter. Walk steadily toward Me through every difficulty.

Now say: I am the Lord God of mercy and justice. I come in power and glory. I it is who commands all of creation. I it is who sits in judgment against the actions of My creatures. I alone am God Almighty. You Evil Ones will come to know Me in all My power. Rue the day you were born into evil.

Now say to My faithful ones: Do not fear the power of the Lord God. My power is also the power of love. My love for you redeems you out of the darkness and terror of My justice and sustains you in the trial. Prepare as I have told you; you will have nothing to fear. Follow My chosen ones. I prepare them to lead you through these evil times. Hear what I tell you. Hear Me the Lord God. Thus says the Lord your God. That is all.

7-26-91 PERSONAL MESSAGE

(. . . What is to come can only be mitigated by prayers and sacrifice. . . The time is very urgent. Pray constantly. Come before Me and beg My mercy for all who dwell on the earth . . .).

7-26-91 THOSE OF YOU WHO REMAIN TO THE END I PROTECT IN A SPECIAL WAY

Say in My name, say in He name of the Lord God: When the power of evil runs rampant throughout the earth I, the Lord God, seek out the remnant and shelter it within the power of My Divine Love. Those of you who remain to the end I protect in a special way. *From this remnant I call forth the Spirit of rebirth to bring forth a new creation of purity and peace. You are given the task of renewing the earth by the power of the Spirit. Your seed will repopulate the kingdom of the Son. You are worthy stewards of the new creation. Your suffering in the trial prepares you for the glorious reign of the triumphant King.* You serve well He who calls you into the restored Eden. Your

91

generations will be holy and upright. You shall see the face of God. You shall live in peace all the days of your life. No memory of the trial will remain, and you shall know the loving presence of your King and Savior in your midst. You shall walk hand-in-hand with the saints, and all your days will be serene. Your hearts will be filled with the fullness of My love, and all creation will live in harmony with its mighty King. Your days will know no strife. All is ordered by My hand. When the days allotted to you are ended, you will enter into the kingdom of the Father — into the special place He has prepared for you alone, for you the most faithful of all His faithful ones. Know that what I tell you through My instrument is truth. Thus says the Lord God. That is all.

7-27-91 PRAY FOR THE SALVATION OF SOULS

Be silent now, I wish to speak. Say in My name, say to My people: Pray for the salvation of souls. So many will enter into eternity in the state of grievous sin. I implore you, My holy people, to offer sacrifices for these who do not know My merciful love. Bring to Me your offerings for your brothers and sisters. So many are lost. So many will not be saved. Help Me, My holy people, for My heart grieves for each soul lost to the power of the Evil One. The darkness increases; they cannot find the way to light. My truth is distorted and rejected. *Man's great folly is to reject His God who creates and sustains him!* Only in Me is life and salvation. All else is death and damnation. Holy is the Lord God of Hosts. I have spoken. Thus says the Lord God.

Now Say: *I repeat — This time is urgent.* The last one is called. Now begins the end of ends. Only a few will remain to serve the Lord God. Glory and praise to the Lord God. That is all. Thus says the Lord God. Pray, My child. Pray much.

I ASK YOU TO PRAY SERIOUSLY THE ROSARY BEFORE MY IMAGE

Now say in My name: Holy is the Lord God. Let holiness permeate your being. With your rosaries in hand approach in humility the Holy of Holies. I ask you to pray seriously the rosary before My image.

In the mysteries of your Mother see her absolute obedience and trust in the Father who chose her from all generations as a perfect instrument in His plan of salvation. One woman — the Woman — she who defeats the Evil One and His works. See the loveliness of her spirit serene amid the trials and incomprehensible suffering she endured as the Handmaid of the Lord God. Rejoice in her triumph and crown her with the crown of your love and loyalty. Give her the honor due one who perfectly accomplishes the will of the Father and who serves as your protectress and mediatrix. Walk with her through the scenes of My life. Experience the hardships she endured; suffer with her at the foot of My cross; endure with her the agony of the Mother for her child so grievously tortured at the hands of despots and sinners. Come deeply into her suffering. Let your love bring comfort to her sorrowing heart. Thus says the Lord God.

Now say: In the mysteries of your brother Jesus understand His complete obedience and trust in His holy Mother and earthly father. See the serenity of His Spirit in the honor He bestows on His earthly parents. See the serenity of His Spirit in His obedience to His heavenly Father. Walk with Him on the path of His agony. Enter into His excruciating suffering. Love Him! Help Him bear the burden He carries for the sins of mankind. Love Him as He loves you.

Come to the glorious reward that awaits you in the triumph of your Mother and Brother. In the mysteries of the triumphant and resplendent glorified Woman and her Son, see what is promised by the Father for each soul who walks in their presence the path they walked to prepare for you the way to eternal life.

Pray each prayer and recognize in them the truth of your faith in the One, Holy, and Apostolic Church of Jesus Christ. Pray then as your Mother asks. Thus says the Lord God. That is all.

7-28-91 MEDITATION FOR THE SORROWFUL MYSTERIES OF THE ROSARY

✝ The Agony in the Garden —
Mankind now enters into its passion in reparation for its sins.

✝ The Scourging of Jesus at the Pillar —
Mankind suffers the scourge of its passion in just retribution for its sins.

✝ The Crowning of Jesus with Thorns —
The thorns of intellectualism bring mankind to the depths of its own helplessness.

✝ The Carrying of the Cross —
Mankind now carries the burden for its sins.

✝ The Crucifixion —
Mankind is crucified on the cross of its own sins.

7-29-91 I WILL PERMIT THE DEVASTATION OF A LARGE AREA OF THE EARTH

Now, My child, I speak to you My words of judgment. Thus shall it be: Say in My name, say to My people: I will permit the devastation of a large area of the earth. I will permit the winds of the air, the waters of the sea, and fires below the earth to converge upon the face of the earth. One country will cease to exist. Its

94

inhabitants will be swallowed in the roaring seas and raging fires. A mountain will be levelled to a flat plain. No sign of life will remain. *The peoples of the earth will tremble in fear and bewilderment before the awesome might of the forces of nature which obey the commands of their Creator. The winds will move over the whole earth. The rain shall fall in torrents until the seas move over the land.* Black clouds will move through the air and large areas of the earth will be in darkness. Buildings will fall and many will perish beneath them. Humans will devour humans for sustenance. Disease and starvation will claim many lives. When the furies of nature have subsided the numbers of dead will be countless; the landscape of the earth will be forever changed. No creature of reason and intellect will be able to account for what has befallen the earth. Unbelievers will despair and curse what they have rejected.

Believers will be sustained by the mighty power of God Almighty. Carry with you at all times your blessed candles and the armor of the rosary. Keep with you the water of baptism. Provide food and drink for yourself and your families. Protect your homes with My image. Bless your homes with holy water. Support your neighbors in need. *Pray!* I, the Lord God, have spoken. *And still they will not turn aside from their evil deeds.* Thus says the Lord God. That is all. (Refer to message of 8-19-91).

7-30-91 LEARN FROM MY PEOPLE OF OLD

It has been a difficult day for you, My child, but now I wish to speak. Say in My name, say to My people: The Spirit of God is upon My servant. Now hear what I say to you in the words I give her. Say thus:

95

"Oh Spirit of the mighty God, fill our hearts with joy. Let our throats proclaim that Jesus Christ is Lord. Oh Spirit of the living God, we call on you to open our hearts to the Word. We pray, oh Spirit of love, for love to transform us. May we accept, as little children, the gentle touch of the hand of the Father upon our fevered brows. Oh kindly Spirit of the Lord God, favor us with an abundance of your gifts that we may serve you and our neighbors for your greater glory. Amen."

Now say: On the morrow after the fourth day look for My sign in the Eastern sky. It is My pledge to My faithful ones that I am their God and they are My people. As in the times of old, My covenant is with those who call Me Abba, Father. *I go before you as a beacon of light. Look for My light and follow where I lead you. Do not be concerned for your daily necessities. I will provide for your needs during the great trial. Learn from My people of old whom I sustained in the desert. You also will I sustain.* Remain faithful to My commands and I, your God, will bring you safely into the kingdom of the Promised One. Follow with confidence those who walk in My light before you. I say to you, I am your God and you are My people chosen for the kingdom of My Son. With you is fulfilled the covenant which I made with the Fathers of old. Now is accomplished what I promised for all generations until the end of time. Thus says the Lord God. That is all.

8-7-91   I DO NOT REVOKE MY JUDGMENT

Now say in My name: The Lord God speaks. In the fullness of time all will be accomplished as I have revealed to those who speak in My name. *I have warned you.* Take heed of My warnings. Mankind is a stubborn species. It chooses to believe only what it wants to believe. This is self-deception. I call you repeatedly to prayer and conversion. I call again. Hear Me, My people, the trial will be severe. Grow strong in My love. Let My peace fill your hearts.

Respond as joyous people secure in the love of their God who cares for them. Your joy must be a light for those who suffer. Let your joy pour forth in hymns of praise and thanksgiving. The Lord God Almighty knows your every need. Trust in My care for you.

Now say: Tell My people to **pray unceasingly.** Tell them to **open their hearts to the power of My Spirit.** Tell them I call each one; let them hear My call and respond. Tell them **I do not delay My judgment. I repeat — prepare well My people, for you know not the hour or the day when the hand of the Father will smite sinful mankind. I do not revoke My judgment!** . . . Thus says the Lord God. That is all.

8-10-91   YOU DO NOT PRAY ENOUGH

Now say in My name, say to My people: My dear ones, why do you fret so? I, the Lord God, bring you peace and joy. How is it that My words bring unrest to your hearts? My words are words of peace; they are words of love; they are words of hope and consolation, for I have told you I do not abandon My own.

Now say: I give you My peace. Be at peace My children. I call you to increase your sacrifices for the salvation of souls. I, your God, ask you to pray for the most destitute of My children. Pray for the conversion of hardened hearts. Pray to hear the voice of My Spirit. I tell you, you do not pray enough. I tell you, your prayers are only on your tongues; they do not come from your hearts. They are spoken in haste without thought. I desire that you come to Me as you would to your most beloved one. Embrace Me in your meditations. Pray with love in your hearts. Offer Hossanahs to the mighty one of heaven and earth. Let Me speak My words of love to you. Can you not spend one hour (a day) with Me? Do not sleep as My disciples did. **The decisive hours are upon you. The struggle for souls intensifies.** I hear your prayers in the struggle. Pray as I have asked. Fortify

97

your souls with fervent prayer. *Do not be deceived — there is always the calm that precedes the storm. I call you urgently to prepare well, for the storm is fast approaching.*

Pray for sinners; pray for yourselves. Pray for all those in need. Pray for those who suffer at the hands of corrupt and evil men. Pray for those who will die suddenly and without warning. Pray for My mercy. *Pray, My people, pray!* I, the Lord God have spoken. Thus says the Lord God. That is all.

8-11-91 WHAT IS TO BE WILL BE

Write My words. Now say in My name, in My name will you say to My people: What is to be will be. Do not doubt that I, the Lord God, act with justice in a world suffering its final assault permitted to the Evil One. His days are numbered. Believe Me when I say to you— be prepared to withstand His vicious persecution. Grow strong in your faith in Me. Pray to My Spirit that you may not falter before the force of His assault. Fortify your souls with the Food of Life; it is the food of everlasting life. *Be not concerned about what is to come.* Receive My peace into your hearts. I am leading you. I provide for your every need. Trust Me; My people, trust that the Lord your God speaks to you words of warning, words of love, words of encouragement. Do not lose heart within the whirlwind of evil deeds that blows stronger and stronger around you. Come to Me who am within the center of the storm. There you will find your refuge.

I, the Lord God, speak now in warning. Be alert, My people, to the dangers that surround you. *Do not be deceived by those who seek a new world order. This is the plan of the Evil One. The promise of a new order created by the hands of man is doomed to fail.* It is an illusion of minds seduced once again by the Serpent — "You will be as gods". Beware, My people, that you do not become unwitting victims of this falsehood. Be constantly on guard that you be

98

not lured by the deceptions and the distortions of My truth so readily accepted by those who seek a new truth. *I am truth!* There is no other but Me. I, the Lord God, have spoken. Thus says the Lord God. That is all.

8-12-91 LET THE JUDGMENT COMMENCE

Let the judgment commence. I, the Lord God, speak. Say in My name, say to My people: I am the Lord God. Now it begins. Thus says the Lord God. That is all.

Now, My child, I wish to say: Now all who have heard these words will come to know that I speak to you My words of truth. Who have heard and believed will walk without fear through the turmoil. I bless them with My blessings and grant them My peace. Know, My child, that this is but the beginning of the woes to be visited upon the earth.

Now say: What is to come is the chastisement of sinful and disobedient creatures. For times and more times have I shown My mercy upon those who continue to ignore My call to love. So many times have I called them back to My fold. So many times have I wept for these creatures who refuse to turn to Me and accept Me as their God. So many times, so many times. Who is there who can save these souls, if not I? There is no one else but Me. They turn away from Me; they are lost. They defile what is pure and holy. If they continue, they will destroy even My remnant. This I do not permit. Henceforth, will I act to safeguard My own. My judgment I bring against you unrepentant ones. You creatures of the night will forever be lost to My light. You have chosen; it is granted to you.

Now say to My faithful ones: I call you to a renewed effort in prayer and sacrifices. I call you to a strong and unwavering trust in My care for you. Do not lose heart in the little trials I send you. Use them to prepare for the great time of trial when you will be sorely tried. How will you endure if you are so easily troubled by what I give you in small meter? My people, prepare in earnest, for I tell you your frail human minds cannot begin to know what My justice will bring. Thus says the Lord God.

Thank you My child. Prepare now for the tribulation of the end time. I, the Lord God have spoken. That is all.

8-15-91 **LET YOUR TONGUES PROCLAIM THE GLORIOUS MOTHER**

My dear child, I wish to speak. On this day when you honor My Mother in a special way, say in My name: I rain down special graces in abundance to those who hold My Mother tenderly in their hearts. She is My most beautiful Virgin Mother. Let your tongues proclaim the glorious Mother. As she consoles you in your times of need, so now your Mother needs you to bring her comfort as she engages the Evil One in the battle for souls. Come to Me, My children. Each one who comes to Me brings joy to her sorrowful heart. Each one saved from the fires of hell is a triumph of her Immaculate Heart. Each prayer you pray for one of your lost brothers or sisters is her weapon that opens My heart of mercy. You must pray very much, My children, that I will continue to give My ear to the pleas of your Mother who sees the depth of My agony which I bear for your sins. My suffering is her suffering. Let your love for our Mother and your prayers for your brethren bring solace to her who suffers so greatly for those who do not know her Son. My dear children, enfold your Mother in your loving embrace. Speak to her words of love and comfort. Honor your Mother. Care for her in her dire need; respond to her call. Do not be one of her lost children who brings so much pain to her heart filled to overflowing with love for you. Each is her precious child. Comfort your Mother, My children — come to Me. Thus says the Lord God.

(Now I wish to say, make many sacrifices, My child. So many grieve your Mother's heart. Offer your sacrifices for those especially who do not honor their glorious Mother, Queen of heaven and earth).

8-19-91 THESE ARE SIGNS OF YOUR TIME

In My name say to My people: The forces of nature bring destruction upon the face of the earth. The ferocity of these forces are increasing in strength. See them as My sign that your time is short. There is severe devastation and suffering in many areas of the earth. What is being wrought upon the earth is a warning for all people — I am coming in all My power to reclaim My kingdom. *These are signs of your time.* Trust in the words I give My little child. *You are called to a firm faith and trust in My care for you. Soon, the upheavals in nature will converge in a single mighty event as I have foretold. You know not when or where.*

Now say: Trust in Me, My people. I cleanse your earth and prepare it for My coming. Those who have ears take heed. What is to be will be.

I give the command — *Commence the judgment.* So it begins. Thus says the Lord God, He who commands what He has formed and sustains. So shall it be. That is all.

(*Note*: Today Gorbachev was overthrown by hard-line Communists in the USSR and returned to power on 8-21-91.)

8-23-91 PRAY TO ME THROUGH THE IMMACULATE MOTHER

I wish to speak . . . Now say in My name: Invoke the hallowed name of the Lord God Almighty in supplication in this time of great trial. Pray that the number of days allotted for the time of judgment will be shortened. Many of My elect will lose heart. My dear children, you must pray for perseverance.

Remember that I uphold you in the trial. Pray that you will not waiver from the path on which I am leading you. It is lighted by My chosen ones. They are My light in the darkness . . .

Now say: Peace to My people. I greet you now with words of preparation for what is about to befall the earth. Grow strong in My love. Increase your prayers to My merciful heart. I am merciful to those who seek My mercy. Gird yourself with the armor of many rosaries. Pray to Me through the Immaculate Mother many prayers with your whole heart, and mind, and soul. Do not be timid in your prayers. Pray boldly with perseverance. Pray with loud voices and with quiet hearts. Pray with confidence. Pray that I do not close My ears to the intercession of the Mother on behalf of her sinful children. Turn away from sin; turn to prayer and sacrifice. Many (prayers and sacrifices) are needed for the salvation of souls, including your own.

Be not afraid, My people. There is no fear where I am. I am with those who respond to My call. Hear and respond, My children. You will find peace amidst the turmoil, courage to endure the trial, and strength to remain true to Me even in the darkest hours.
. . . Thus says the Lord God. That is all.

8-27-91 PRAY SERIOUSLY, MY CHILDREN

Say in My name, in My name say to My people: I have called you, dear people of My heart, to reparation and prayer. I call you now for sacrifices on behalf of those who bring shame to My Church. These are not My faithful ones. They sin before the eyes of the world and mock what is sacred and holy. Many follow them into sin and perdition. Their souls are in grave danger. I call you to pray for these lost children. Place your prayers at the feet of My Mother. You are her children. Come before her as little children to plead for your lost brothers and sisters. Pray thus:

"Dear Mother of My heart, I come before you with trust that you will hear your child. I offer you My heart with love for those of My brethren who do not love and honor what is sacred and holy. Open your compassionate heart to My pleas on their behalf. Grant them the grace of conversion. Touch their hearts with your motherly love. I, your humble child, ask this for the salvation of souls and the greater glory of God. Amen."

Now say: I do not close My ears to the pleas of My faithful ones when they come before their Holy Mother. Always she brings your prayers to Me. Always I hear her. Always I answer those who pray. *Pray seriously, My children. Your Mother needs your prayers in her struggle to win back souls out of the clutches of the Evil One. You can bring her many souls with your prayers and offerings.* Respond faithfully to her need. Help her in her efforts to bring many souls to Me. She needs your constancy, she needs your firm commitment in the battle against evil, she needs the love of her children. I call you to respond with hearts open to your Mother. I, the Lord God call you. Thus says the Lord God. That is all.

8-29-91 **THEIR FAITH IS BUT A DYING EMBER**

Now say in My name: I speak this day to warn you that so many are lukewarm in their response to Me and to My dear Mother. There is no fire in their hearts. There is no zeal in their souls. Their faith is but a dying ember. Speak to them My words of love. I desire their unreserved commitment to conversion of heart and reparation for their sins. My graces can fan even dying embers into renewed flames of the gifts of My Spirit. Pray that My Spirit of love will open their hearts. . . Thus says the Lord your God. That is all.

9-5-91 **PERSONAL MESSAGE**

(My child, I wish to speak to you. Pray 15 decades of My Mother's rosary every day. Her heart grieves for her beloved Jugoslavia . . .).

103

I wish to speak. In My name say to My people: The hour is at hand. I speak now to prepare you now to withstand those forces of evil that bring upon mankind the agony of its purification. I tell you now what is your fate.

The Evil One now embarks upon His plan to subjugate all the nations of the earth. *Be thou warned of His plan to make himself the emperor of all nations and all peoples. His peace is a false peace. His minions create havoc and turmoil, doubt and confusion. The leaders of the world are puppets in His scheme of world domination.* His name is Anathema. His presence is death. Know that His hour is at hand. He begins now His final assault. From the holy place does He begin the final conflagration. Keep alive the faith. He desecrates My holy tabernacles. He spills the blood of My holy ones. He sustains himself on the blood of the martyrs. He violates what is pure and chaste; he ravishes the maiden; He crucifies without mercy the undefiled. He is the carnivorous beast who feeds on the flesh of His enemies. I tell you He is the beast of the Apocalypse.

Now say: I the Lord God speak. I say to you sinful creatures, your sins are blacker than ebony. The whole earth is black with the abomination of your sins. You are a scourge, a vile stream of filth that covers the whole of the earth and all that it holds. You are the sepulchers of the walking dead. You are evil personified. I can no longer permit this desecration to continue. Now I act. Now I let fall My arm. Now is My judgment come. You creatures of the earth wail and weep but My ways are just. Suffer now My justice. You reap what your sins have wrought. I, the Lord God have spoken. Thus I say; thus shall it be. That is all.

Now say: I do not forsake My own. Be strong and faithful followers of the Lord God, Jesus Christ. The

crosses you bear in My name are your salvation. I call
you to pick up your cross and come follow Me. Come,
My loyal and faithful ones, I the Lord God call you.
Now are you called, My brothers and sisters, to put on
the yoke of the Lord your God. Thus says the Lord
God, the God of justice and mercy. That is all.

**9-21-91 TAKE UPON YOURSELVES VOLUNTARY ACTS OF
REPARATION**

Now I wish to speak, My child. Say in the name of the
Lord your God: praise to the Lord God on high. Sing
praises to the holy God.

Now say: Of My chosen ones, I ask you to offer many
sacrifices in reparation for your many sins that so
offend your God of hope and mercy. Offer many
sacrifices for those who sin without remorse. Offer
sacrifices for those who are redeemed in the purifying
suffering of purgatory. *Take upon yourselves
voluntary acts of reparation. Each day offer to
the Father an act of self-denial. Come before Me
on bended knee and seek My forgiveness and
mercy on a world on the brink of self-destruction.
Do not scorn even the smallest offering. Each act
of expiation performed with love has merit before
the justice of the Lord your God.* Presumption is a
grievous fault that denies My justice. My mercy I give
to those who repent of their sins and come before Me
with a sincere promise of conversion. They receive My
graces. My hands lift them, My heart receives them.
They grow in My love. They know My peace. They
grow strong by the power of My saving graces. Do
thou then become souls of reparation. Make amends
to the Almighty God. Open the doors of mercy for
those closed to My mercy. The Father's wrath is let
loose. Many will perish because they refuse My
mercy. Pray in My name that these, the lost ones, will
open themselves to My graces. I ask this of you, My
dear children. The Lord God asks this of you. This is
not such a difficult task I ask of you. Many can be
opened to My saving grace. Hear and respond My

dear ones.

Now say, My peace I give you. I bless you with My blessings. I, the Lord God of justice and mercy, have spoken. Thus says the Lord God. That is all.

9-23-91 WHEN ALL SEEMS LOST WILL I COME IN POWER AND GLORY

I wish to speak. In My name say: Hail to the Almighty God. Your children await your coming.

Now say: I, the God of power and might, recall the Queen of Peace to the heavenly realm. Now the false peace of the Evil One descends upon the earth. Prideful men seek to displace the hand of God in the events of human creatures. They do not see that they are instruments of Satan. If they know not Me, neither do they know My adversary. They walk blindly upon the path of My justice. My poor deluded creatures, everywhere is My power evident; they see it not. Everywhere is My love manifest; they do not recognize it. They cannot know Me if they reject the signs of My presence in My creation. They are so filled with themselves they can see nothing but themselves. These creatures command vast armies and peoples. *Terror and suffering is the lot of their victims. Terror and suffering are the fruits of the Evil One. Where He is there is death, destruction, lies and deceit. Let all with eyes to see recognize the signs of the Evil One. Pray that your eyes may see the signs of this perilous time.*

Say to My people: All is in readiness for the coming of the Lord God in power and majesty. *When there seems no hope, will I come. When all seems lost, will I come in power and glory to lift you out of the earthly hell. What a glorious people you are who persevere; what a glorious triumph awaits you.*

Now say: The Lord God speaks. I the Lord God tell you what is to come. Be prudent, My people, and attend to the words I give My instrument. I love you.

106

I act to save My own. Thus says the Lord God. That is all.

9-25-91 THE SPIRIT OF RENEWAL IS COME

. . . Now say to My people: The Spirit of renewal is come. By the power of the eternal Trinity I act through the children of the Mother whom she has called. Now is the triumph of her holy people manifest. Now do they participate as instruments of the Spirit to renew the kingdom of the lost. Recognize the signs of the Spirit in the darkness. I come again like a mighty wind. All hail the mighty God. Thus say I, the Spirit of the living god, one God eternal. That is all

---

9-26-91 RENEW YOURSELVES . . . IN THE FIRE OF DIVINE LOVE

Yes, child, I wish to speak. Say in My name: The Lord God calls you to a sincere effort of conversion of heart. The struggle for souls is fierce. Satan has no power over those souls who have opened their hearts to My love. Sincere conversion is the domain of the Spirit. He who is open to the Spirit hears the voice of the Lord God cry out . . . *renew yourselves, My children, in the fire of divine love*. Come to Me with hearts open to My saving graces. In My Spirit do you know the power of My love for you. You are steeped in the fragrance of holiness. Your eyes are opened to the being of the Lord your God. The power of the Spirit breathes into your soul and moves it to respond to the love of its Creator. From gentle stirrings the awakened soul rushes to embrace the life—giving streams of redemption that flow from the merciful heart of its Redeemer. It responds joyfully with songs of praise and hossanahs, for it knows the loving mercy of its Creator.

Come, My people. Let joy fill your souls. Sing out the mighty anthem — Jesus Christ is Lord. Thus says the Lord God. That is all.

107

I wish to speak. Say in My name, say to My people: Where justice reigns is My kingdom. All are created equal in My image. Why do you create divisions among yourselves? Are you not all My children? I am the Father of all. All are one in Me. My dear children, the Father cares for each one. He does not cause divisions among you. Each one is His creation. Each one He holds tenderly in His heart. Each one He calls to His mercy. Each one He sustains in His love. Each one is precious to your loving God.

I say to you: When each one is united in Me there can be no divisions. I call each one to union in My heart. You are brothers and sisters united in the love of the one God. You are the one body of the one Lord and God. *Become one in love. Become one in My mercy.* Bear no animosity towards your brothers and sisters. I am the one Father of all. Turn your eyes to Me. *When you see Me, you cannot see the shortcomings of your neighbor*. When all eyes see Me, they see perfection. I the Lord God call each of you to perfection. Now say: *My dear children, strive for perfection.*

Your Lord God Almighty calls you to heal the rifts that separate you from your brothers and sisters. Look to Me and My Word. We are three but one. You are many but one in the Lord God. I call you, My children, to give your hand each to the other. With your hands clasped raise your voices and proclaim the one God, the one God and one body united in the one heart and the one Spirit. That is all. Thus says the Lord God.

10-3-91 **WITHOUT ME YOU ARE BUT HELPLESS BABES**

I wish to speak. Say in My name, say to My people: See what evil inhabits the earth. There are wars and persecutions, hatred and unforgiveness, apostasy and heresy, famine and death, cruelty and savagery. My dear people of My creation, what have you become?

You revert back to your primitive state. Do not delude yourselves into thinking that you have advanced to a new enlightened state. You advance backwards into the darkness of paganism and the worship of false gods. There is but one God, and you deny Me. I am the one God worthy of your love. There is no other but Me.

Now say: Your false gods cannot fill your emptiness. They cannot bring peace and mercy. You fill yourselves with illusions and deceptions. They are but fantasies that evaporate like the mist in the clear light of the sun. You grasp, and your hand is empty. You seek but cannot find what is hidden in the fog that clouds your minds. What you seek eludes you. You stumble blindly along always searching for what can only be found in the clear light of My truth. My light dispels the darkness. In darkness there is confusion and ignorance. In My light there is truth and serenity.

Now say: Come to My light, My children. Come to Me, My children. I am before you, not behind you. If you wish to progress, you must look forward to My light. Accept that I am here among you leading you forward to your destiny in the kingdom of the Father. Only in Me and with Me can you become the new man. Put away the old and put on the new. By the power of the Spirit clothe yourselves in the saving love that is given to you by the Father through the Son. Leave the darkness behind you. In My light you will find what you seek. In My light will you become the fulfillment of the holy, pure, and illuminated creatures you seek to be with your own power. I say to you: You have not the power if you reject Me. I, the one God, the Creator, the Redeemer, and The Spirit of love and wisdom, am the power, and the glory, and the majesty by which you become the glorified creatures you were created to be. Without Me you are but helpless babes who perish without the sustenance of their parents. Foolish people of the earth, you perish because you have rejected your parent, the One who created you, the One who sustains you, the One who brings you to eternal life. You know not your one God; you are doomed. Thus says the Lord God, the one God of heaven and earth, the one God of all created beings, your one and only God. That is all . . .

10-5-91 MAKE MANY ACTS OF PENANCE

My dear little child, I wish to speak. Say in My name, say to My people: I, your God say, I do not revoke My judgment against sinful mankind. The peoples of the earth have refused to heed My call to conversion and repentance. I, the Lord God, call you to repentance. I call you to make reparation for your sins and evil deeds. *The actions of man against man cry to heaven for vengeance. Vengeance is mine says the Lord God. My people's suffering will not go unanswered. Do you take heed, for My wrath is immense; My justice fierce. My fury cannot be contained. The cup of My mercy is empty; the cup of My justice runneth over.* You refused the cup of mercy, now you taste of the cup of justice. Repent all you who have ears to hear. Make many acts of penance — your sins offend Me mightily. Thus says the Lord God. That is all.

10-11-91 I CALL YOU URGENTLY TO REPENTANCE

Say in My name, say to My people: My dear children, I call you urgently to repentance. Forsake not My words. My dear children, I am the Spirit of the living God. I am the voice of truth in the midst of lies and deception. I act in the power of the Father to bring new life where life has succumbed to sin and evil. Through Me the life of the soul is restored. Through Me love replaces hate; the soul is moved to charity. The heart filled with love exalts in the presence of its Creator. It sings the joyous songs of praise and thanksgiving to the Almighty God of justice and mercy. It celebrates in joyous jubilation its freedom in its redemption from the darkness of the eternal pit into the light of the everlasting salvation of the Lord

God of light. Come then, children lost in the darkness, open your hearts to the Spirit of the living God. Receive the Spirit of light. Do not remain in the darkness. Renew your fidelity to the one God; Father, Son, and Spirit. Open your ears once again to the truth that I have revealed through My instruments in ages past and in the Word of the Lord God. My Word is the Word of scripture. My Word is the revealed truth of the Father given to all generations until the end of generations. The end of generations *is soon. Seek the truth of the Lord God; seek Me. Walk in the Spirit, and you will walk through the turmoil and the distress of these times with peace in your heart and the understanding of the fateful events wrought in the heavens and on the earth by the hand of the Almighty God of heaven and earth.* In My power, granted to Me by the Father, I restore the purity of creation. I act now to bring about the rebirth of creation into the glory of its Creator. I am the living Spirit of the living God, Three in One. Now is My time come. I say to you, if you possess Me, you possess the Father and the Son. You possess your salvation. Thus says the Lord God. That is all.

10-17-91 DO NOT SCORN YOUR CROSSES

I wish to speak, child. Say in My name, say to My people: Pray for the souls who have been called to their final purification.

Now say: What you suffer in your earthly life is but a grain of sand compared to the suffering of eternal damnation. The suffering of the earthly life is soon ended; the suffering of eternity never ends. The suffering of the earthly life, though seemingly excruciating, is the fire of mercy by which souls are purified for eternity in the eternal kingdom of the Father. In suffering is compassion born. In suffering is expiation made before the justice of the Father. Who seek to enter into the kingdom seek also the cross of the suffering Son. Accept your suffering with peace in your soul and joy in your heart, for you know that the hand of salvation has touched you.

Now say: Understand the blessed grace of suffering in the plan of salvation for your soul. Suffering is not to be despised but welcomed as a sign of My special favor. I suffered to prepare the way for you into the kingdom. My suffering was necessary to open the gates; your suffering is necessary to enter through the gates. You never suffer alone. I sustain you in all that you are given for your purification. Look with confidence to the Mother of Consolation, to the uplifting arm of the Lord God, to the beckoning light of glory that waits at the threshold to enfold you in the everlasting life of the eternal kingdom.

Now say: Come then, do not scorn your crosses. You carry them but a short time to gain for yourselves the endless time of eternal happiness. I the Lord God have spoken. Thus say I. That is all.

10-24-91 LOVE

. . . Now I wish to speak to My people. Say in My name: The Lord God speaks. I wish to tell you, My people, of My love for you. My love is the purity of your soul. My love is the warmth of the summer breeze that blows gently upon your bruised and broken spirits. My love falls softly like the morning dew and refreshes your tired hearts. My love flows like the clear mountain stream and fills your souls with pools of the water of life. My love flows over you like the mighty water fall and carries you to the safe harbor. My love is as deep as the sea and the breadth of the heavens. My love is the soft caress and gentle embrace of your beloved. My love is passionate; My love is unending. My love is yours always and forever. I give you My love, My dear people.

11-9-91 MEDITATION FOR THE JOYFUL MYSTERIES OF THE ROSARY

Mother Mary speaks:

✝ The Annunciation —
Announce to the world that the Lord, Jesus Christ, is coming. He comes to reclaim His kingdom. Pray for His swift return.

✝ The Visitation —
I, the Mother, the Woman of the Apocalypse, prepare the way for His coming. Pray that all mothers prepare with prayer for the coming of their offspring as did My kinswoman Elizabeth and I.

✝ The Birth of Christ —
Give praise and thanksgiving for life — for the child in the womb, for those who breathe their dying breaths, for the life of all His creatures.

✝ The Presentation of Jesus in the Temple —
Know that the children given to you come from the hand of the Father. Raise them up in the knowledge and the love of the giver of life — their Creator, their one God.

✝ The Finding of Jesus in the Temple —
As My Son went about His Father's business, so must you be obedient to the will of the Father. Do not rest until the evil of abortion is defeated. Pray the mysteries of life to bring about the end of death. Your Mother asks this of you.

11-12-91 PRAY THUS

(I wish to speak to you My little child. I, the Lord God, say to you: Increase your prayers on behalf of My suffering children. When you pray, kneel before My image. Offer your discomfort in reparation for the evil committed against all those who profess the one God of heaven and earth. Pray thus:
✝ Offer each sacrifice of My beloved Son for those suffering persecution for My name's sake.

✝ At the consecration of the holy sacrifice, offer My

113

body and blood in reparation for the offenses that
bring My judgment against My sinful creatures.

✝ Pray My Mother's prayer (the rosary) before My
image.

✝ Pray the Novena of Divine Mercy continuously.

✝ . . .

✝ . . .

✝ Study seriously now My prophet Isaiah.

I, the Lord your God, ask this. That is all. I ask
special sacrifices from those of My chosen ones. It is
necessary, for My wrath is so great I would wipe away
all this sinful generation, even the remnant. I have
spoken. Thus say I the Lord God.)

11-19-91 I CALL YOU TO SINCERE EFFORTS OF REPENTANCE

. . . Now, in My name say to My people: Hear the
words My daughter speaks to you. I call you to
sincere efforts of repentance. Confess your sins. Do
this quickly. Cleanse your souls. Your sins pollute
the holy tabernacle (individual souls). I find no
dwelling place; I search in vain. Only a few in all of
My creation have prepared well for My coming. Open
your hearts — I come soon to take up My dwelling
place among you. The time you do not know.
*Recognize the signs I place before you, and you
will know that the coming of the Most High God,
triumphant Saviour, is imminent.* In all ages I
reveal to certain of My chosen ones that which is My
will from all eternity. In each sinful generation I call
My children to return to My presence. I call out to you
in a loud voice —
*Repent of your sins. Pray unceasingly for My
mercy.*

In a loud voice I say to you: Return to My fold.

114

Raise your eyes and open them; see My hand in the affairs of men. Let not your arrogance blind you to the reality of My presence among you. Let not your evil deeds continue. Turn aside from evil. Seek out My mercy. Put on love. Put on the cloak of salvation. Put on the Lord God Jesus Christ, merciful God, triumphant King.

Now say: I call you again, My children. Will you still persist in your stubbornness and self-delusion? Come, My children, I wait but a short time longer. I, your loving God, call you. I have spoken. Thus says the Lord God. That is all . . .

12-3-91 I AM INFINITE BEING

I wish to speak. In My name say to My people:

✝ **I am the living God**. I live in My word. I live in My Church. I live in souls open to My saving grace.

✝ **I am the all powerful God.** My power is in My hand. My power is in My Word. My power is in My love and in My justice.

✝ **I am the all knowing God.** I know what is in each heart. I know each thought before it is present in your mind. I know the beginning and ending of time and of all that occurs in time and out of time.

✝ **I am the God of mercy and justice.** My mercy is for all generations; My justice is for those who forsake My mercy.

✝ **I am the God of love.** In My love are you sustained in the trials. In My love are you redeemed for the kingdom. In My love are you protected from the furies that seek to destroy your soul.

✝ **I am the eternal God.** There is no other, nor shall there ever be. *I Am* before time, *I Am* in time, *I Am* without end. *I am infinite being!*

115

Whosoever doubts Me as I reveal myself is filled with arrogance and pride. He places His trust in His own intellect, which is woefully deficient even in its capacity to understand the smallest details of mortal existence. I say to you mortals of the earth: When all knowledge of the earth passes away, what knowledge will you have if you do not know Me? All things mortal pass away — I, only, remain. Only I, the one God of heaven and earth, do not pass away. *I Am!* Thus says the Lord God.

Now say: Little minds have little. Minds open to the Spirit of the Living God grow and expand. The horizons of their minds have no limits. Be open, My children, to the fullness of My presence. Be filled with My limitless graces, My endless love, My infinite mercy. Only when you possess what is limitless are you freed to grow in love, and knowledge, and wisdom, and understanding. Only when you possess Me, My children, are you truly free. I am the Lord God. Thus say I, the Lord God. That is all . . .

12-4-91 HAVE YOUR LAMPS READY

I wish to speak, child. Say in My name, say to My people: In this holy time of preparation for My coming as the infant Son of the Father and of the Woman, I bring you tidings of the good news of My coming as the King of Glory. How will you greet Me when I come? Will you be immersed in the fruitless pursuits of merrymaking and an over—abundance of material possessions? For the coming of the infant you spend endless years of frantic activity to celebrate His birth. For the coming of the King of Glory you take little heed. Have I not told you I do not delay My coming? Have I not told you My coming is imminent? Why, then, do you not prepare as well for My second coming as you do for My first? I tell you, the time is short. I tell you, make haste to respond to My call for conversion and reparation for sins. Have your lamps ready and be clothed in the garment of My mercy. The foolish delay their preparation; the wise take heed and are prepared. In the infant recognize your King, recognize your Saviour, recognize He who will judge your deeds. From the seed comes the mighty tree. From the babe comes the Redeemer King, the God of power and might. As you make welcome the infant, make welcome your Almighty God, He who comes soon to rule with justice in the new heavens and the *new earth. Be vigilant, My people; do not be caught unawares at My coming. The Lord your God gives ample warning before He acts.* I warn you now. I call you to repentance, to prayer, to reconciliation. Waste no more time. Thus say I, the Lord God.

Now say: Thank you, My faithful children, for preparing a room for Me in your hearts. There I dwell; there I find welcome; there do I take up My abode. Thus says the Lord God. That is all.

12-9-91 THE TIME FORETOLD BY THE PROPHETS IS NOW

I will speak now. In My name say: Dear children of My heart, I the Lord God speak. Hear My words. You enter now into the time of the beginning of the end. Tragic events are about to occur in the world of men. Do thou take heed of the voices of My chosen ones who warn you in My name. You know not the hour when you will stand before Me. I tell you, many will perish without warning. I tell you these things because you are a stubborn species. I tell you this because too many refuse to take seriously the promise of My justice. Too many refuse to remove the scales from their eyes and (they) fail to see their iniquity. Too many ridicule those whom I have called to speak My truth in this time. *But, I say to all My children, the time foretold by the prophets of old is now. It is the present time, the time of the great apostasy. Mankind knows not its God. I tell you, the apostasy is not only in My Church but in every heart that refuses to acknowledge Me and the laws I gave for your salvation. The majority of mankind knows not its God. I have spoken. Thus*

117

says the Lord God.

Now say: You must remain strong in My peace My children, if you are to survive in the turmoil brought about by unprecedented events in your world. Remain serene amidst the confusion and fear which will be all about you. Many will perish in an instant; there will be no time to flee. Please, My children, take heed. I call to you through the voices of many I have called to speak in My name. Be forewarned. Thus says the Lord God. That is all.

12-10-91 BE BORN AGAIN IN THE FIRE OF THE SPIRIT

Dear little child, I wish to speak. In My name say to My people: I am the Spirit of the living God. Receive My gifts. Love, peace, greetings to the people of God.

I am sent by the Father through the Son to reawaken in souls the knowledge of the one God of all. Say to your brothers and sisters: Renew the Spirit that was given to you in Baptism. Be born again in the fire of the Spirit. I breathe into your souls a new life of the Spirit, a life of zeal for the word of God. Mine is the breath of life, the eternal life. I breathe life into the soul when it is formed in the mind of the Father. The living soul is the image of the living God. It is the life of the body. The body is no more than an inert mass of the elements of nature given form by the hand of the Creator in the womb of its mother. I, it is, who gives life to the elements of nature in the form given them by the Father. I am the Spirit of Life who comes from the giver of life. I am He who sustains the life of the universe. He who has not My life possesses not the life of the Kingdom of the Father. They are souls possessed of death; they know not eternal life. Thus say I, the Spirit of the Living God. That is all.

12-20-91 PERSONAL MESSAGE

(. . . Now begins the darkest of the dark days in your world. From now until the end My light will be extinguished except in the hearts of those who have heard My Word. They are but a few. You must keep My light burning for the few. . .Thank you child. Do as I ask in all things. I, the Lord God have spoken. That is all.)

12-24-91 **I ANNOUNCE TO YOU THE REIGN OF PEACE AND JUSTICE — 4:00 p.m.**

I am with you child. Now I wish to speak. *By the power of the mighty God proclaim the coming of the Lord Jesus Christ in power and glory.*

This message must be announced to all the earth. I, the Father, have set the day for His return. This is the task I will for you. Today begins the final days of this age. The Almighty Lord, Jesus the Christ, King of Glory, reigns supreme over those He has redeemed for My Kingdom.

I, the Father, announce to My creation the end of your days as you know them. I announce to you the reign of peace and justice. I tell you — the reign of the God-Son is at hand.

On this joyous night of His birth into your world, I, the Father who sent Him, foretell to you His second coming. Rejoice, oh people of God! The King comes! I, the Lord God, Father-Creator, so proclaim and announce to My creation. Go now and proclaim the good news. Let all My creatures sing joyfully hossanahs and alleluias to the Living God, He who fulfills His promises of old.

Now say: Little daughter of My heart, glad tidings do I announce to all of My creatures on this most holy night when all creation bows in humble adoration before the awesome God-Son, King, and Redeemer. Thus do I say to you: Rejoice, He comes again! I have spoken.

9:15 p.m. I wish to continue. My dear child of My

119

heart, bring forth by the power of My Spirit the news of the coming of the God-Son in power and glory, the triumphant and resplendent Holy Son of the Father. This is what I enjoin you to do. The peace of this holy night is granted to you. That is all. Thus say I, the Lord God, Father-Creator.

12-31-91 THAT WHICH IS UNCLEAN MUST BE MADE CLEAN

I wish to speak. Say in My name, say to My people: Dear children of My heart, face the year to come with courage in your hearts. Let not the events which are about to occur disturb your peace, the peace I give you. I, the Lord God, speak to you words of comfort. Know that the hour is at hand when I act in the fullness of My power to purify My creation. No stain of sin will I permit in the restored kingdom. Who remain will be cleansed in the fire of the Spirit. Restore purity to your souls. That which is unclean must be made clean. Only the pure, in all their splendor, will find a place prepared for them. Cleanse yourselves. Prepare for He who comes to claim His inheritance. He is the pure and holy Son who bears only the light and the radiance of the Father. There is no stain in Him. Where He is all must be clean as He is clean, light as He is light, holy as He is holy; united to the Father as He is united to the Father. Let no man seek to enter into the kingdom unless He has made himself clean beforehand. Make recompense to the Father for your many sins. The kingdom awaits the coming of those who have made themselves clean in the blood of the Risen Christ. Hear, oh people, your God. I tell you, no one who is not clean shall enter in. Thus say I, the Lord God. That is all.

Tribulations and Triumph
Revelations on the Coming of
THE GLORY OF GOD
1992
"NOW IS MY JUDGMENT UPON YOU"

"Now very shortly I will pour out My wrath upon thee, and I will accomplish My anger in thee: and I will judge thee according to thy ways, and I will lay upon thee all thy crimes."

(Ez 7:8)

1-6-92 **THERE IS NOT ONE IN ALL THE EARTH WHO DOES NOT OFFEND ME**

I wish to speak child. Say in My name: At the beginning of this very decisive year in the history of mankind, I call each one of My children to a renewed effort of heroic acts of reparation for sin. *The severity of My judgment, which you bring upon yourselves, will depend on the response of mankind to what I tell you is necessary to open My heart of mercy. I tell you: Only heroic efforts on the part of all My people will shorten the time I have marked for your purification.* I tell you: My judgment is now come upon you. There is not one in all the earth who does not offend Me — *not one!* The sins of most of My creatures are grievous in My sight. Only a few do not grieve Me greatly. I tell you, My children, of the immensity of My just anger. You are creatures created in glory to return to Me in glory. Instead, My created ones wallow in sin and corruption. You do not

121

shine with My glory; your glory is covered with the filth of your corruption. No sign of My glory remains in you. You were created to return to My kingdom at the end of your days. My kingdom is left empty because so many fill the pit of the serpent. You have forfeited your inheritance; your eternity will be damnation, not glory. Thus say I the Lord God.

I wish now to speak to My faithful ones. Say in My name: **You are My remnant! I call you also to reparation.** In this time of severe trial I say: Study My Word that you do not follow the false teachers who are all about you. **Know My truth!** The darkness descends upon My Church. My priests reject My Word — they teach falsehood; they permit gross violations of My law and commandments. They lead My flock astray. I say to you: Stay firmly on the path I have shown you.

✝ **Do not** deny Me!

✝ **Do not** follow the false teachers!

✝ **Do not** stray from Me and My Word!

✝ **Do not** follow those who choose the path to eternal damnation!

The time is coming when My faithful ones will find no truth in My Church. In that time the truth, My truth, My Word, must be fully fixed in your heart. The days ahead will be infinitely difficult for My faithful ones. Remain totally consecrated and committed to My Sacred Heart and to the Immaculate Heart of Mary, our Mother, and we will bring you safely into the kingdom. Endure, My children. Remain faithful. Remember — I am your God; you are My chosen ones. I do not forsake My own. That is all. I, the Lord God, have spoken.

I ONLY AM GOD

My dear little daughter, I wish to speak. Say in My name, say to My people: Hear, oh children of the Lord God, what I tell you through My instrument. Why do you close your ears to My words? There is no falsehood in My Word. If you do not hear My Word, you follow the lie. You follow the great deception of your age that each is God. I alone am God! I have commanded that there be no other God but Me. All other gods are false gods created in the minds and hands of prideful creatures. Whyfore do you accept the delusions of your own imaginations, which have no power, and reject He who is your strength? I, it is, who have created you; you have not created Me. Unless you know Me, you have no God. There is no other beside Me. I only am God. I tell you, My creatures, you cannot know Me if you remain creatures of the earth. I have told you, heaven and earth shall pass away, but My Word shall not. If you remain creatures of the earth, your fate is to remain creatures of the nether world. Your hearts are so hard, My children. Would you risk damnation because your pride admits of nothing but your own idolatrous self? Foolish creatures! What folly to choose damnation over salvation.

Dear children, I seek for you, My lost ones. Will you not soften your hearts? Will you not come to Me? Come, My children, I call you again. I wait but yet a little time. Thus say I, the Lord God. That is all.

WOE TO THOSE WHO REJECT MY MERCY

I wish to speak. Say in My name, say to My people: Be serene amidst the turmoil. The peace of Jesus Christ be with you. I come to tell you, My children, of great events which will soon change your world for all time. Do thou take heed of what I tell you through My instrument. I grant but yet a short time this time of great mercy. Woe to those who reject mercy. Woe to all creatures. Woe to all that is in My creation.

123

Suffering is your lot. Pain, and death, and destruction is come again. The one who is My enemy (Anti-Christ) is now visible upon the earth and in the affairs of men. He has not yet revealed himself. In but a short time the earth and all that it holds will know the scourge of His presence. My dear people, you must not remain closed to the signs of His presence that are all about you. Admit of His existence, admit of His power, know that He is evil incarnate. I tell you, do not turn away from this knowledge I give you. Accept what is truth — Satan now walks the earth in visible form. The evil He plans will bring to an end this age. I have foretold this; so shall it be. Thus says the Lord God.

Now say: Hear, My children, My voice. Attend to My words. No one will be spared. I tell you again in My name: What is to come will come. I bring My hand against you, I do not delay My judgment. Thus say I, the Lord God. That is all . . .

1-22-92 MY CREATURES DESTROY THEMSELVES WITHOUT A SECOND THOUGHT

This message is in response to prayers and pain offered to end abortion.

(Thank you for what you offer. Abortion is the greatest of all evil. How can abortion end if My people do not know Me? Pray that My people return to Me. My child, you begin to glimpse the enormity of My justice. My creatures destroy themselves without a second thought. Pray very much, My dear little child. Only a few will be left. So few, My child. How My heart grieves. Console Me with your prayers and your love. Love My children. Offer many sacrifices. I am so weighted down by the sins of My creatures. Help Me, child. I can no longer bear the weight by myself. I have spoken. Thus say I the Lord God).

1-23-92 YOUR FAITHFULNESS IS REWARDED

Say in My name, say to My people: Here am I the Lord God. I bring you tidings of great joy. Hear, oh My people, the voice of the Lord your God.

Now say: Do not weep My faithful children. Tears are for those who have no hope. Your hope is in Me. You see about you the evil that runs rampant in all My creation. You see all about you death, and disease, and suffering. You see despicable acts committed by one human being against another. You hear the cries of the poor and homeless. Everywhere in My creation do you find every kind of abominable deed. Mankind rushes headlong toward its own destruction. Satan wishes to delude you with talks of peace. Satan cannot know peace — He is the angel of death. Satan is the cunning deceiver.

Children of My Heart, will you choose life or death? I am life. Choose for life dear children. Act swiftly. The time to act will end suddenly for many. What events are to come, My children. That which is hidden will be revealed one by one. The first is about to be made known. Ask for My graces to persevere. Ask for My graces to restore your souls to purity. Ask for the grace of a repentant heart. Ask for My mercy. Ask, My children, ask. I give abundantly to those who ask.

I tell you the glad tidings of My coming. Be filled with the Spirit of joy and anticipation. You are ransomed out of evil. The day of your deliverance is at hand. Your faithfulness is rewarded. Thus say I, the Lord God. That is all . . .

1-25-92 WHEN YOU CALL MY NAME I ANSWER YOU

Dear little child of My heart, I wish to speak. In My name say: I tell you, My people, of great events that are about to overtake your world. My love for you is infinite, My children. I wish no one to be lost from the kingdom. Fill your souls with My love. Rest in My peace . . .

Now say to My people: My children, why do you wander so far from Me? I call you each by name, but you turn your ear from Me. I, the Lord God, call you loudly, I call you softly, I call to you to all the ends of the earth. You have turned a deaf ear, all you My creatures. I speak to the stillness of quiet hearts. The hearts of men are filled with the sounds of their own voices that resound in the emptiness of their hollow hearts. They make a fearsome din; they cannot hear My words. They will not hear. Howsoever I speak, they refuse My Word.

Now say: I do not turn My ear from you, My children. When you call My name, I answer you. Though even the last should turn from Me, I do not turn from you. Seek Me, and you shall know Me. Come before Me with repentant and contrite hearts, and I reach out to embrace you. My arms are empty. My children do not return. I cry in bitter anguish for those who remain deaf. I stand lonely and alone, and watch My precious children suffer the loss of their eternal joy.

Stand with Me, My faithful ones. Reach out to your brothers and sisters with prayers and sacrifices. They will not hear, but I will hear and I will rescue them. Thus says the Lord God. That is all.

1-27-92 STAND IN READINESS TO GREET YOUR KING

I wish to speak. Dear little child of My heart, say in My name: All hail to the mighty King-Redeemer.

Now say, so say I to My people: Stand in readiness to greet your King. Cleanse your hearts from all evil. Satan works diligently to ensnare My faithful ones. He spins His web and traps the unsuspecting in the gossamer threads of His evil intentions. Be alert, My children, for the strands of His deceptions are not easily broken. That is all for now. I have spoken. Thus say I the Lord God . . .

PREPARE WELL

Dear little child of My heart, I wish to speak. Say in My name, say to My people: I speak to you My words to prepare you for My coming. I repeat to you often the message of My coming in power and glory. I tell you again the same message. Many of My children rebuke those of My servants whom I have called to speak this truth. I tell you, hear the words they speak. They are My words. *I do not leave My children unprepared. Therefore, I call to you again, My children. Prepare well. The wise will take heed. I, the Lord God, send My servants before Me. They prepare the way for My coming. Satan wishes to delude you. He whispers in your ear that I will not come. How easily you believe the lie and reject the truth. I tell you: I come! My coming is soon. Now must you prepare. There will be no time left at My coming.* Now is the time of My great mercy. Now do I tell you is the time of preparation. Now must you do as I ask; you do not know what the morrow holds.

Now say: Trust in My words, My children. Better to hear and respond than to be left in the darkness knocking to enter. Thus say I the Lord God.

WHY DO YOU GRIEVE ME SO?

I wish to speak. In My name say: Oh My poor children, why do you grieve Me so? Here am I, the God of love and mercy. There is no separation between us if you would but turn your face to Me. You turn to Me your back. How can you know Me when you look away from Me? What do you see, My children, when you look into darkness? You see nothing but the darkness. You must turn to the light if you will see what the darkness hides. I am not in the darkness. You will not find Me there. What is in the darkness is sin, and evil, and ignorance. I am the Light, the Way, and the Truth. Open the door of your heart and let My light enter your darkness. Come, walk through the door. Banish the darkness. Receive the graces of My mercy. Keep your eyes fixed on My way. If you look to either side, you will not see Me; you will lose your way. So many have turned and walk away from Me. They walk again toward darkness and apostasy.

My children, walk no further. Stop and look about you. Can you not see that the direction you have chosen leads you to perdition? Call My name, My children, and I will come and show you the way back to My love and mercy.

Now say to My faithful ones: Help your errant brothers and sisters. Call on Me to open My heart of mercy to them. I hear and answer your petitions for each one of My lost children. No prayer is in vain, no sacrifice unacceptable when offered with a pure intention. Thank you, My children, for your response to My call. That is all. Thus say I, the Lord God.

2-19-92 MAKE YOUR HOMES HAVENS OF PEACE

I wish to speak. Dear little child of My heart, say in My name, say to My people: Open the door and welcome Me into your home. I, the Lord God, bring you greetings of peace. Make your homes havens of peace.

Now say: It *is My wish that in each home a place be prepared where My image and the image of the most Holy Virgin of Virgins, Mother of Mothers may have a place of honor. In this place let father and mother and all members of each family gather for prayer and meditation. Bring to Me your babes in arms, your sons and daughters, your friends and relatives. Pray first and foremost the prayer of the Mother (rosary). Ponder My Word. Give to each other pardon. Sing songs of praise and thanksgiving, for the mighty God has saved you in His merciful love. This I ask of all My children.*

Grow up strong shoots, for the time of trial will be

128

severe. Become the sturdy branches upon which the fruits of faith, and hope, and love will ripen to feed the godless, the hopeless, and the forsaken. From these families I will call forth loyal shepherds for My flock, holy servants to My children. In the flowering of the new time these families will be like the flowers of the field that perfume the air with the fragrance of their holiness. How beautiful is the family formed in the image of (God) the Father, and nurtured by the hand of the Mother (Mary). I have spoken. Thus says the Lord God. That is all.

▬▬▬ MOTHER MARY SPEAKS
2-21-92

Dear child, come before Me now. I am the Mother who wishes to speak. Soon, My children, I, your Mother, must cease to plead for you. The great hour of mercy will be withdrawn. . . Oh My children, avail yourself of mercy now. I cry bitter tears because so few have returned to My Jesus. His heart is sorely wounded, for once again His own have rejected Him. My Mother's heart grieves for His anguish. I can no longer console Him. The Mother once again walks with the Son the painful steps of His cruel sacrifice. The weight of the cross cannot be lifted because your sins are multiplied innumerable times and bring upon Him a crushing weight. He lies exhausted beneath its weight. He cannot rise. There are too few to lift the weight.

Oh My beloved Son, the sins of your creatures are so great that even I, the Mother, can only stand silently now and let My tears fall.

(Pray, little daughter. You must pray with your whole heart and soul. Make every moment of every day a prayer. Remain united to the suffering of Jesus. Love Him with your whole being. Tell to My children that they must *pray, pray, pray*. That is all).

Now say in the name of the Lord your God, say to My people: I love you with an unending love. As I lie beneath a cross now too heavy to be borne, I look to you and with the last ounce of My strength I call out for the last time — *I love you, come to My mercy.* I have spoken. That is all. It is finished.

2-23-92 THE FULLNESS OF GOD'S POWER

I wish to speak, child. In My name say to My people: Thus says the Lord God — I have numbered the days which now remain to My fallen creatures. Do thou take heed, for I act in the fullness of My power. When I tell you of the fullness of My power you are to understand it as the unrestrained exercise of every element of the structure of My being united as one omnipotent action against the forces of evil. The forces of evil smother the whole of My creation with a blanket of abominable deeds. My creatures cannot free themselves from the stranglehold of sin and evil. They struggle feebly but have not the will to resist the enticements that bring about the demise of their souls. Thus, I act in the fullness of My power in the fullness of time to release My helpless ones from the bonds which hold them captive to the Evil One. The battle for souls is waged in the arena of the infinite reaches of the universe from whence the forces of evil battle the forces of justice in mortal combat. The sword of My justice strikes at the head of the serpent. The just are rescued for the kingdom of the just. The armies of evil pursue their prey with unrelenting attacks, for their days are but few to enslave the captives who fall victim to the diabolical onslaught of the end time.

Glory to God on high, for the victory of the just is assured. Thus says the Lord God. That is all

3-5-92 MINE IS NOT AN IDLE PROMISE

Dear little child of My heart, I wish to speak. Say in My name, say to My people: *Mankind now enters a most critical period in its history. Nations form alliances, but I tell you there shall be no alliances*

130

when the Son of Evil announces his dominion. All
nations shall be as one, and he will rule with an
iron fist. He does not offer mercy as your Father
in heaven offers mercy. He shall call himself
Messiah. My children of the earth will pay Him
homage and raise Him up upon the throne of infamy.
My children of My Spirit will He raise up upon the
cross of persecution. These are of the kingdom of the
Father. Suffer to come unto Me, My children, for I
uphold you in the trial. Be forewarned, for what I tell
you will be, will be. I speak not words of falsehood.
My word is truth.

Now say: I the Lord God speak. Mine is not an idle
promise. Your God fulfills each word that flows from
His infinite being. Now is to be fulfilled all that has
been spoken since the beginning to the ending. I do
not speak in jest, neither do I break My promises. I
am a faithful God. I keep My word through all
generations. This generation is soon to end. The final
holocaust for this generation, at the hand of the Son
of Evil, will fulfill what My servant, John of Revelation,
announced at My command for this generation. Thus
have I spoken, so shall it be.

Now say: At the appointed time shall the creatures of
the earth be brought to judgment before the tribunal
of the Evil One and His minions. Who refuse His
dominion will be put to the sword. Who pay Him
homage will perish in the fires of hell. Who proclaim
the Lord Jesus Christ will I claim for the Kingdom.
Who are My faithful ones to the end, the Kingdom is
theirs. So say I. Thus shall it be. I have spoken.
That is all.

3-8-92   CURSED IS THIS GENERATION OF EVIL DOERS

Hear My voice. I wish to speak. Thus say I the Lord
and giver of life: Wheresoever there is one who speaks
in My name, there also are those who speak in the
tongue of the Evil One. If there be one who does not
falter in proclaiming the Lord Jesus, there are also

those who revile His holy name. Proclaim the Lord Jesus!

Now say, if there be but one who tells of the glory of the Risen Christ, there shall I pour down graces in abundance upon those whose hearts are cold and hardened by sin. Proclaim the Lord Jesus Christ!

Where there is but one who dies to self, I raise up many as the fruits of the labor of that lowly one. Where there is but one who comes to My living presence, there will I gather together My true and faithful followers and welcome them into the abode of My Sacred Heart. Where there is not one to pay Me homage, I shake off the dust of that place from My feet and leave them. They are left destitute and forsaken, without hope. Thus say I, the Lord God.

Now say: Cursed is that place where there is not one found who proclaims My holy name. Cursed are they who torment and persecute My lowly ones. Cursed be they who deny their God. Cursed is every generation where evil runs rampant and the just cry out for deliverance. Cursed is this generation of evil doers. Thus say I the Lord God. That is all.

3-19-92 I WHO AM LOVE AM REJECTED

I wish to speak. Dear little child of My heart, tell to My people, say in My name: I the Lord God bring you greetings of peace and joy.

Now say: I call each one. Many have heard, but so few have responded. It grieves Me greatly that love is rejected. So easily do My children invoke the name of love in the performance of sinful and evil deeds. I speak in a loud voice and I say to you: If evil results from actions performed in the guise of love, you have not acted with love. You have acted from the motives of self-interest. Love seeks always for the welfare of the ones loved. Love must have no limits; it must be given unconditionally. Love must not be reserved for

132

a chosen few. As the Father loves you, so must you love one another. As the Son revealed the love of the Father through the redemption of the cross, so must your love give witness to the God of love. Receive the Spirit of Love. Let the Spirit of Love be a strong light for all to see where now there is only found bitter disputes and violence.

I who am Love, am rejected. Love is rejected. The cornerstone will crumble without the mortar. As the mortar binds stone to stone, so it is that love binds each to the other and all is bound upon the altar of My infinite love. If love is not the cornerstone, if love is rejected by the builder, if love is not the binding force in human relationships, the edifice which man has created upon His altar of wilful self — interest will crash down upon Him. My children, build your lives upon the altar of love. I am the cornerstone — I am love. That is all. Thus say I, the Lord God.

4-2-92   YOU ARE LOST IN THE MAZE OF HUMAN ENDEAVOR

Now I wish to speak for today. In My name say: I the Lord God must act now in justice to bring to an end the abominable deeds of creatures who follow the dictates of the Evil One. My heart is weighted with grief for the multitudes who will enter into eternal damnation. What misery you have brought upon yourselves, My children, all because your pride and your intellect have led you on the byways of secularism and atheism. These paths lead you into dark caverns and dead ends. Still you seek other paths and wander aimlessly; you are lost in the maze of human endeavor. Even those lost in the maze can find their way out, if they choose the right pathway. I am the Way. Come, follow Me and I will lead you on the open path, the path of truth and knowledge, the path of wisdom and understanding, the path that transcends what is limited by human frailty. Then will you be freed from the bondage of the restrictions you have placed upon yourselves. Cast off the bindings of pride, remove the blinders from your eyes, open the gates that enclose you within the confines of your self-delusions. Unless you cast off that which keeps you bound to the earth, you are doomed to wander aimlessly and without hope in the endless paths from which there is no door that frees you to find what you have lost in the realm of human endeavor. Seek for Me, and I will show you the way. Reach for Me and I will open the door. Free yourselves, My children — come to Me and you will find all that you seek. I the Lord God have spoken. That is all.

4-7-92 . . . THE BEGINNING OF THE END

Dear child of My heart, hear My voice. This is not the end, but the beginning of the end. Henceforth, I plant My foot upon the firmament and My hand moves over the face of the universe. From this day forward do I act, and no longer will mankind know it (the universe) as it has been since the beginning of time. In My power I wipe away all that went before, and bring forth from the travail of My sons and daughters in this present age the restoration of the heavenly kingdom in the new time of grace. I have spoken. Thus say I the Lord God.

4-7-92 THESE ARE THE SEED ON THE BARREN GROUND

. . . My children turn from My love and My commandments, even those who have heard the good news of salvation. These are the seed on the barren ground. They wither and die on the lifeless soil of materialism and secularism. My faithful ones must not lose heart. Neither must they follow their brothers and sisters lost in the world of man. My judgement is just. What is to be must be. Mankind has made its choice. I have spoken. Thus say I the Lord God. That is all.

4-12-92 TURN YOUR HEARTS TO PRAYER

I wish to speak. In My name say to My people: Do not be concerned for your welfare, My children. So many are concerned not with the status of their souls, but with the practical issues of survival in these end times. I, the Lord God, will provide for your every need. Have I not sustained My people in ages past? So shall I sustain My faithful ones in the trial of the present age. Rather, turn your hearts to prayer. I hear and answer My people's prayers. Pray, My children, for it is in prayer that the Word of the Most High will come to enlighten you. That is all. I have spoken. So say I, the Lord God.

4-15-92 THE HOUR OF MERCY IS SOON TO BE WITHDRAWN

Dear little child of My heart, tell to My people that I desire that they come to My presence and pray with fervent prayers. This is what you must tell them:

"The hour of mercy is soon to be withdrawn. Who have made themselves clean in the sacrament of mercy need have no fear for what is about to befall mankind. Who waver I say to them: You do not know the hour or the day. I grant but only a short time before My judgment in all its power is unleashed upon the earth. Who refuse My mercy cannot be saved. I speak My final warning. Thus say I, the Lord God . . ."

4-20-92 THE LORD GOD DOES NOT ENTER WHERE THE DOOR IS CLOSED AGAINST HIM

I wish to speak, little daughter of My heart. Beloved child, tell to My people, in My name say: How is it that the Lord God of heaven and earth has become a pariah and an outcast from what He has created by His own hand? Will not My creatures give praise and honor to the One? Do you still not know that My hour is upon you? I send My messengers before you; do you still close your ears to My call? How you have hardened your hearts, My children. Who can soften them if not I? Who can bring you to Me if not My holiest Mother? Who can bring you to salvation if not the Son in the power of the Spirit? Who is there left? There is no one, and sinful creatures have not the power to save themselves. Oh My poor children, what have you wrought — you condemn yourselves to the eternal fire.

So many times have I spoken. *I have remained with this generation in all the tabernacles throughout the world, in My revealed Word, in the hearts of the holiest of the holy, in the visible presence of My Vicar on earth, in the signs and wonders I have performed throughout the ages and to the present day, and still you deny Me. You seek for answers for mortal existence in every methodology, but you do not seek them in Me. Because you reject Me, I block your intellects and you will not find the cures to the evils of this generation until you open your hearts and your minds to My saving grace. If mankind wishes to restore peace and harmony, kinship among peoples, health of body and soul, triumph over sin and evil, it must turn back to Me, the one God, I Who Am the Answer.* By its own free will mankind has closed the door to its salvation. The Lord God does not enter where the door is closed against Him. Thus have you chosen, thus is My judgment against you. Thus say I, the Lord God.

4-21-92 THERE IS STILL YET A LITTLE TIME TO RESPOND TO THE CALL OF THE MOTHER

Dear little child of My heart, speak to My people and say, in My name say: I, the Lord God, commence the judgment. There is no turning aside until the last vestige of sin is cleansed and the whole of My creation is purified for the reign of Jesus, the Lord of all. Let no one of My creatures doubt that what mankind now suffers is My judgment. And yet, there is still yet a little time to respond to the call of the Mother who

136

restores you to My loving care, for the final hour is not yet upon you. I say to you, My children, know that the hour is at hand when the fullness of My judgment will fall upon you. You have not yet tasted of its fullness. I say to you: The time of mercy is now but a second; after that begins the final hour before the coming of the Son of Man. Do thou tell to My people in My name that I, the Lord God, restore My kingdom as a woman labors to give birth. First is the seed planted in the receptive womb. As the seed grows so grows the discomfort of the mother. At the time of birth the mother struggles in pain and suffering to bring forth her child. And when she gazes lovingly at what she has brought forth, joy fills her heart and the pain is forgotten in the beauty of the new life which she holds gently to her breast. So shall be the coming of the kingdom. So say I the Lord God. That is all.

4-22-92 MEDJUGORJE — 9:15 a.m.

I will speak to you today of a matter of great urgency. In My name speak and tell to My people that the forces of evil plan to destroy the holy site of My Mother's visitation. The sign of My suffering and death which stands upon the highest peak will be pulverized into dust. Nothing will remain of the villages. The temple of sacrifice will be destroyed. My Mother's presence in this holy place is ended. Now, My people, you must adhere to what she has asked of you. My people must trust in Me and be strong in their faith. In but a short time the first of her secrets to My daughter, Mirjana, will be revealed to the world . . .* see editoral note, p. VI, #2.

4-22-92 CELEBRATION OF DIVINE MERCY

Dear child of My heart, this night I speak to you My words of mercy. In My name bring greetings of peace to My people. In this hour of mercy I embrace each one here present. I rejoice with you in your joyful celebration. From My heart I bathe you in the rays of My radiant love. With My hand do I raise you up and clothe you in the garments of purest light. You are My radiant and resplendent children. I hold you tenderly, My precious ones. You bring joy to the heart of mercy.

Hosanna and Alleluia to the Risen Christ, He who stands among you, He who is glorified in pure hearts, the King of Peace, the King of Kings. Glory and praise to the Almighty God who receives you into His merciful heart.

Rejoice, My people, for you rest in the light of the Risen Lord. I stretch My hand over you and bless you with many blessings. Thanks be to the Almighty God for His wondrous gift of mercy. Alleluia! Alleluia! I have spoken. Thus say I, the Lord God. That is all.

Dear child, these are My words to all those who drink of the cup of mercy:

✝ **Be merciful** as I am merciful.
✝ **Love one another** with My love.
✝ **Be My joyful witnesses,** My bright and shining
  flames in the darkness, My royal people.

I, the Risen Lord, raise My voice in joyful proclamation — Thanks be to the Father, for He has brought you into the light of salvation. Alleluia! Alleluia! So say I, the King of Peace, King of Kings. That is all.

4-25-92 YOU HAVE BEEN SEDUCED BY LIES AND DECEPTIONS

Dear child of My heart, in My name say to My people: Glory and praise to the living God.

Now say: Behold! The risen Christ stands at the threshold of His inheritance ready to enter and take claim of all that is rightfully His by the hand of the Father. How will you greet Him when He comes in glory? Seek within your soul for the Word. Do you find the Word of the Father, or do you find only the meaningless words of the world? The words of the world are devoid of meaning in the kingdom, they are empty promises in empty hearts. My Word is the

Word of truth. The words of the world are words of lies, of slander, of blasphemy.

Now write: Oh hardened hearts, oh children of evil, I speak to you these words. You have been seduced by lies and deceptions. If you continue to follow the Prince of Darkness, your only light will be the fires of eternal damnation. The Son of Evil holds you spellbound by the promise of worldly power and material possessions. You sell your souls to possess what has no value and soon passes away. You have accepted the lie that freedom consists of no restraints on human behavior. You follow blindly the path of death — the death of your unborn children; the death of those by their own hands; the death of those who are deemed to have no value; death by disease, starvation, and abuse. He has so blinded you that you cannot see what is before your very eyes — that you destroy yourselves! And when this scourge is ended multitudes of My children will be lost to the kingdom of darkness. This Son of Perdition places a veil over your intellects so that truth may not enter. You follow Him like one mesmerized. You follow passively, for you have surrendered your wills into slavery. This, My people, is the bondage of Satan. No power can release you from this bondage. Only in truth will you be set free. My Word is truth. I am truth. If you wish to be set free, you must return to Me. Come, My people, understand that only in Me, and with Me, and through Me can you be freed from the chains that bind you to the Evil One. Ask for deliverance, and I will set you free.

(Speak, little daughter, these words to those who have turned away from truth, to those who have not heard the truth, to those who falter before the onslaught of the Evil One, to the hopeless ones, to the mighty and the lowly. So say I, the Spirit of the most high God. That is all.)

I wish to speak dear child of My heart. Glory and praise to the Risen Lord.

Now say, in My name say to My people: How is it that My people have strayed so far from the path of truth? My truth is My Word. If there is no truth, there can only be lies and deceptions. If the first (truth) is rejected, the other must, perforce, become the life force of human existence — lies and deception are accepted as truth. This cannot be. Truth is truth, lies are lies and one cannot become the other. Truth is in My Word and in those who follow My Word. My children, do not follow the lie! You can recognize the lie only if you once again seek the truth. I am Truth; I am the Word. Seek Me. Thus say I the Lord God.

Now say: The Father of Lies hovers beside you waiting patiently to fill you with His venom. This is why, My children, I call you to vigilance. This is why you must become strong with My strength and fortified with My living presence. This is why I call out loudly and urgently — *Return, you creatures of the earth, to the One in whom is all truth, all power, all mercy. I call repeatedly; I call urgently, for the hour of wrath is upon you.* So say I, the Lord God. That is all.

Later in the evening: My children have a choice — they can heed My call, or they can be handed over to the Son of Perdition.

4-29-92 HOW IS IT THAT YOU NO LONGER KNOW ME?

Dear little child of My heart . . . Now say, in My name say to My people: Hossanah, Alleluia. Give praise to the living God.

I live! I Am! How is it that you no longer know Me? How is it that I, the Lord God, cannot be comprehended? I do not change. If you do not know Me, it is because the minds of human creatures have changed what does not change. You have created a false image of what I am, have been, and always will be. You confine Me within the limits of what is limited; you form Me in your image. If you see only yourselves, you cannot know Me. I am not mortal, but immortal and transcendent. If you refuse to see beyond what is limited and look to the limitless, you

are bound to the imperfect knowledge of your imperfect intellects. I say to you: Whatever is created by the hand and mind of man is imperfect. When you create Me in your image, you see Me as imperfect and limited as are all human creatures. I say to you: If you are to know Me, you must look beyond your self and beyond the limits of mortal existence. Humans are powerless to know Me unless they fill their emptiness with My Spirit.

Now say: I, the Lord God, am not of the things of the world. You cannot know Me in worldly possessions, in inanimate objects, in pursuit of worldly past-times. There you will not find Me. You will not know Me until you remove the barriers of the world that keep us separated. you will not know Me until you accept that you are transcendent spirit as well as mortal body. You will not know Me, My children, unless you seek for Me beyond the horizon of human endeavor and mortal existence. Thus say I the Lord God. That is all.

―――――――

5-7-92   CONTINUE TO PRAY

I wish to speak. Dear little child of My heart, tell to My people in My name: The cries of My suffering ones resound imploringly in the heavenly courts, yet so few are they who hear their cries in the worldly courts. I hear the cries of My people. Oh, if mankind had but listened to My Word. If mankind had but responded to My call, if mankind had but turned back to My mercy. It has not and it continues to reject its only hope. How tenaciously it clings to hatred and revenge, to self-glorification and the false freedom of self-gratification. Mankind prefers to wallow in its misery, not recognizing the immensity of its own despair. I hear the prayers of My faithful ones, and I say to them: *Continue to pray. Raise your voices to the Almighty God that the days of My justice be shortened.* I do not remove My judgment against My creatures, for your rebellion has destroyed the holiness of My creation. There is no place in all the earth that is not tainted by the sins of this generation of rebellious and disobedient creatures. *Your prayers can no longer stay My hand.* Now must you suffer what you have freely chosen — war, famine, death, disease, destruction, immeasurable suffering — all because you have refused My commandments of love and mercy. As you have chosen, so shall you reap. Thus say I the Lord.

Now say: Dear child of My heart, I speak to you words of comfort. My people do not understand what My justice demands. They have been lulled by the false teaching that all sins are forgiven by My suffering and cruel death. Sins are forgiven when they are confessed to My priest-sons. Those who do not ask for My mercy will not know Me, for I rescue only those who ask to be rescued. My people who do not know Me can find salvation in the prayers and sacrifices of those who do know Me. I ask each of My faithful ones to accept one soul (who does not know Me) and offer for that soul the graces they (the faithful ones) receive from their own confessions. I ask each (faithful) one to come to My sacrament of peace once each month. My graces will flow abundantly to those who respond to My call and to those for whom this sacrifice is made. Bring many souls to Me, My children. I am a merciful God. I grant mercy if you but ask. I have spoken. Thus say I the Lord God.

5-16-92 THE TRIUMPH IS LIFE OVER DEATH

I wish to speak, dear child of My heart. In My name say to My people: Here stand I at the threshold, here I stand and survey My inheritance. That which I died for is lost to the Evil One. His is not triumph. Though the whole of creation be black with sin, His is not the triumph. The triumph is life over death. I am Life, He is death. Satan brings death to all that has life, but He has no power to bring death to the giver of life. Who possess Me will have life everlasting, for I am life without beginning or ending. I give you My life in the power of My Spirit. If you have not life, you are dead. When I speak of My life you are to understand this to mean My living presence within you, If anyone denies that I am God, the one sent by the Father through the power of the Spirit, let that one understand that He denies the Father and the Spirit; He denies the one God. If the Three-in-One is denied, life is denied. What remains is death.

Now I say to you all you creatures of the earth: I speak to you of eternal life. If you do not possess My life in mortal existence, neither will you possess My life in eternal existence. This which I tell you is My truth, this is My promise. Heed well the words I tell to you, for no one who does not possess My life will enter into the kingdom. Thus do I say, thus shall it be.

Now say, praise to the Almighty God, infinite being, source and giver of life. Holy is His name. Holy is Jesus, My life present in My body and with My Spirit — eternal Unity, immortal God. Thus say I the living God. That is all. Go in My peace, little child of My heart.

5-20-92 YOU ARE CRUCIFIED BY YOUR OWN SINS

I wish to speak little child of My heart. In My name say thus: Holy is the name of God.

Now say: Hear, oh people, your God speaks. Beloved ones, you enter now into My passion. Dear children, I have carried the burden of your sins. Now you must take up the cross of your infidelity. I am a just God. If you reject the God of mercy, you reject the Lamb of

143

God who takes away your sins. If there is no one to take away your sins, the burden of your sins falls upon your own shoulders. My children, you are crucified by your own sins. If you reject the Lamb who takes away your sins, you have no recourse but to bear the full burden for your sins. The Son of Man relinquishes to the Father His cross of salvation. All is accomplished as the Father has commanded.

Now say, in the name of the God-Son say to My people: I endured My passion and suffering so that you might have life everlasting. I, the God of heaven and earth, so loved you that I gave My life for you. If you are to save your life but reject My mercy, your cross of salvation must be My cross of justice. The cross of mercy was freely taken upon My back for your salvation. Do thou, by your free choice, take upon your backs the cross of justice. Suffer now what you have freely chosen. I have spoken. Thus say I the Lord God. That is all.

5-28-92   **MY MOTHER'S HEART IS FULL TO OVERFLOWING WITH GRIEF**

(Mother Mary speaks): . . . My Mother's heart is full to overflowing with grief. I cry bitter tears and I am weighted with sorrow. My little ones are so far from My Jesus. They refuse My Mother's touch and fly from My call to conversion. Oh what pain do they inflict upon themselves. My Son's arm rests at His side; He has lowered it in judgment as He has foretold. His way is just . . . I have called to all My children but so few have answered. Thank you, little daughter, for having answered the call of your Mother . . .

6-9-92   **THEY ARE JUDGED UNWORTHY STEWARDS . . .**

Dear children, I, the Lord God, command My instrument to reveal to you certain of My hidden truths. Hear her, for she speaks in My name.

In but a little time there shall come upon the face of

the earth a scourge, a pestilence, the magnitude of which has not been since the beginning of time. I permit this as a consequence of man's interference in the order of nature. By the stubbornness of His heart and the seduction of His intellect by the forces of evil, man will become the victim of His own perverted nature. Where there are many, only a few will remain. Of the few, many will curse the day of their birth. Those who do not curse their God will mourn in the depths of their souls and cry out in loud lamentation, and I will open My heart of mercy to them. Those who seek to make themselves gods by the power of their intellects will fall before the power in the hand of God which is unleashed against them. Neither will the innocent be spared. The earth and all that dwell therein stand naked before the mighty God who judges their deeds. They are judged unworthy stewards and corrupters of the goodness of creation given into their hands at the beginning of time. Thus are they called to account and found wanting before My justice. Thus are they rewarded for their stewardship. I have spoken. That is all.

(Note: This scourge does not refer to AIDS but to something in addition to AIDS. This message refers to all of creation including human life.)

6-11-92 I LET FALL THE SWORD OF MY JUSTICE

Hear Me, little one, I wish to tell you more. In My name say: Here am I, My people, ready to comfort you in this time of trial. Who are they who turn to Me? Those whose hearts are open to My Word. Who are they? They are My faithful ones. They fill My ears with sounds of joyful praise. They return to Me with hearts open to My Spirit. They uphold My statutes and proclaim My mighty name. Those who seek to advance their own causes are not My faithful ones. They cry out against that which I established for your salvation. But, I say to you, if any are they (unfaithful ones) who hear My word and believe, they shall be saved. Is there not one among you (unfaithful ones)

145

who will hear and respond? Have you so hardened your hearts that you cannot hear your own desperate voices submerged beneath the sounds of your arrogant self-will and prideful self-righteousness? Will you not understand that you can do nothing unless the power is given to you by My hand? Each breath you breathe, each beat of your heart, each moment of your life is given by My hand. There is nothing in all of creation that does not move except by My hand.

If there be anyone who hears My voice and yet rejects the call to conversion, let that one be anathema. I, the Lord God, will not be mocked by those He has formed in His own image and likeness. What do you seek, My children, that you cannot find in Me? I have spoken. Thus say I, the Lord God.

Continue and say in My name: Now is My judgment upon you. Because you have hardened your hearts and turned from My commandments, I let fall the sword of My justice. There is no turning aside My wrath. Ungrateful creatures, you defy your God and look proudly at the efforts of your own hands. You take pride in your defiance and find no shame in committing the evil acts which I have forbidden in My commandments. I, your God, see every evil deed and do not withhold My judgment against you. Thus say i the Lord God. That is all . . .

6-24-92 FORGIVE!

. . . Now I wish to speak to all My suffering sons and daughters. In My name say: Give praise to the mighty God. Praise must be in your mouths and in your hearts. Praise and glory to the Living God.

I, the Living God, say to you — *Forgive one another. Forgive those who torment and persecute you. Forgive!* Free yourselves from the atrocities of bloodshed and death. Let the fetters of hopelessness and despair be replaced with the bonds of trust and faith. Each must be tested in the fire.

146

Now say: I am the Lord God. I speak My words and tell to you this message of urgency. *If there be any among you who harbor within their hearts unforgiveness towards even the most barbaric and inhumane instruments of divine justice, the number of days allotted for your purification will not be shortened. I give you My command — Love your enemies.* Refuse to be caught in the unending circle of hatred and revenge, heaping one atrocity upon another and perpetuating the myth of sovereign rights from one generation to the next. Hate begets death. Love begets peace. Hear, oh people, the words of the Lord your God. I have spoken. That is all.

6-25-92 MOTHER MARY SPEAKS

The Mother speaks to all of My children. Thank you, My precious ones, for your faithful response to My call. On this day, which marks My presence among you for these many years, I call you to a renewed effort of prayer and fast. In these decisive days before the coming of the Son in power and majesty, the struggle with the forces of evil intensifies. Many falter and fall before the force of His attack. Your prayers and fasting are mighty weapons in the hands of your Mother that bring defeat to the Serpent and His seed. Respond, My dear ones, with love to what I have come to ask of you in these recent years. Your Mother speaks. That is all.

6-25-92 THE CHURCH OF SATAN

I wish to continue (Message of 6-24). There is one within the ranks of My cardinal prelates who works seditiously to destroy what My chosen vicar (John Paul II) seeks to affirm as the revealed truth of My Word. This son of Satan, and His cohorts, stands poised to step into the shoes of the Fisherman. This one is not My successor, but one who usurps the place granted only to the legitimate heirs to the throne of Peter. I spit this one out of My mouth and condemn Him to the fires of hell. His plotting and scheming will usher in the abomination of the apostate church. Every aberration will be condoned, every blasphemy permitted. This abomination is the church of Satan. The desecration of My holy temple will be complete. There must be no compromise with this one, for He exalts himself and extinguishes the light of My truth and makes of My Church a mockery before the eyes of God and man. Prepare well for the hour of His infamy is upon you. I have spoken. Thus say I, the Lord God.

Now say: This is what My faithful ones must do if they are to withstand His reign of terror.

✝ Hold within your heart true devotion to Mary, the Mother.

✝ Understand that persecution is the lot of all of My faithful ones and martyrdom the lot of many.

✝ Protect one another in the time of persecution. You will know who are of Me by the mark I have placed upon My own.

✝ Pray constantly the rosary of My Mother — 24 hours a day. Let there be no time when this prayer is not prayed day or night.

✝ The true sacrifice and the living Eucharistic Presence will disappear from My churches. You are not to partake of the bastard spawned out of the diabolical seed of heresy.

✝ Sustain and protect My faithful priests and religious. Their lot will be especially difficult and perilous.

✝ Believe with firm faith and sure hope that I sustain and protect you in all that is to come.

I have spoken. That is all. Now My Mother will speak.

(Mother Mary speaks): Dear Children: This is the harsh reality that is planned for the Church of Jesus the Christ. I have gathered you under My mantle. I am permitted to bring you consolation and graces during the time of your purification. Not one who is consecrated to My Immaculate Heart will be lost. This is the promise of the Father granted to you by My hands. This is the promise of the Mother to each of My children. I bless you with My blessing. Your Mother has spoken. That is all.

6-30-92 I SPEAK TO YOU A STERN WARNING

. . . Now say: My children must be brought to an understanding of the gravity of the events that will accompany the reign of the Evil One. I speak to you a stern warning of the immensity of the suffering He brings upon you. Lo, His star is on the horizon. Recognize it not at your own peril. I have spoken. That is all.

7-7-92 YOUR SUFFERING IS NOT IN VAIN

I will speak now. Hear well what I tell you. In My name say to My suffering ones: Dearest ones so close to My heart, I do not abandon you. All must be made clean in the suffering of the cross. As you join your cross to mine, My blood washes over you. As our tears mingle, your eyes are cleansed to see the glory that awaits you at the end of this tribulation. As the water from My side pours over you, it washes away the diseased blood of sin and corruption. The pure blood of My sacrifice flows through your veins. It is the blood of My life; it is the transfusion of purity and holiness. Thus say I the Lord God.

Now say: With sure hope endure your suffering with peaceful hearts. Give praise to the living God, for your suffering merits for you the reward of eternal life. Hope in the Lord God. Open your hearts to My compassionate mercy, your ears to My words of love, your eyes to the eternal kingdom, your mouths in praise and thanksgiving, for by your suffering I bring you into the glory I have promised to My faithful ones.

149

Your suffering is not in vain. So do I tell to you that you may not lose heart in the trial. So say I, the Lord God. That is all . . .

7-13-92 SOON I CEASE TO CALL

Come to Me, little one, I wish to speak. In My name say thus: I, the Lord God, call to all of My children loudly and urgently. Soon I will cease to call. I call you to repentance. I call you to myself. This hour of mercy comes to an end. In but a brief moment begins the hour of tribulation that marks the minutes left before I come to reclaim the kingdom. I have said it, so it is.

Now say: Woe to those who heed not My call. These are blind to My presence, deaf to My Word, and dumb to prayer. They see no evil in what is evil. They hear only the sound of their own voices spewing forth a river of unholy pronouncements that would bring glory only to themselves. There is no glory in sin, yet they sin with impunity and denounce what is of God. They are motivated by the selfishness of individual self-interest. There is no room in them for any but themselves. They see themselves as self-sufficient, yet

> *"Holy Lord God, by the power of your Spirit, through the intercession of the Mother of Mercy, open the eyes, the ears, and the mouths of those who refuse to acknowledge that you alone are God and deserving of our love and adoration. We ask this with confidence in your love, with trust in your care for all of your children, and with faith that you will hear and answer us. Oh Father of goodness and mercy, we praise you, we thank you, we love you. Our tongues proclaim your holy name. We look to the promise of your glory, we listen for your voice. Have mercy on us, we pray. Amen"*

see not their dependence upon all manner of human addictions. They are the servants to their passions, the victims of their self-delusions. These are they to whom I call out loudly and urgently — *will you remain blind, and deaf, and dumb?* Will you not recognize the peril in which you have placed your souls? Will you not come to My mercy? My mercy is for all of My children; My mercy is for you. Thus say I, the Lord God. Now say: I, the Lord God, have spoken. That is all. Go in My peace, little one.

_____

7-17-92 I TELL YOU CLEARLY THAT I COME

Take up your pen. Now write: Through this instrument whom I have chosen to speak in My name I say to you these words. Attend well to My instructions.

Now must My faithful ones find solace in My wounds, for the time of your passion is at hand. Were I to come without warning, all of My created ones would be lost in the eternity of hell. Were I to come without warning, the kingdom of the Father would welcome only a few from all the inhabitants of the earth. The mansions of the kingdom stand empty. I speak to each of My children and call you each by name, yet you hear not My voice. I tell you clearly that *I come — I come in power and glory, I come with justice and peace, I come to rescue My own for the kingdom. I tell to you that I come!* Thus must My faithful ones be purified in the blood of martyrdom. Remain pure and grow in holiness, for you know not the moment when I come to claim you. Thus say I the Lord God. That is all. Now say:

✝ **Blessed are they** who hear and answer Me, they shall live in My eternal presence.

✝ **Blessed are they** who invoke My name in the trial, I will rescue them.

✝ **Blessed are they** who keep My word and do not falter from My way, they walk with Me into the glory of the kingdom.

So say I the Lord God. That is all . .

THOSE WHO POSSESS LIFE POSSESS ME

I wish to speak, little one. In My name say: All hail the mighty King. See the glory of His countenance radiant as a thousand diamonds shimmering in the brilliance of a thousand suns.

Now say: Eyes have not seen, the mind cannot comprehend that which lies beyond the senses. Man, in His limited nature, cannot know the fullness of My glory. Even the most sainted ones who know Me fully in the mortal realm; even they, while in the body, fall short of complete knowledge of I Who Am! How can you think to make yourselves gods when you know not the one God? If you reject Me, what can you know of that which is God-like? If you know not that which is God-like, what is it that you make of yourselves? I only am God. You make of yourselves the golden calf, the pagan symbol of idolatry and faithless corruption. I wish to say to you, rejoice not! Your so-called liberation from the constraints of discipline bring upon you your own downfall. The cloak of civilized behavior falls from your shoulders and reveals you as the spiritless and soulless corpses of the walking dead. What is the power of the dead? Where there is no life, there can be no power. Those who possess life possess Me. Mine is the power and the glory. All else is illusion. So say I the Lord God.

7-22-92 **MESSAGE FOR THE UNITED STATES (Abortion)**

Now for today say in My name: I wish to speak to the inhabitants of the American states. This I say to you: *Unless this people once again turn back to Me, return to prayer, return to belief and faith, this mighty nation will crumble and fall never to rise from the ashes of its downfall.* I warn this people that death and violence will overtake them. I warn them that the voices of their children, stilled before their births, cry out for justice before the throne of justice. These innocent ones are betrayed as I was betrayed by the godless ones who cried out "crucify Him!" The innocent lamb was handed over to His executioners as these are handed over to theirs. Theirs is no less an execution by lawless masses as was mine. For this massacre of the innocents just retribution is about to be exacted from this people who flaunt My law in the dung heap of carnal desires and unrestrained passions. The proud land grovels in the ashes of its lost heritage. Its voice is but a whisper in the affairs of nations. So I decree. So shall it be. Thus say I, the Lord God.

7-30-92 ALL IS EVIL; ALL IS DARKNESS

Take your pen in hand. I wish to speak. In My name say . . . Now say: In the days to come what is hidden will be revealed. The holocaust of the earth at the hands of the Evil One is upon you. The holocaust of My faithful ones begins. All is evil; all is darkness. My time of mercy is ended. Weep tears of joy, for from the fires of the holocaust do you enter into the life-giving water — cleansed, purified, resplendent, glorious souls, My beloved sons and daughters. Enter in. Thus say i the Lord God. That is all.

8-1-92 NOW I AM THE GRIEVING MOTHER

Tonight the Mother wishes to speak. These are the words of your Mother.

Dear children My heart is burdened with grief. I cannot speak for the sobs that I cannot contain. How I long for you to open your hearts to My motherly care. Like the childless woman, My arms ache to hold My babes, but My arms remain empty. The time of My visitation is ended. I have gathered under My protection the ones who have responded to My call. Now I am the Grieving Mother — so few have answered My call. My tears fall for My lost children. Goodbye, My children. My work (of gathering) is ended. Now the Woman of the Apocalypse must take her army into the final battle for men's souls before the coming of the Son of Man. Be My valiant army. Persevere in the struggle. You have received My words. Let them be your battle plan. The Mother has spoken. That is all.

153

LOVE ONE ANOTHER WITH MY LOVE

I, the Lord God, wish to speak. In My name say: Hear, oh children, of the dawning of the new age of grace . . .

In My name tell to My people of the scourge that I visit upon them if they do not turn away from evil. In the name of compassion the human beings of My creation commit the most bestial acts against one another. Beasts do not have the capacity to love. If you have not love, you act like the beasts neither understanding nor forgiving your transgressions against each other. You are greater than the beasts. The beasts devour each other. Do you (if you) deny your humanness and turn viciously on your neighbor, then you become less than the animals who obey My commands. I have commanded you to love. Unlike the beasts you turn aside from what I have commanded for your peace, prosperity, and salvation. If you do not return to love, then the beasts of the earth will know more peace than My creatures of reason and intellect. In you, of all My creatures, have I given the ability to love. Hear the word I speak to you — *Love one another with My love.* Come to love and you shall know love. Come to Me — I am the fountain of love. Drink deeply, My children, thirst no more. Thus say I, the Lord God. That is all.

8-11-92 THE TIME OF GREAT PERIL QUICKLY APPROACHES

Write these words: Heavenly Father, we implore your mercy. Fill us with your Spirit.

Now say: Do you, oh peoples of the earth, hear My voice, for the time of great peril quickly approaches. The furies from hell are released from all restraints. They hurl themselves in ferocious attacks against the unsuspecting. They are everywhere seeking to undermine My law. They preach falsehood as truth. Truth is spurned and each one speaks His own truth.

My children refuse to understand that there is only one truth — I am Truth. Those who abandon Me, abandon truth. They follow the mother of lies, for out of this one is born every deception, every evil, everything unholy in the sight of the Father. He schemes always to bring ruination to all that is good and to all that is holy.

Beware, My faithful ones, that you too may not fall before the subtleties He parades as truth. I, the Lord God, implore you to turn a deaf ear to all those who would deny the Father as Father-Creator, the Son as Son-Redeemer, and the Spirit as Spirit-Giver of Life. These ones will not withstand the trial. So say I, the Lord God. That is all.

8-23-92 I DO NOT WISH TO CHASTISE

In My name say: I wish to speak to My children with the words of a father. I do not wish to chastise. I would not chastise if My children would but turn back from their sins and evil deeds. My command is not difficult to understand, yet so many seek in it every interpretation but that which I intended when I gave it. Love is unconditional self-giving first to Me, who am love, then to your brethren. Unless you know My love, you cannot understand the full meaning of love. Love is sacrifice. It seeks not for self-comfort but to the needs of neighbor. Each is neighbor. There is not one who is not neighbor to another. If My children would understand that love is not self-serving but seeking always for the well being of others, the evils that result from self-indulgence would disappear from the face of the earth. There would be no hunger, no wars, no bigotry, no prejudice, no barbaric inhumanity visited one upon the other, nation upon nation. Love demands self denial and self-control. Love is freely given to any and to all to uplift, to nurture, to sustain, always in the light of My love. Thus say I, the Lord God. That is all . . .

155

I . . . ASK . . . SINCERE ACTS OF PENANCE AND REPARATION

Take up your pen, I wish to speak. In My name say: There is no turning aside My hand of judgment. My child, tell to My people that I, the Lord God, ask of all My children sincere acts of penance and reparation. They must mortify their appetites. They must offer of themselves many sacrifices for their sins. No head must remain unbowed, no knee unbent in humble supplication before the saving power of the Triune God. Let your tears flow from hearts open to true contrition. Re-form your hearts and make them like unto mine. My heart beats out the tempo of the end times. Join your hearts to mine and our hearts will beat as one. We will enter together into the kingdom of the Father. That is all.

Now say: The Father calls each of His children to respond to His call for conversion of heart and reparation for sin. Sin is everywhere. Sin blackens each soul, and the light of mercy cannot penetrate the darkness. Prayer, confession of sin, conversion of heart, and many acts of reparation will open My heart of mercy. I tell you what will shorten the time of your purification. Hear Me, My people, and respond to your God, for many will be lost to the kingdom if the time of My judgment is not shortened. So say I, the Lord God. Thus shall it be. That is all.

9-20-92 MY FAITHFUL PRIEST SONS MUST BE STRONG. . .

Pick up your pen. Now I wish you to write these words: The Lord, your God, speaks. Infinite wisdom of the mighty God, fill us with your presence.

Now say: I wish to tell you a message of urgency. *I ask My children to pray on bended knee for certain of My priest-sons whose faithful witness to My truth will being upon them the wrath of the lawless forces of evil.* These, My faithful priest-sons, must be strong with the power of My Spirit if they are to withstand the diabolical scheme to destroy the last vestiges of My presence in My creation. They must speak, loudly and clearly, My words which I give them in defense of My truth. Speak, My loyal sons, the words I put into your mouths. Let not the raucous voices of the ones lost to Satan be the only voices heard in the land. Let My cohort, formed in the silence of the Immaculate Heart of Mary , now come forth fearlessly to proclaim My name in all the earth. They must be stalwart defenders of Jesus, My Son, and Mary, His Mother. Seek after the kingdom first, My beloved ones, and all else will be given to you in the earthly realm to restore My fallen children to My saving grace. Let your voices be heard proclaiming that Jesus Christ is Lord. Proclaim the name of the Virgin, Mary, as the triumphant Woman, she whom I chose from all generations, she who perfectly cooperates in My plan of redemption for all of My fallen creatures in all ages in time. My priest-sons, know that you will not be spared great suffering. Know that you will be abandoned and forlorn in your quest to re-establish My truth in the far reaches of souls long dead to My presence within them. You will engage the Evil One and His minions, and the battle will be fierce. Know that I sustain you in the battle. Refresh yourselves daily in My presence. I have called many to support you and sustain you. Ask of them when you are in need. All is in readiness. *Come forth!* The Lord, your God, has spoken. That is all.

9-22-92 LISTEN

Now for today I wish to say, in My name say: Behold your Mother, behold her Son. See the beauty of their countenances as they gaze with loving tenderness upon those who seek rest and repose in their two hearts. What more fitting a place is there to find the quiet stillness of the heart than in that of the pure and serene heart of the Immaculate Virgin and the radiant and merciful heart of the Son of the Mother. In every trial, within the quiet of their hearts, they knew My voice speaking words of love and encouragement. So do I speak to the hearts open to My voice. Be at peace, My children. Peace is My gift to those who permit the silence in their hearts to be filled with My voice speaking My Word. Hear My Word, My children. You will be filled with knowledge, and wisdom, and love.

Now say: My beloved ones, if you are to walk through the great trial with peace in your hearts, you must be open to My inspirations of the heart. My voice cannot be heard in hearts filled with anxiety and fear, and the bombardment of the senses with the incessant clamor of the world. Close your ears to the sounds of the world and listen with care. I do not always speak in a loud voice, but in quiet whispers and a soft touch. Hear Me, I speak softly to your hearts — *listen!* That is all. Thus say I the Lord God.

10-5-92 DELAY NO LONGER!

Come to Me now, I wish to speak. In My name say: I call out to you, My people, and tell you of My love for you. Let My love console you in the time of trial which is now upon you . . . In the days that lie ahead catastrophic events will be visited upon the whole of My creation. If the souls of My children are not prepared with the gifts of My Spirit, they will be as the foolish virgins, unprepared to meet Me at My coming. The day is upon you when I will cease to warn you; you will not withstand the trial. Please, My children, I the Lord God tell you urgently — delay no loner. Be awake to the signs that are all about you. Daily grow strong in My love. Pray unceasingly. Keep your souls pure that there may be no blemish at the time of our meeting. The time is upon you. I have spoken. Thus says the Lord God. That is all.

10-11-92 BE MY OBEDIENT PRIESTS

I wish to speak, little one. Now there comes darkness into the heart of My Church. The Evil One attacks with impunity the Holy of Holies. The mystery of redemption is masqueraded in the cloak of renewal. In truth, the mystery of redemption is denied. The sacredness of the sacrifice is defiled on the altars of false ideologies. My priest-sons have forgotten that I have chosen them to be servants to My people and shepherds of My flock. I wish for My priest-sons to reclaim their rightful inheritance in the temple of sacrifice. I speak to those of My priests in words of anguish, who relinquish with increasing frequency, My Church into the hands of those who will not serve Me. My side is pierced with the sword of their betrayal. Think you not of the day that is fast approaching when I will judge you for your betrayal? Have you no thought for those who seek for My truth and find in your mouth falsehood? What of those who seek in your priesthood the mystery of redemption and find only the shell of your lost faith? My brothers, I address you with love to tell you of My stern warning if you persist. Woe to those who lead My flock astray. Seek ye not what the lost sheep seek, seek only Me. Seek Me in prayer, seek Me at the table of the Eucharist. Seek Me in the truth of My Word. Seek Me where I am. Be My obedient priests in the service of your one God. Hear well, for My justice is swift. So say I the Lord God. That is all.

10-20-92 SEE HOW I HAVE PREPARED FOR YOUR FLOWERING?

. . . Now I wish to speak to My creatures of intellect. In My name say: . . . Whyfore do My creatures wish to destroy themselves? I see the evil they plan to rid My creation of the helpless and the burdensome. I, your God, permit what you choose. But, even they who seek to rid the earth of the unwanted, will themselves fall victim to the cleansing from the earth of all but the seed protected for their flowering in the new age of grace. My seeds of renewal, lie silent and still in the furrows where I have planted you among the brambles and weeds soon to be harvested from the earth. Take nourishment from the streams of grace that flow abundantly to feed you for the time of your flowering. You will not flower until the last weed and the last

159

bramble is cut down and their roots removed out of the soil of apostasy. See how I have prepared for your flowering? . . . I have spoken. Thus say I the Lord God. That is all.

11-1-92   SEE HOW I LOVE YOU

I wish to speak, little one. In My name say: See how I love you, My children. Your God loves you with an unreserved love. All the powers of hell cannot destroy My love for you. Howsoever far you place yourself from Me, still I love you unconditionally. Howsoever far you stray from truth, still I wait patiently for your return. You do not return. My love is unanswered and still I love you. Love is betrayed, love is refused. Love stands empty and desolate. It cannot be found in the dark emptiness of souls dead and buried in the wasteland of their godless existence. Your hearts have turned to stone. A stone cannot love. A stone remains fixed forever as an element of earth. In time the stone becomes nothing but dust and is carried away by the winds. Weep for yourselves, My children, for you are buffeted by the winds of godlessness that lay waste the rock of faith. Weep like My daughter Rachel who mourns the lost children of Israel. Weep, for you are children lost to the covenant of My love for you. Weep. Thus say I the Lord God.

Now say: Praise and glory to the ever-living God. Mourn not, My faithful ones, for the God of glory and majesty rescues you from the children of Rachel. Praise to the Almighty God for His love endures forever. I have spoken. That is all. Thus say I the Lord God.

11-3-92   UNITED STATES (ELECTION DAY)

(I wish to speak to your heart, little one. You must pray unceasingly, for the hour of darkness has come upon this land (United States), and it shall reap the fruits of its apostasy. You understand well the magnitude of what is now unleashed in the name of freedom. The voice of freedom is stilled, and the voice of oppression is raised in a mighty roar. The hour of judgment is come. So say I the Lord God.)

11-11-92 LET A NEW LIFE OF LOVE BEGIN

Now say in My name, I command My instrument to tell to you these words. Oh Holy Spirit of the mighty God, pour forth your gifts upon the barren desert. Let the seeds of renewal which lie silent and still, send forth the tender shoots of the vineyard protected for the new age of grace. What seems barren and desolate is filled with the life that waits My command to renew the face of the new earth. Those who seek to destroy what is created by My hand do not understand that I am Life. Life begets life. What has no life has no power to renew or restore life. Foolish creatures — they have no life; they perish and have not the power to flourish in the soil of faith. They die and are seen no more in the kingdom. All who wish to have life must receive My life — My life of love, My life of faith, My Spirit of life — ME. Thus say I the Lord God.

Now say: Little seeds of love, I call you forth. I call you forth first from among My seeds. It is love that heals the wounded hearts, the suffering souls, the aching spirits. Love defeats hatred and transcends death. Love begins new life. Let a new life of love begin. So say I the Lord God. That is all.

11-15-92 BE DISCIPLES OF PEACE

I wish to speak. In My name say: To My faithful ones I wish to tell you that the time of great suffering is come. My dear ones, I assure you that though it seems that all of hell is let loose upon the earth, still I am with you even in the darkest of the dark days of

161

your purification. In the time of your greatest suffering you will find solace in the knowledge that the Mother and her Jesus enfold you in their loving embrace and sustain you in every trial. In the midst of the fear and despair that will be all about you, you will know serenity and a peaceful heart which is our gift to those who trust completely that we are caring for them. Those who have responded to the call of the Mother and the warnings of the Lord God and have prepared well know the sweet comfort of the Mother's hand in theirs and the strong arm of the Lord God about their waists holding them firmly through every moment of the great trail. My faithful ones, you are not to fear what must be endured before I come in glory. There is no need to fear for you will be granted all that is necessary for your faithful endurance. In the depth of your suffering I will fill your souls with joy for you are deemed worthy to see the face of God. I have spoken. That is all.

Now say: My children, you must be disciples of peace. Live peace, pray for peace, give peace each to the other. Those who are now freed to bring persecution to My faithful ones are the instruments by which you will earn eternal peace. The Lord God, Prince of Peace, has spoken. That is all.

11-19-92 NO PORTION OF THE EARTH WILL BE SPARED

Take up your pen. Write these words: In the name of the Almighty God speak to My people. Tell them that the raging forces of nature will once again be set free to bring devastation and suffering upon those peoples and places which have not yet tasted of My wrath. I have foretold and so shall it be. The forces of nature obey My commands. No portion of the earth will be spared. This too is My judgment — in but a short time from north to south, from pole to pole a mighty tremor will split apart east from west. As in the days of pharaoh the sea will be parted; its waters will engulf the land. What is submerged will remain submerged, what is opened will remain opened. By the power of the Almighty God will this be accomplished.

Now say: The mountains roar, the heavens quake, the winds howl — all of nature proclaims the awesome power in the hand of the Almighty God. Take heed you who claim My power, your hands are empty. By My mighty proclamation I say unto you: I am your God, Supreme being, infinite being, eternal being. I proclaim My judgment against you — not one will escape My judgment. Thus is My word spoken. Thus shall it be. That is all.

11-22-92 MY FAITHFUL ONES, YOUR NUMBERS DIMINISH

Received at Franciscan Retreat House - Marian Day of Reparation.

Take up your pen, I wish to speak. Say in My name to all My children: Now must you prepare with sincere and a full commitment to conversion of heart and actions. I no longer open My ear or My heart to any who refuse My mercy. For them My time of mercy is ended. My Mother is no longer permitted to intercede for them. The harshness of My judgment is just. These are they who have heard the good news of salvation and have turned away. Without the graces granted through My merciful love they are left destitute of hope. The darkness grows darker, the light of mercy is extinguished.

My faithful ones, your numbers diminish. I do not close My heart of mercy to you. Pray that you also do not follow those lost to mercy.

Oh My poor children, grieve for yourselves. You do not know what you have relinquished. I cry for you, but you do not cry for yourselves. So say I the Lord God.

Now say: My beloved children, how I long for you to return to love. You must return freely of your own free will. What you choose is given. Choose love, come to forgiveness, make reparation for your many sins. Then I will be freed to grant mercy. Please My children, respond to My call. You have not the imagination to know what awaits you in time and eternity if My wrath is not turned aside. Hear Me well for your sins demand My justice. That is all. So say I the Lord God.

12-11-92 BEFORE THE FATIMA STATUE

(Prepare well little daughter. Increase your prayers. Pray the prayer of the prophets: Lament oh Israel, you have forsaken your covenant. Your cities are laid waste, your people led into captivity. Mighty one of Israel, I call your name. May it please you to have mercy on us. Let your face shine upon us.

"Seek ye first the kingdom of God.")

12-22-92 PREPARE! PREPARE! PREPARE!

I wish to speak. In My name say: Children of the royal throne of the most high God, I address you with words of love. *Prepare with full dedication of heart and soul for My coming which is not delayed.* Each day is a day closer to My coming in power and glory. The days remaining are few. Prepare with prayer and fasting. Open your eyes and see the signs I place before you. Be My children in trust and hope, for that which I tell you is imminent. Turn your ears away from those who scorn the words I place in the mouths of My prophets. I am Truth. I speak truth. In this present age, My creatures have refused the hour of mercy. As in the days before My first coming, My people endure great suffering. As they prayed for the coming of their Messiah so must you pray for the coming of the triumphant King-Messiah. *Prepare! Prepare! Prepare!* Oh yes, I say unto you prepare with your whole mind and heart and soul. Be ready to greet Me clothed in the garments of purity and holiness.

164

Tribulations and Triumph
Revelations on the Coming of
THE GLORY OF GOD
1993

"SEEK YE FIRST THE KINGDOM OF GOD"

"For the kingdom of God is not meat and drink; but justice, and peace, and joy in the Holy Ghost."

(Rom. 14:17).

1-1-93 YOU ARE MY SEEDS OF HOPE

My dear children, I am the Lord God. I speak to you through My instrument . . . I wish to tell My children to face the trials of this year with sure hope in My mercy and justice and with peaceful hearts. Each day brings its own joys, its own trials. Those who have faith in Me, those who have prepared as I have asked and stand in readiness to greet Me, will not fear the events that are about to unfold in the history of human endeavor. My faithful ones, you are My seeds of hope amidst despair, My seeds of love amidst hatred, My seeds of peace amidst war and strife. You are planted in the fertile soil of faith. In faith will you become the blossoms of hope and love and peace. I have spoken, so shall it be. Thus say I the Lord God . . .

SEEK NOT AFTER THE WORLD BUT SEEK YE THE KINGDOM OF GOD

Now for today I wish to speak. I am Jesus the Lord, obedient Son of the Father and son of Mary. In My name say: Seek not after the world but seek ye the kingdom of God. This I tell to all My faithful ones: so many have become lax in the commitment to peace, prayer, fasting, and the sacraments. I call you to renewed fervor. I call you to *live your consecration to My Sacred Heart through the heart of the Immaculate Mother.* I call you from the gentleness of My Merciful Heart. The time of mercy is soon to end. The time ahead is tortuous and a time of great suffering. *I do not tell to you these words to cause you fear but to inspire you to greater effort in seeking first, above all else, the kingdom of the Father.* What you seek in time will be granted to you for all eternity. So say I the Lord God. That is all.

LET EACH VOICE SPEAK MY TRUTH

. . . In the Spirit of the Living God awake from your slumber and see about you what chaos is wrought by the hands of those who have turned aside from faith. In every sector of society, in the churches, in most hearts the abomination of desolation has entered in. While My children slumbered in sweet oblivion the agents of Satan have worked seditiously and persistently to introduce thoughts of rebellion and censure against all that is of God. *Why have you been silent before the onslaught of this brood of vipers who instill their poisonous venom into the heart of all that is holy?* To give witness to My truth is not the realm of only a chosen few. I call each one of My faithful ones to break the silence that exists in the midst of the clamoring sycophants (base or servilely attentive flatterers or self-seekers, minions,) who spew from their mouths streams of denunciations against Me, Son of the Father, second Person of the Trinity. These voices of Satan denounce all that I have revealed as truth and introduce in the minds and hearts of the trusting false doctrines. *Let each voice speak My truth.* Your voices united in truth will soon silence the liars and the purveyors of heresy. *You must not remain silent. Speak My truth, defend My truth, give witness to My truth.* I have spoken. Thus say I the Lord God.

1-11-93 BEFORE THE TRIUMPH MUST COME THE SUFFERING

I wish to speak. In My name say: I am Jesus obedient Son of the Father and son of Mary. In but a short time the son of Perdition will be made known. Then all that has been foretold for this age will be fulfilled. Now is mercy granted to all who seek mercy. Then will the judgment be visited upon you through this agent of Satan. *If any doubt My word, you need only open your eyes to the evil that grows stronger about you. This is but a foretaste of what is to come. Before the triumph must come the suffering.* Oh My dear ones, if you would but turn back to Me, the tide of evil would find no shore upon which to deposit its corruption. You stray even further from Me, and the tide of evil moves unchecked to engulf the whole of creation. The tide will not turn until each one heeds My call to conversion of heart and actions, prayer, and donning the sackcloth and ashes of repentance. Heed My words well for, as in the days of old, mercy is granted to those peoples who hear the Word of the Lord and repent. Thus say I the Lord God. That is all.

1-13-93 WILL YOU STILL REFUSE MY MERCY?

I wish to speak. In My name say: I am Jesus obedient Son of the Father and Son of Mary. Now must My people recognize the tribulation of the end times. My people, will you still refuse My mercy? Have I not called you to repentance? Have I not offered My mercy endless times? Do you still fail to understand that if My offer is refused, My mercy must, perforce, be withheld and My justice must prevail? My brothers and sisters, your hearts are

167

hardened like flint. When flint is struck it produces the sparks to ignite the flames that burn away all that is in its path. The fire of My love has left you untouched; the fire of My justice will not. My message

I am the Lord God. I grant mercy to all who ask for it. If My mercy is refused and My people continue to sin without remorse or repentance, then they will suffer the consequences of their evil deeds.

is so simple:
I have said it. Thus say I the Lord God.

Now say: To you who remain faithful to My Word, to you who follow always the light of My truth, to you I grant My special favor to uphold and sustain you through every ordeal. Seek not after signs and wonders but seek to be united to Me in faith and truth. Thus say I the Lord God. That is all . . .

1-14-93 BE HEALED IN MY LOVE

I am Jesus the Lord. I bow in humble obedience to the Father. I wish to speak. Sons and daughters of the eternal Father, I address you with words of love. Such is the will of the Father that those who speak in His name go forth to proclaim the royal Godhead - Father, Son, and Spirit, Three-in-One.

Now say: I am Jesus. I speak to bring solace to the wounded hearts bleeding into the crucible of purification. Faithful hearts, rejoice in your suffering, for you are purified for the New Age of Grace where all will live in the light of My presence. Do your days seem an unbearable burden? Do you languish in despair? Can you see no promise for the future? I tell to you your hope is in the name of the Lord your God. Seek for Me in the depths of your suffering. I am your Suffering Servant come to wipe away your tears and bind up your gaping wounds. I enfold you in My loving arms and hold you tenderly to My heart. My love is the precious balm of healing. All who come to Me receive the healing grace of My love. So say I the

168

Lord God.

Now say: Be healed in My love. Look with hope in your hearts to the dawning of the new day. If (on condition that) I uphold you in the trial, be glad and sing joyfully for you will see the face of God. That is all. Thus say I the Lord God.

1-19-93 PRAY FOR PEACE

The day before the inauguration of Bill Clinton as President of the United States.

I wish to speak. I am Jesus the Lord, obedient Son of the Father and son of Mary. In My name say: Children of the Father, children of Mary, I speak to you words of great urgency. In this time of great peril increase your prayers. Pray as you have not prayed before. Pray on bended knee and with bowed head. **Pray for peace!** Pray with full attention; pray from the depth of your soul. Pray with hearts full of love and compassion for the terrible suffering of your brothers and sisters. Pray for yourselves, for neither will you be spared great suffering. **Pray, children of Mary, pray!**

Now say: The major instruments of My justice are now in place. You have been warned. Thus say I the Lord God.

2-3-93 I AM THE SAFE HARBOR

. . . Remember My words: "The first shall be last and the last shall be first in the kingdom of the Father". You see about you many who gloat over their apparent triumph in grasping the reins of power. Their triumph is short-lived, and the hollowness of their victory is soon to be exposed. The winds of change blow stronger and these hollow reeds will not withstand their strength. Only those rooted in fidelity to the moral law of the one, holy, and living God will not be uprooted. These are they who profess the name of Jesus the Lord. These are they who, in their lowliness, seek refuge from the storm in My loving heart. I am the Safe Harbor. I carry them in safety through the tempest. They are preserved for the kingdom. These who are least before the exalted of the world are they who remain faithful to My word. These are they who shall be first in the kingdom. Thus say I the Lord God. That is all.

2-8-93 THE PROPHECIES MUST NOW BE FULFILLED

Now I wish to speak. I am the Almighty God, Triune God. Speak in My name these words: Let all who have ears to hear listen well for that which has been foretold in ages past will find completion in these years of the last decade of this century. Mankind does not wish to understand this message, but I tell to **them, it is so decreed. Seek ye not after the world for the world will be forever changed. You will lose all that is of the world. Nothing will remain of the world as you now know it.** Would that you open your hearts to what has been prophesied for this age, but you hide from truth and cower in fear and refuse the hour of mercy. Hard-hearted people, the prophecies must now be fulfilled for you have refused the covenant of love. I have spoken. That is all.

Now say: (If you) Refuse the hour of mercy, then you must accept the judgment. By your own hands will you suffer the consequences of your choices. I grant what you choose. My poor children, how you grieve Me. So be it. Thus say I the Lord God. That is all.

2-18-93 SEEK YE NOT AFTER THE WORLD

I wish to speak, little one. I am Jesus the Lord and obedient Son of the Father. In My name say: Courage, My faithful ones. Seek ye not after the world. I tell you this again for what is of the world is fleeting. Swiftly does time come to an end. Swiftly do the forces of evil gather for their final assault. Even more swiftly do the unsuspecting fall before the allurements of fame, and wealth, and power. Yet,

170

these are but wisps of smoke that disappear in the slightest breeze. Be like the mighty oak tree - firmly rooted in the earth, strong before the storms of nature. Plant your feet in the soil of faith; stand firm before the storm of apostasy that seeks to uproot the faithful from My truth. Howsoever fierce the storms that blow about you, remain fixed where I have planted and nourished you. Soon the storm passes and once again the sun shines upon that which has not been swept away by the storm. My people, do you understand that unless you take shelter from the storm in the truth of My Word, you too will succumb to the storm? Beware of the teachers of heresy, of false prophets, of the wolves who hide in the skins of the faithless shepherds of My flock. They devour My poor helpless lambs who turn to them in trust. Poor lost souls, you are easily deceived because My Word as I gave it no longer bears the truth of revelation. The Spirit of the living God is rejected and the spirit of darkness has entered into the soul of the church. Woe to the deceivers of the innocent and trusting. Woe to you I say, for the souls of those you lead astray must be redeemed upon the Cross of My merciful justice. So say I the Lord God. That is all.

2-22-93 YOU SEE NOT THE EVIL . . .

For today I wish to continue. In My name say: My people, in this day (a period of time, not a specific day) you hear of death, disease, wars and rumors of wars. You see about you the increasing ferocity of the forces of nature. *Still you see not the evil that is breathed into the very structure of your world. You resist not the evil deeds and persecute those who seek to open your minds and hearts to the desperate hours of your purification which you now live. Unless you hear and see these signs that are all about you, you will not be prepared for that moment when the reality of hell confronts you.* So say I the Lord God. That is all.

171

3-1-93   MY WORD THIS DAY IS ONE OF ENCOURAGEMENT

I wish to speak. Take up your pen. Little one, tell to
My people that Jesus brings them greetings of peace
and love. My word this day is one of encouragement.
I wish to tell those engaged in the struggle to keep My
Word pure and My Church undefiled that I keep My
promise and the gates of hell shall not prevail. They
must know also that the struggle has only just begun.
They must not falter or grow weary. Nor must they
lose heart for I carry them through the battle and
shield them in adversity. I am their strength. Who
come to Me are fortified for the battle, and I do not
forsake them. Be peaceful and trust that though the
battle seems lost, in truth it is already won for My
Mother has succeeded in raising up her loyal children
into a mighty army of prayer and reparation for the
sins of the world. The forces of evil stand defeated
before these chosen ones. Rejoice then and be glad for
the hour of your deliverance is at hand. The struggle
is fierce, the battle intense but in the end only the
faithful will remain to join Me in the inheritance of the
Father. I am Jesus obedient Son of the Father. Let
these words bring you consolation and joy. That is all.

3-6-93   IN SUFFERING IS COMPASSION BORN

Let us begin. Take up your pen and write these
words: The Son of Man speaks to the children of the
Father. In My name say thus: Rejoice children of
God, I come upon the throne of justice to bring you
My compassionate understanding of your sufferings.
Still, what you suffer for My name's sake is a sin
offering in recompense for the unspeakable crimes
committed by human against human and nation
against nation. Were suffering to be taken from you,
My human creatures, you would not come to know the
strength of My mercy and the power of My love. In
suffering is compassion born. In the stillness of your
hearts let compassion for the suffering children of God
speak of the need to bring solace and comfort to the

172

desolate and afflicted. Compassion in and of itself is but the stepping stone by which justice for the downtrodden must be pursued from the fullness of the love and mercy granted by My hand to My suffering children. Then shall your suffering be turned to joy and your hearts rest peacefully in the knowledge that justice has been served. Let no man sit idly by so long as His brothers and sisters are subjected to the greatest inhumanity inflicted one upon the other in this evil age. I the Lord God say unto you - unless mankind acts with justice for all, and especially for the least and most helpless of My children, will it then suffer the loss of My compassionate understanding and suffer the justice of My wrath. Thus say I the Lord God. That is all.

3-9-93   I HAVE HEARD MY PEOPLE CRY

Take up your pen, I wish to speak. In My name say: The Lord God brings you greetings of peace. I the Lord have heard My people cry. I have heard their mourning and weeping. Their anguish and suffering do not fall on deaf ears. I do not forsake them. *Tell My people, in My name, that the birth pangs of their deliverance have only just begun. What has begun must continue to the final end. Think not that the travails that will give birth to the New Age of Grace will cease. As in all births, new life does not come forth until the process is completed. So it must be for the coming of the Kingdom.* This I tell to you that you may not lose heart in the struggle. Thus say I the Lord God. That is all.

3-15-93   THE UPHEAVALS OF NATURE ARE A SIGN OF THE TIMES

I wish to speak, little one. I am Jesus, obedient Son of the Father, born of the Woman Mary, My Mother. In My name say: Dear ones, the destructive forces of nature which have been visited upon certain areas of the American states are but a foretaste of the upheavals of nature which I have foretold to My instrument who speaks in My name. There will be those who will seek to explain these upheavals as **natural processes. I say to you they are aberrations of the natural order and are a sign to My people that I do not delay My coming.** Those who are open to the signs I place before them recognize the time spoken of by the prophets before My coming in power and glory. Be peaceful, My people, for the Spirit of the Living God renews and restores all of creation in preparation for My coming. Be My joyous and faithful followers for it **is given to you to know the time of your deliverance. Give praise and thanksgiving to the Almighty God whose merciful love grants you these signs that you may not be unprepared for the coming of the Kingdom.** Thus say I the Lord God. That is all.

Now say: Open your hearts to the presence of My Spirit, and you shall not be left unwarned or unaided in the time of great trial which is upon you. I have said it. Take heed. That is all.

3-31-93 THE WOMAN CLOTHED IN THE SUN

I wish to speak, little one. I am Jesus obedient son of the Father. In My name say: Behold in the rising of the sun the dawning of the new day. Behold in the Woman clothed with the sun the dawning of the New Age of Grace. I wish you to remember that the darkness of the night precedes the light of the new day. So too will the light of faith and truth follow the darkness of this age of apostasy. I grant the light of the Woman to illuminate this age as a sign of My love and mercy. Those who respond to her light, I grant the graces of conversion and repentance. Who would be lost to the kingdom are restored to life in grace. Those who refuse the Woman, My Mother, do not recognize the sign for this age which I place before all creatures. **She who is the radiance of the universe is the sign granted to mankind by the hand of the Father by which souls are ransomed out of evil. If** *anyone doubts the role of the Woman, Mary, in the salvation plan of the Father, let that one understand that salvation history began with Mary and will end with Mary. This Woman, the Mother, brought salvation into the world in the human form of her Divine Son, Jesus. So too do I come again through this Woman, the Woman of the Apocalypse, who prepares the way for My coming in glory.* It is I, Jesus, who say to you, refuse not the sign of the Woman, Mary, for it is through her maternal care that you are restored to kinship with her Son Jesus, your brother, in the kingdom of the Father. This is the age of the Woman. Recognize the signs for this time and respond to My request - **return to Me.** Let My Mother show you the way. I have spoken. That is all.

4-9-93   GOOD FRIDAY - FEAR NOT THE TOMB

I wish to speak. Take up your pen. In My name say: The awful deed is accomplished. My body rests in the dark and silent tomb. What man has sought to destroy, the body torn and mutilated, lies still awaiting its transformation into glory. Let those who mourn be comforted. Let those who see the face of death look beyond death to the sure hope of resurrection. Fear not the tomb; it is not the final resting place. It is but the entrance into eternal glory. The body shall come forth transformed in the glory of its God just as did mine. Suffering is the prelude to glory. Death releases the body from suffering and frees the soul to return to Me. Death must not be viewed as a terrible scourge but as a gift of My merciful love by which you are granted release into eternal life. From the moment of its creation the soul prepares the body for the moment of its death. How the body responds to its soul determines its entrance into eternal glory or eternal damnation. Those who follow in My footsteps will rise glorified and triumphant as did I. All the rest molder in the stench of eternal damnation. On this day when My body is laid to rest in the tomb, I call you to rejoicing My beloved ones, for your glorious resurrection awaits you beyond the door of death. Thus say I the Lord God. That is all.

YOU ARE CREATED IN THE IMAGE OF LOVE AND MERCY

My dear one, I wish to speak. I am Jesus obedient Son of the Father and Son of Mary. I wish to say this day that you, My brothers and sisters, must cease the abuse and scorn you heap upon each other. This is not My love but rather the work of the Evil One who goads you into bestial acts of depravity. If I had wished for you to act like the wild beasts, the Father would have created you as they are created. Rather, you are created in the image of love and mercy. If you turn aside from that image, you cannot know of what love and mercy consist. I am the pure image of all that is holy. If you but once again turn your gaze upon what is revealed by the Father through His Son, you will come to know your stature as a child of God. No more will you respond from the depths of depravity, and once again will you become the image of goodness and purity, the resplendent human creature reflecting the goodness and glory of God by whose hand you were placed in the world. Is this not the better choice? How is it that you have deluded yourselves into the belief that love and peace can be brought forth from hatred, and war, and self-gratification? The seed must perforce become what is contained within its kernel. *So will you become what is in your heart, and the seed in your heart will scatter and take root in the hearts of those around you.* Soon the seeds of faith, hope and love are uprooted by the weeds of sin and evil, and your souls cannot be nourished in the grace of My love. Is this truly what you prefer, My dear ones? Is war and strife, disease and corruption, butchery and bestiality truly what gives you peace and happiness? If this is so then you have made of yourselves monsters such as those who inhabit the nether world of the Evil one. You are not My created ones (i.e. you are no longer as

God created you); you have no place in My kingdom. You have become the image of the Evil One whom you follow into eternal damnation. Thus say I the Lord God. That is all.

4-18-93 BECOME MY DISCIPLES OF MERCY
Feast of Divine Mercy - Franciscan Retreat Center

I wish to speak, little one. Please take up your pen. In My name say to these My faithful ones: I seek reparation for the sins of the world. You who know My mercy and respond in faith and love to My Feast of Mercy, must become My Disciples of Mercy in a world that increasingly turns away from mercy. I ask each one here present to show mercy to all by whom you have suffered injury. I ask you to forgive from your heart, forgive in My love, forgive any and all transgressions. Forgive each other as I now forgive you. Go in My love to love with My love. Only when you love Me and then turn to your neighbor with My love will mercy flow like a river into the parched souls of those who do not know My merciful love. Thank you, My dear ones, for responding to what I ask of you this day. I am Jesus, merciful Lord, eternal love. I have spoken. That is all.

4-28-93 THE SON OF CORRUPTION

I wish to speak dear little child of My Heart. Thank you for coming to Me as I have asked. Now say in My name: I am Jesus the Lord who comes to bring you the good news of your deliverance from this age of Satan.

The diabolical plans of this Son of Corruption slowly unfold and soon He will claim His place as undisputed leader of the world. His scheme for world domination has long been evolving, and the time for its fulfillment is at hand. My poor deluded creatures cannot see what is before their eyes. The fruit of a world corrupted, secularized, apostatized and organized under a union of nations is ripe for His plucking. He holds in His hand the fruit from the Eden and tempts you with the promise that you are like unto God. The sweet fruit is in truth rotten to the core and the maggots of His lies and deceptions have consumed the seeds of truth and justice. Once again My creatures partake of the fruit of disobedience and self-will, and once again their reward will be no less than the first. Those who succumb to His wiles will follow him to perdition. Those who refuse the bitter fruit are the ripe fruit harvested for the kingdom. Thus say I the Lord God.

5-7-93 EUCHARISTIC EXPOSITION
First Friday Eucharistic adoration.

(. . . Dear child of My heart, I wish My Eucharistic presence to be exposed in all My churches so that My people may come to know Me more fully. Pray for this intention. Thank you for honoring Me this day. I bless you abundantly and grant you My peace. So say I the Lord and savior.)

5-11-93 WHERE ARE YOUR HEARTS?

Come little one, I wish to speak. In My name say: Where are your hearts My children? I seek and find your hearts so cold and so hardened to any but your own selfish desires. The hearts of your brothers and sisters are bruised and broken, yet you see not their pain. Why is it so hard for you to love one another as I have commanded? Can you not see in the hearts of your brothers and sisters the same pain and suffering that is in yours? If this is so, then why can you not reach out to one another in love? Why do you persist in fracturing the garment of your shared humanness into splinters of factions opposed to each other in hatred and divisions? I tell you from a heart filled with anguish that unless you heal the divisions among you; unless you set aside your petty jealousies, your delusions of self-empowerment, your grandiose schemes of self-autonomy, the divisions among you will grow wider and deeper. Have I not told you that a house divided against itself will fall? How can any

178

family, any nation, the world itself close the great chasms among peoples without loving as I love you? *Do not be deceived by those who claim that love permits evil and sinful deeds to ease the suffering of their brothers and sisters.* I say to you, this is not love. This is a great deception visited upon you by those who do not understand love. Unless you know Me, you cannot know My love, and if you do not know My love, you cannot heal the rifts of your fractured and splintered world. My dearly beloved people, please learn to love one another with My love. Come to Me once again so that I may teach you how to love. Then shall peace be restored in your hearts and in your world. I am Jesus the Lord, the loving Son of the Father and of the Mother of Love. So say I the Lord God. That is all.

Spirit of truth, Spirit of the living God, thou who restores and refreshes us and makes all things new come and fill us with your holy presence. Speak to us that which will renew us and fortify us in every trial. Come Holy Spirit, take possession of our darkness that we may become children of the light, holy and faithful people of the Lord God Jesus Christ. Praise to the Holy Trinity, Three-in-one, through whom is salvation given in the name of the Father, Son, and Holy Spirit. Amen

5-19-93 PRAY TO MY SPIRIT

I wish to speak, little one. Please take up your pen and let us begin. In My name say:

Now continue thus: In My name say to My people pray seriously and with hearts open to My Spirit that you may know the fire of love by which you will burn with zeal for all that is holy. Become My holy people and by the power of the Spirit your holiness will bear witness to those who walk in the darkness of apostasy and disobedience to My Word. If you strive for holiness, you will be blessed abundantly with the gifts of My Holy Spirit. You will grow in virtue, and in the depth of your soul you will hear My voice and know that I am present. Seek after holiness, My people, if you wish to restore faith, hope, and love to an unloving, uncaring, and hopeless generation. My beloved Mother has called you to become holy people. I tell you in these words to hear and respond to what the Mother asks. Be My holy people. Let the power of the Spirit overshadow you in this perilous time that you may become My holy and faithful disciples for the end time which you now live. You shall become the disciples by which the New Age of Grace in the restored kingdom will flourish and nourish the generations to come after this time of the great trial. I, the Lord God, ask this. Hear and respond. I have spoken. That is all.

5-24-93 MEDITATION ON THE JOYFUL MYSTERIES OF THE ROSARY

Mother Mary Speaks

† The Annunciation
I come to announce the coming of My son Jesus in power and glory.

† The Visitation
Visit My son often in His presence in the holy tabernacle of the Church. My poor Jesus, they have sealed him in the tomb. He is removed from the body of the Church, but He will come forth glorious and triumphant.

† The Birth of Christ
Come and visit Jesus in His home (church) as did the lowly and exalted at His birth. The door of our home was always open to those who sought him.

† The Presentation of Jesus in the Temple

Receive My son from My hands as the Father received him from My hands in the temple.

† The finding of Jesus in the Temple
Find My Jesus where He is - in the Eucharist, in the tabernacle, in His Word, and in the hearts of your brothers and sisters. If you seek for him here, you will find him. I come to help you find him.

(. . . My days on earth are now but a few, yet I do not leave My children orphans. In prayer (i.e. if you continue to pray) will I continue to bring My children My protection. Therefore, I ask you to pray without ceasing until you are brought into the Kingdom of My son Jesus. I, the Mother, ask this.)

6-1-93   **REFUSE NOT THE HOUR OF MERCY**

. . . Now I wish to speak to My faithful ones. In My name say: Now will your hearts be filled with great suffering. Offer this suffering for the conversion of your brothers and sisters who are led by means of lies and deceptions deeper and deeper into the dark abyss of the secular and humanistic goals of those who seek to govern the whole world. My people do not recognize the plan of these sons of Satan to abolish My presence in My creation. Do not be seduced by the promise of power, and glory, and honor as are these, but remain My humble and obedient children. Refuse not the hour of mercy which now comes to an end, and plead My mercy on behalf of those who trustingly accept the lie that each one is responsible only for himself. This is not so for I have said that in the fullness of time, I will call each to account for His response to the needs of His brothers and sisters. The souls of many of your brothers and sisters are in jeopardy. Please respond to My request for these who would be lost to the kingdom if you, My faithful ones, do not seek My mercy for them. Ask and it shall be granted. So say I the Lord God. That is all.

181

6-4-93 THE STAR OF THE EVIL ONE RISES
First Friday Eucharistic adoration

I wish to speak now, little child of My heart. Hear Me well. In My name say to My people: The star of the Evil One rises higher and more brightly as the time for His triumph quickly approaches. I speak of this event often to warn you of His impending appearance upon the world as supreme ruler. I warn you urgently to prepare your souls in purity and your hearts in love. You do not understand the enormous evil He will bring against all those who profess My name. Be assured, My faithful ones, that I the Lord God do not spare My justice against those who will not spare their brutality against the innocent and the faithful. What say you, My people? Are you prepared to stand before Me? Think hard upon this, My dear ones. **Respond now to My plea - return to Me, convert your lives, make reparation for your many sins.** Do not think to put this off for another day, another day may not be granted to you. So say I the Lord God. That is all . . .

6-9-93 TEACHING ON THE BOOK OF REVELATION

Let us begin. When My son, John, received My words they were clouded in mystery. Throughout the ages men have attempted to unravel the mystery without success because it was not yet the time spoken of for them to be revealed. Man, of himself, cannot decipher what is hidden. Thus, I speak now to reveal to mankind what it must know, for now is the time spoken of by My servant John. I wish now, as I did then, to address the churches.

First to the Roman church who follows faithfully and obediently My vicar on earth I say to you: You are My loyal and faithful remnant. You uphold My statutes and have not strayed onto the path of apostasy. Hold fast with loyalty to this My one true church which contains the fullness of My Word and the fullness of the power of My Spirit. Be consoled and know that the gates of hell will not prevail against it.

182

I say unto you the purity of this, My holy temple, is stained by the deeds of those who proclaim loyalty to this, My church on earth, but seek to destroy it from within. **Thus, My Church, which I formed and placed on the rock of Peter must undergo its hour of purification before it rises resplendent and glorified, cleansed from these and their deeds.**
I speak now to those churches who profess My name. I see in you a deep faith and a great love for My Word. Yet, I say unto you this is not the fullness of the Church I established on earth. Each contains a portion of the truth but not the full truth as I have revealed it. I urge you to re-examine what is contained in the fullness of My revealed Word. Understand that I am truly present - Body and Blood, Soul and Divinity under the species of bread and wine. Understand the fullness of the truth of the person of the Woman, Mary My Mother, and her role in the salvation history of the world. Understand that I desire all of her children to honor their Mother as the Father, the Spirit, and I her Son honor and love her. Though you honor and reverence all that is holy, still you do not honor and reverence her who is the holiest of all that is holy. This I desire from you.

To those who reject any belief that I exist and place your trust in the churches of atheism, secularism, humanism, materialism, and egoism, I say to you *I EXIST. I AM.* I love you still. But unless you turn away from the world and the gods of your own creation, My justice will come against you. I say to you, set aside the pursuit of your worldly gods and open your hearts and your minds to My presence that I may shower upon you the grace of conversion and the gift of faith. Then will you be freed to find Me where I am - in My Church, in My Word, and in your heart.

When I speak of **My Church** you are to understand this to mean the living entity which proclaims that Jesus Christ is Lord, that Jesus Christ is Savior, and proclaims the fullness of My revealed word by the power of the Holy Spirit.

The priestly ministry of My son Jesus began with His baptism by My servant John (the Baptist). The beast who rises from the sea are the priests who follow in the footsteps of Jesus in accepting the priestly ministry but betray their vocation by betraying the Word by their dissent, disobedience to the visible head of My Church on earth (the pope), by their rejection of My truth as handed down for all generations through the Church I formed on the rock of Peter. These are they who destroy My Church from within. These are the **Beasts of Betrayal**. As the water of the sea contains infinite droplets of water, the beast from the water brings countless souls into the water of life polluted by false doctrine, untruth, blasphemy, heresy, abandonment of My commandments, and loss of faith.

(Note: For a continuation of teachings on the Book of Revelation see the messages for 7-6-93, 7-20-93, 8-15-93, 9-1-93, 10-15-93, 11-13-93).

6-21-93 VIRTUE IS YOUR STRENGTH

9:15 a.m. - There is silence now in heaven (Rev.8:1).

3:30 p.m. - I wish to speak little one. In My name say: Receive My Spirit My dear ones. In the days to come you will witness the fall of the great nations of the world. No nation can be strong unless the life of each citizen is deemed valuable and worthwhile without exception. Strength is not in armaments, in wealth, in the use of force or the attainment of fame or fortune. Nor is power strength. Open your hearts to My Spirit that you may come to know that to be strong in the Spirit one must be weak in the flesh. To be weak in the flesh, one comes to recognize that power is in the will conformed to the will of the Father. Then does the will subdue the passions and one is freed from the chains that bind the human spirit in bondage to every obsession and every addiction. It is not the passions that make you human, but My spirit of love and mercy

184

and forgiveness. Then do you come to recognize the worth and dignity of each precious person without exception. Do you see, My dear ones, that love, humility, forgiveness, obedience to My commands, faith and trust in My care for you are your strength? Did I not possess these virtues and by them triumph over death? So too are they your strength to triumph over your weaknesses. When you become strong in My strength then nations can be converted and peace restored to the world. Thus say I the Lord God. That is all.

6-25-93 THE FATHER DOES NOT REVOKE HIS JUDGMENT AGAINST YOU

"Subject us not to the trial".

(Jesus speaks) - My dear children, today I wish to speak to you of the trial which you now live. In My name say: I plead with you My dear ones to take heed to My call to mercy. Oh My dear children, the Father does not revoke His judgment against you. If you were to know what you must suffer for your willful stubbornness in refusing the offer of mercy, you would die in an instant with the horror of what is now upon you. *Can you not understand that if I had not warned you of your danger, if the Father had not sent the Immaculate Virgin Mother to all parts of the world to prepare you for My coming, if He had not sent out His messengers and prophets of this age among you, My heart of mercy would have been closed against you long ago.* I, the Almighty God, call you each by name. I offer you again and again every means to return to faith and a life of virtue in accord with the commandments. If you would but open your hearts to My voice. Many have heard and responded. To these do I grant My merciful love and protect them in the trial. But to those who refuse to turn aside from their abominations, I say - the hour of mercy is come to an end. It is ended! I have said it.

To My beloved faithful ones I say: You will not

endure the trial unless you remain faithful in prayer, loyal to My Pope, John Paul II, and fully surrendered into the safekeeping of the Immaculate Heart of Mary the Mother and My Sacred Heart of Mercy in whose rays you are protected.

† Pledge your allegiance to no man lest you sell your soul to the devil.

† Remain steadfastly fixed on My truth which has been safeguarded in the Church of Peter.

† Make no compromise with the false teachers and their false doctrines.

† Keep alive the faith in your hearts.

† Return to the catacombs.

† Fear not persecution or martyrdom for I am with you and do not leave you.

† I grant you peace (interior) for you have faithfully prayed for peace.

My heart is heavy as I speak these words. My tears fall and I tremble in anguish for what must now fall on mankind. Would that you had heard and responded. What must be must now be. I have spoken. That is all . . .

7-6-93   HEAVEN IS SILENT (The Seventh Seal)

Be still now little one, I wish to speak. Know that I am God and I speak to your heart. Now say: In My name speak to My people these words.

† Heaven is silent before (at) the opening of the seventh seal (Rev. 8:1).

† Heaven is silent before the proclamation of the Almighty Father that the final holocaust in all of its fury is come to unsuspecting mankind.

† Heaven is silent before the awe-full and awful events that are to bring this age of human history to an end.

186

† Heaven is silent before the fullness of the power in the hand of the Almighty God which is unleashed against the powers of evil that seek to destroy all of created goodness.

† Heaven is silent before the multitudes who will wash their garments in the blood of martyrdom.

† Heaven is silent so that the merest whisper of repentance may be heard before the final onslaught of the Evil One (occurs).

Heaven is Silent! Prepare! Prepare! Prepare!

So say I the almighty and all powerful God who proclaims to you the time of the Seventh Seal. I have spoken. That is all.

7-20-93 THE FIRST TRUMPET

I am the Lord God. Thus do I say to My people: Hear, oh children, that which I speak and hearken to My voice. I speak to you the message of the first trumpet (Rev. 8:7) which is soon to be sounded throughout the universe. The angel of the first trumpet stands poised to sound the first note. The first note begins the refrain of calamities which will devastate one-third of all created matter. This I say unto you - refuse My warning at your own peril.

I say and proclaim that truly one-third of creation shall perish. Already this judgment has begun. Humans perish in greater and greater numbers from plagues, incurable disease, war, starvation, torture at the hands of despotic rulers, and self-immolation. That abomination of abominations - the holocaust of the unborn generation - claims this number (1/3) from your future. Everywhere does mankind fall in greater and greater numbers, and so it shall continue until the fulfillment of the prophecy is accomplished.

The heavens proclaim the glory of the Lord God, but the heavens will be darkened and the glory of God will

187

be hidden behind the darkness. The demons of darkness snatch away the precious life of the number allotted for this period of the great trial. It has been prophesied; it is so. (See 9-1-93).

7-23-93 WHAT FOLLY TO DAMN YOUR SOULS!

I wish to speak, little child of My heart. In My name say: . . . Now say: In the fullness of time there shall come to the human condition the one who will fulfill the prophecies that bring to an end this sinful generation that began with the first parents. Sin entered into the world; sin was defeated by the death and resurrection of the holy and pure sacrifice of Jesus Christ, the Lord and Savior. I say to you sin is defeated yet My creatures continue to follow the voice of the one who brings about ruination and damnation. I am Jesus who came into the world to free you from sin and lead you to the kingdom of peace and justice. There is no peace and there is no justice in the world, yet you fail to see why this is so. Your hearts and your intellects are enclosed in the darkness of the lies and deceptions of those who seek to re-create My creation by the feeble efforts of their own intellects and by their own hands. The measure of their intellects is but a particle of dust that they pit against the infinite and supreme intelligence of their all mighty God. Throughout all of the history of mankind only this tiny particle has been granted to mankind. What folly, what colossal pride to think that without Me, your God, you have the power, the intellect, the means to create what you cannot create. Folly! This is folly! This is doomed to fail, and it shall fail for you cannot and will not succeed in any endeavor unless it is granted by My hand. You then become the pawns of the evil forces who are My enemies. Folly! I say to you, all is folly for you bring about your own destruction and have not the ability to recognize what your grandiose pride will not permit you to recognize. Fallen creatures, you will continue your fall to the fiery pit because your pride does not permit you to humble yourselves. Pride is your downfall as it was in the beginning. Folly! What folly to damn your souls.

188

Truly, I say unto you, you have come to know evil but you have refused to know Me, the living God, the creator of all that is good. Thus are the fruits of the first sin ready for the harvest. So say I the Lord God.

7-31-93 FORGIVE ONE ANOTHER

Take up your pen, little one, I wish to speak. In My name say to My people: A short time of peace will once again be granted to My brothers and sisters who have engaged in brutal warfare, one against the other. I have heard the prayers of My people, and I answer them. Come unto Me you who are weary; you who are heartbroken; you who are scarred in body, mind, and spirit. Come unto Me in the midst of desolation and destruction, and I will heal you with My love. Understand in your hearts and in your souls My desperate plea in My agony - "Father forgive them for they know not what they do." You must do no less - forgive one another. Let there be no hatred in your hearts for hatred will only continue the cycle of revenge. This cycle can only be broken if enemies refuse to be enemies, if peace is restored to each heart, and if each soul is cleansed of its grievous sins committed against the most inviolable of all human rights - the right to life of every human creature. *The dignity and worth of each person, from the moment of conception to the moment of natural death must be upheld and protected. Inhumane brutality will cease when the worth of every person is recognized and when My creatures recognize the truth and live My command to "love your neighbor as yourself."* Will you not learn this most important lesson from what hatred has taught in the most brutal conflicts everywhere in the world? Look to these and see what hatred has wrought, then turn from hatred to love and forgiveness. Please, My people, use this time well. I have spoken. That is all.

(Note: On 9-13-93 Israel and the PLO signed a peace agreement.)

8-15-93 THE HARVEST OF THE EARTH

I wish to speak, little one. Now I wish to speak a message of great urgency. You must say to My people I have given the command to the angel of death to begin the harvest of the earth. The trumpet sounds the fateful dirge. The fulfillment of the prophecies commences. Oh creation, you groan and shudder and you quake with trepidation for the old order quickly passes away and the new is not yet born. That is all I wish to speak for this day.

8-20-93 SO FEW UNDERSTAND MY TRUTH

Now I wish to speak little one. The hour is late. So few understand My truth. So few accept fully what has been given for your salvation. I, the Lord God say to My people - accept with faith and trust that which is preserved by the Church of Peter as necessary truth given by My hand to bring My children to their glorious reward for their faithful adherence to My revealed Word. So say I the Lord God. That is all.

8-27-93 FIGHT THE GOOD FIGHT

Now little child of My heart, I wish to speak to all of My children. In My name say: Your faithfulness to My Word as preserved in the Church of Peter is rewarded. In the stillness of your hearts you hear My voice speaking words of encouragement. Fight the good fight, My children. The battle intensifies, and I call to you to wage the battle in My truth and with love in your hearts. Look with eyes of pity upon those who scorn what I proclaimed as necessary for salvation. Let your pity move you to offer many prayers and sacrifices for them. Speak out My truth boldly and without fear. Be willing to accept abuse and persecution. Remember My words (paraphrased) - blessed are they who suffer persecution for My name's sake; theirs is the kingdom of heaven. Thus say I the Lord God. That is all.

THE SOUNDING OF THE TRUMPETS

Now I wish to speak little child of My heart. I the Lord God proclaim and announce the sounding of the trumpets. I have given the command to commence the purification of the earth. Let there be no doubt in the minds of My creatures that what has been prophesied by John of Revelation is now being accomplished. You must recognize My command in the furies of nature that roar the mighty anthem *Jesus Christ is Lord, Jesus Christ is King, Jesus Christ is Master of the Universe.* Thus do I say unto you the earth and all it holds, the heavens and all they contain: My human and nonhuman creatures will be decimated by the forces of nature which will destroy a full one-third of created matter as I have foretold. All of nature is in revolt because My human creatures of intellect and power have usurped what rightfully belongs to Me. That which I command as the harmonious order in nature becomes disordered when rebellious mankind usurps My authority and seeks to subvert and control that which is My dominion alone. You who would be gods, look about you and see the massive death and destruction that is all about you because you have sought to make yourselves masters of the universe. I tell to you again, *You have not the power!* Only I, the Lord God, have the power you seek. Only in Me and with Me can peace and harmony be restored. Therefore, children of the Father-Creator, turn once again to a life of faith, restore My presence in your hearts, and respond to My request for conversion and repentance. Seek first the Kingdom of God for the Kingdom is what you seek — peace, love, harmony, justice, and integrity among all people. That is all for now, little one.

9-3-93 **COME TO THE REFUGE OF THE SACRED HEART**
First Friday Eucharistic adoration.

Thank you for coming to Me as I have asked. Now I wish to speak. In My name say: Peace to My children. I come with greetings of peace. By the power of Almighty God proclaim the mighty name of Jesus. Proclaim His sovereign majesty. Proclaim the Word who is your king and savior. Seek in the heart of Jesus your safe refuge. Come to the refuge of the sacred and most holy and pure heart of Him who seeks to gather you in. Let the peaceful stillness of His Heart enfold you. Let its soft beating soothe you like the lullaby sung to a restless child. Softly it murmurs the sound of love and refreshes you and restores serenity to hearts and minds weary from the strife and struggle of the world. If you seek for the kingdom, seek for it in the Sacred Heart of Jesus. Come to My Heart. There you will find refreshment, there you will find what you seek. Thus say I the Lord God. That is all.

9-7-93 **UNITE**

Please, little child of My heart, get your pen. I wish to speak. In My name say: Though the hour is late, still there is time for My faithful ones to form the temple of God into a united church. I call each one to stand united in faith against those forces that mark the final assault against My Word. Unite your voices, unite your hearts, unite your efforts in order to reestablish the primacy of truth and justice in the affairs of men. Once again I admonish you that a house divided against itself cannot stand. Speak with one voice, My people, in defense of My truth, in defense of My pope (John Paul II) who works tirelessly to proclaim My Word to all peoples, and in defense of the one true church of Peter. With one mighty voice defend your faith and your one God before the powerful tribunals of the world. With one voice united in faith let your prayers resound in every corner of the earth. Fill the farthest reaches of the heavens and the infinite chambers of the heavenly kingdom with your prayers. With one voice give praise and thanksgiving to the Almighty God, for peace and justice, mercy and love are granted to those who ask. With one voice ask and it shall be given to you. Thus say I the Lord God. That is all.

THE STAGE IS BEING SET

I wish to speak, little child of My heart. Today begins the rapid unfolding of the events which will usher in the final holocaust of the end times. My people are lulled by a false security. My people must understand that the agreements of peace between peoples and nations are but the prelude to great deceptions by those who seek to rule the world. *I solemnly tell you that the stage is being set for the one who will step forth as the great deceiver of all mankind. He orchestrates this masterpiece of deception, and those open to My Spirit understand the meaning of the events that are about to befall mankind.* Give praise to the Almighty God for He rescues you for the kingdom.

Now say: Quickly now do the puppets of Satan dance to the tune of their master's diabolical scheme to destroy the world. See to it that you also do not become actors upon this stage of infamy. *The curtain for the last act is drawn, and when the grand illusion comes to an end, the curtain will close upon this age of Satan. I call upon you now to choose where you will stand for the grand finale - with the satanic puppets or with your God who will triumph and alone stand victorious at the dawning of the New Age of Grace. I tell you the plot, I tell to you the ending.* Thus shall it be. So say I the Lord God.

HELL IS ETERNAL REALITY

I wish to speak, little one. To those who seek refuge in My Sacred Heart I bring greetings of peace and joy. You have heard My Word and responded.

I speak these words to those who have heard My Word but have refused the hour of mercy. To these I pronounce My judgment. Salvation is in the Word of God made flesh. Were I to come now, you who have rejected the Word in its flesh and in its inspired revelation, would forever be lost to the kingdom of darkness. You scoff, you mock My Word, you persecute those of My faithful ones who proclaim and uphold the Word of your salvation. I solemnly tell to you hell is eternal reality. Scoff though you will, (if you) refuse the truth of My revealed Word, blaspheme all that is holy, then for all eternity will you suffer the reality (hell) which you now reject. I pronounce this judgment against you and not one who persists in willful abandonment of the Word of God will be spared eternal existence in the reality of the damned. I Am Who Am have spoken. Thus say I the Lord God. That is all.

10-3-93 BE STILL MY PEOPLE

I wish to speak, little one. In My name say: There must be no fear in the hearts of My people. Rather, peace must reign supreme for where I am there is peace. If you wish to find peace, you must convert your lives. There is no peace in violence, hatred, promiscuity, and the evils resulting from power, greed, lust, and self-debasement. Your peace must be My peace. You will find My peace in the quiet stillness of your heart. Be still My people. Cease your incessant searching after peace in evil, and vice, and gross and obscene violations against the dignity and person of your brothers and sisters. ***Stop your evil!*** I warn you solemnly that the world now stands at the brink of disaster. ***Beware of those who plot to secure a world confederation of nations. Beware, for these agents of Satan will succeed in destroying all of creation. Beware of the one who beguiles you with the promise of world peace.*** This is a peace forged out of lies, deceptions, brutal inhumanity, and ruthless enforcement of lethal laws and policies. I solemnly tell to you that this peace is a delusion which is the prelude to the annihilation of the world. Therefore, My people, you must keep vigilant and seek your peace in Me. If you know Me, you will not be seduced by the promises of the false prophet of the Apocalypse (Rev. 16:13-15). I am your Safe Harbor of Peace. Thus say I the Lord God, Prince of Peace. That is all.

10-6-93 THERE WILL BE GREAT SUFFERING

Dear little child of My heart, I call you to My service as an apostle of the end times. Seek out My lost and frightened lambs. Announce the good news that Jesus is coming. My children must not be frightened. If their souls are maintained in purity and they have prepared to stand before Me at any moment as I have asked, there is no need for fear. *In the days to come there will be great suffering throughout the earth. Because mankind knows not its God, it will follow the beast.* My faithful ones find solace nowhere in the human realm. That is why, My children, I have called you to the rock of faith and unwavering trust in My care for you. These will be tested sorely. Truly I say unto you, the fires of hell will devour the earth, but the fire of My love will sustain you in the holocaust. The earth and all it holds, the heavens and all they contain begin their death throes. So be it. I the Lord God so pronounce My Word.

10-15-93 RECALL THE WORDS OF THE PROPHET ISAIAH

You are to write these words in the name of the Holy Trinity. In the name of the one God tell to My people this message of great urgency. Recall the words of the prophet Isaiah. Recall His condemnation of the haughty and mighty who lived in splendor while their subjects lived in squalor and destitution. Recall His condemnation of the kings who sought to wage war one against the other. Recall the images of the destitution of the earth. Recall the woes to be visited upon mankind if they refused to abide by My covenant which I made with the Fathers of old. Recall all that this prophet speaks, for I say unto you (that) what is contained in this prophecy is fulfilled in this day and this age. This age refuses the covenant of the new sacrifice and offers once again the holocaust of wars, genocide, the aborted fruits of the womb, and the plagues and pestilences which devour My creatures in hideous deaths.

† I condemn this age.
† I condemn your apostasy.
† I condemn any and all who seek to bring about the ruin of souls.
† I condemn those who seek to destroy My creation.

I pronounce My condemnation and I announce to you the woes of the end times (Rev. 8:13). Woe I say unto you for the mighty arm of My wrath is fallen. Woe unto you, My creatures of pride and self-will, for your moment of glory will end in the ashes of your delusions and godless schemes of self-empowerment. You too will become the victims of your own grand illusions which come from the source of all evil - Satan himself. Woe I say unto you My creatures who turn to pagan gods and the practices of the occult. You shall die in great terror for at the moment of death you shall stand face to face with the evil one - Satan and all the horrors of hell. Woe, woe, woe, I say unto My creation. I am the mighty God of heaven and earth, Three-in-One by whom is salvation granted. Thus say I the Lord God.

10-26-93 THE NEW JERUSALEM

I wish to speak little one, take up your pen. By the power of Almighty God proclaim that Jesus Christ is Lord; that Jesus Christ comes in power and glory; that Jesus Christ, Son of god, eternal with the Father and the Spirit announces all that is final in the affairs of mankind. Do you doubt that this is so? I tell to you that all that the Father has deemed necessary for the salvation of mankind now quickly approaches the final days granted for this age of the fallen Eden. So often have I foretold this time and sent My prophets out *among you. What has been foretold now comes to pass in these last days before the power in the hand of God refashions the new heavens and a new earth. What has been since the beginning of time, ushered in under the power in the hand of the Evil One, will cease to exist.* Hear Me well you who dwell on the earth, you must be aware that Satan does not willingly release His hold on this corrupted Eden, and defends ruthlessly and with all His cunning that which rightfully belongs to the kingdom of the Father. All that the Father has created in time is despoiled at the hands of the master of destruction. What has been given into your stewardship has been wrested from you because you refused the covenant of mercy. Thus, what has been taken out of your hands undergoes its violent purification in preparation for the coming of the Son, the pure Lamb, whose pure

O Sanctissima, o Purissima, the fairest Queen of Heaven, you who prepare the way for the coming of the triumphant Son in His resplendent majesty, pray for us in the hour of trial. Oh Mother of the incarnate God grant us your protection and deliver us from the powers of evil. Grant that we may know the love of your Son and the everlasting joy of heaven. Amen.

sacrifice was a necessary step in the restoration of the kingdom from the grip of Satan. He clings tenaciously to that which He has usurped from the stewards of the kingdom. Thus is the battle waged between the Prince of Darkness and the Legions of Light, **and thus must the old order of sin and evil give way to the New Age of Grace, the New Jerusalem** (Rev. 21). Thus say I the Lord God.

11-2-93 THE MOTHER OF ALL SOULS
All Souls Day

I wish to speak, little one. In My name say to My people these words:

Now say: The holy virgin, Mother of God, Mary, My Mother remains upon the earth to recall to your hearts the urgency of the times in which My faithful ones are tested in the fire of great suffering. She is the heavenly prophet come down to earth at My command. If you hear her, you hear Me.

Now say: The Mother of All Souls is arrayed in the garment of her royal motherhood as she joyfully receives the souls of her triumphant children into the royal homestead. Children of Mary, what joy fills the heart of your Mother for each child who responds to her call and faithfully seeks the eternal kingdom. Seek ye the kingdom, children of Mary, and what you seek you will find. Thus say I the Lord God.

11-5-93 **PRIDE IS THE GOD FROM WHICH ALL EVIL FLOWS**

I am the Lord God. I wish to speak. In My name say: My dear children, you have not heard My voice, you refuse the hour of mercy. You have become depraved in your violations against My covenant of love. However many the times I have called you to love, you have chosen pride as your covenant, the covenant for the self by the self. Now must I remove pride for in My creation love will conquer all evil. The hearts hardened in pride will perish. My kingdom is a kingdom for the redeemed. Those who refuse redemption refuse the covenant of love. They perish in the bitter anguish of their unrepentant egoism. Oh poor children enslaved by the sin of Satan, I mourn for you for pride once again banishes you from the Eden, the new heavens and the new earth.

Now continue thus: I the Lord God say from the heart of My wrath no idols, no other gods will I permit. I have said it. *Take heed for pride is the god from which all evil flows. Thus say I the Lord God.* Hear and repent. That is all.

11-13-93 **IT IS FINISHED**

The Glory of God, the work of the Lord proclaimed for all mankind. This is My word spoken through My little child, the child of the Heart of Peace. I have said it.

My peace be with you. In My name My child speaks to you these words: Thus is the moment of your deliverance upon you. Thus do I proclaim in a loud voice the judgment of the earth. The angelic host raise the trumpets and sound the warning notes (Rev. 8:2, 6). Woe, oh woes - to My sinful creatures do I lament the dirge of woes. (Rev. 9).

My mouth opens; the earth trembles.
I speak. My tongue is the two-edge sword (Rev. 19:15 Douay Rheims) - the sword of justice, the sword of mercy. The heavens and the earth tremble.

I wield the sword; the kingdom is restored.

I open the gate; the Son of Man comes forth for all to see. For all eternity does the gate separate the two kingdoms - those within and those without. All creation trembles. All is silent. None is heard but the voice of God thundering forth the proclamation -
"It is finished" (John 19:30). *Now do I open My mouth!*

11-30-93 UNJUST LAWS AND GOVERNMENTS

Get your pen little child, I wish to speak. In My name tell My people these words which I speak. I speak to their hearts words of comfort for I see in their hearts the suffering of the persecuted. More and more the laws that are meant to govern peoples are in fact the laws of injustice by which the helpless and the weak, the innocent and the God-fearing are chained and silenced before the tribunals of unjust governments.

I speak specifically of those laws which seek to stifle all opposition to the grand illusion, the master deception (see 9-19-93) of governments which seek to establish the kingdom of humanity. What kingdom is this? - the kingdom of the enslaved. In this kingdom the ideologies of the godless take precedence over the people of faith; where under the guise of individual freedom, the freedom of the just is subjected to harsh repression. I say to you, this begins for this time the persecution of those who uphold the truth of My Word and refuse the yoke of the political domination of their godless and perverted leaders. I tell to you that though the voices of the just are stilled before the powerful of the earth, their voices are heard before their God by whose hand will justice be restored, though injustice now reigns supreme.

Take heart My faithful ones. Though all seems lost, still I am in your midst urging you onward in the battle against the forces of evil. Bring to Me what seems hopeless and I will raise up before you those who will lead you in the darkness of the great trial. I prepare them in the silence of My heart, and I send them forth as My apostles to lead you into the New Age of Grace. Thus say I the Lord God.

12-2-93 THE KINGDOM IS AT HAND

Dear little child of My heart, I wish to speak. Tell to My people to use this season of Advent to prepare as I have been asking over these many years, for My coming will burst forth as a blaze of love purifying all of My creation for the coming of My presence among you. Rejoice at these words, My beloved ones, for the kingdom is at hand when your pain and suffering, your tears and anguish will be wiped away and you shall finish your days in the radiance of My love and glory. "Glory to God in the highest" the angels sang at My birth, and their song is repeated at My coming as King of Glory. Glory to the King of Glory.

Let your spirits rejoice and your hearts be glad for soon the gates (of heaven) will be opened and you *shall see Me coming with the multitudes of heaven, coming upon the clouds of justice, coming to bring you into the Kingdom of the Father. Sing out the triumphant song of praise - Christ the King comes. I come!* Thus say I the Lord God . . .

12-3-93 COME TO THE EUCHARISTIC PRESENCE
First Friday Eucharistic adoration.

(Prepare! I am coming. Let Me speak to your heart, little one. Swiftly do the days pass. You must understand that all must be accomplished in the world of men as has been foretold. See how peaceful is My dwelling place (the chapel where the Eucharist was exposed). This is the peace I wish for each heart. The peace of this place where I am present before you is but a foretaste of what is to be in the time beyond the tribulation of the great trial. Tell to My people I wish for them to taste of My presence when I stand before them in My Eucharistic presence. In My presence they will come to know what is to be in the kingdom of the Father. Tell My people I long for them to come before Me that I may fill them with every blessing. Thus say I the Lord God . .)

12-6-93 THE REMNANT

. . . Now say to all people of faith, soon now must the Son of Man raise up the remnant. Soon now will you flower in the fields left barren by the harvest of the weeds of apostasy and heresy. Soon your seed shall scatter and take root. See to it that the seed remains pure in truth, nourished by faith, and rooted in My Word. Thus do I say to you these words that you may not falter on the path where I am leading you. Soon now, your faithfulness will be rewarded and you and your seed will be as the lilies of the field - clothed in beauty and fragrant in holiness. Thus say I the Lord God (see message of 10-20-92).

12-7-93 REPENT! REPENT! REPENT!

I wish to speak little one. Hearken to My word which I place within the heart of this My chosen one. In the name of the Lord God do the prophets speak lest the Word of God find no ear in the din of godless pursuits. Now do I call forth the prophets for this age to recall to the godless masses the imminence of My sword of justice which will bring to an end this evil age. **The prophet speaks urgently My word - Repent of your sins!** Repent oh lost children of Israel. Repent you upon the heights and in the depths. Repent you powerful and you lowly. Repent all sinful creatures. I cry out in a loud voice - **Repent! Repent! Repent!** Hear the voices of the prophets warning you of the Word of God placed on their tongues - **Repent!!!** **I the Lord God raise My voice in urgent warning that each one must hear My message and understand that what I speak must be heeded immediately lest the sword strike.** Thus say I the Lord God. That is all.

12-10-93 THE SECOND COMING OF JESUS

(Mother Mary speaks) - (Thank you for responding to My call. Stand with Me, little child, in the bitter cold of this dark and dank shelter which is chosen by the Father as the throne room of the tiny babe, His son. This is no kingly palace; it is little more than a hovel. There is no soft pillow upon which to lay down our weary heads.

The child stirs in My womb, and I know that this dreary place is soon to be transformed into a holy tabernacle by the glorious God-child who dwells therein. A stillness settles over the starry night, and the presence of My Lord, My Son, becomes manifest in the cold still of the night. The heavenly host surround the shivering Babe enclosing him in the warmth of their presence. They stand in wondrous awe adoring the Son from heaven come down to earth, then raise their voices in jubilation announcing to the world - **Christ the King is Born.** The angels sing their hymns of praise for from the lowly servant has come forth the Savior, the promised One of Israel.

Rejoice with Me in the birth of My Child for the world grown as cold and dark and dreary as the place of His birth, is soon to see the God-man, triumphant king, Lord of lords, the glorious God come in all His power and glory. Join with Me in preparing for His coming which is upon you. *In the heavenly stillness of His first coming wait with Me in joyful anticipation of His Second Coming.* As I received the God-child into My arms, I receive you and hold you close under My protective mantle until the day of His coming. Your Mother blesses you with My blessings. Go in peace.)

12-18-93 REPENT NOW, IMMEDIATELY

Take up your pen, little one, I wish to speak. This day I speak this word to your hearts. I am the Lord God. Hear Me now and let not mockery or derision cross your lips against My word which warns you of imminent calamities. Rather, let your hearts accept My word and your mouths open with sincere and heartfelt prayers. Children, I plead with you to do as I ask. Before this year is ended (1993) I will speak a message of great warning. Quickly now do events unfold. My faithful ones, you now enter the period of greatest danger, and the urgency of My warning must not be lost upon you. I say again - *Repent Now, Immediately* (See message of 12-7-93). Please, it is I your God who knows all that is upon you who pleads, who implores, who begs from the depth of My grief if you do not repent, to open your hearts and accept My merciful love. *Wait no longer. It is imperative that you wait no longer.* I have spoken. That is all.

12-21-93 THE MESSAGE OF URGENT WARNING

Take up your pen the Father wishes to speak. My dear and faithful daughter now must you write these words which I give in urgent warning to all people. Thus say I:

As this year (1993) comes to an end I warn you that My wrath can no longer be contained. Thus begins the calamities of My justice. Understand that sin and evil have triumphed throughout creation, and for the sake of the faithful remnant *I announce to you this day the day of My justice.* Be forewarned that calamity shall follow calamity, disaster follow disaster, and no area of the earth will be spared.

    † I announce to you a fearful persecution of any and all who profess My name.
    † I announce to you the imminence of the martyrdom of My beloved and loyal priest-son, My chosen pope of the end time (Pope John Paul II).
    † I announce to you unspeakable atrocities; the war to end all wars.
    † I announce to you death and devastation unparalleled in human history.
    † I announce to you it is come, and it comes at the hands of the one who now steps forth to rule the whole world. ***Now begins the day of Anti-Christ.*** Now it begins.

This is that time for which you have been preparing and why I have called you to repentance. Now do I wield the sword of My justice. Thus do I pronounce My word; thus it is so. I have spoken. So be it . . .

Tribulations and Triumph
Revelations on the Coming of
THE GLORY OF GOD
1994

"I ANNOUNCE TO YOU THIS DAY THE DAY OF JUSTICE'

"And the heavens shall declare His justice:
for God is judge."
(Ps. 49:6).

1-1-94　　**BE MY OASIS OF PEACE**

I wish to speak little one. In My name speak these words: Tell My people — *Seek Peace.* You see all about you those who speak of peace, but I say to you peace must not be spoken but lived. However much My people speak of peace, however much they wish for peace, however well intentioned their efforts, peace eludes them for peace begins in the heart. A heart conformed to My heart of peace creates an oasis of peace. Like the oasis of the desert, these hearts of peace exist amidst the desert of strife and warfare. If each heart would but become an oasis of peace, soon the desert would flower and grow into a lush paradise in which peace would flourish and strife and warfare would forever be vanquished. My dear children, I call you to live peace. Aggression will not bring peace. Softly, gently, with great patience and forbearance be peace - be My oasis of peace. Let not one grain of sand remain. Vanquish the desert. Let peace reign. Thus say I the Lord God.

BE WHAT I ASK YOU TO BE

Heaven wishes to speak, little one. Take up your pen. I am the Father of the living. Who live are those in grace filled with My presence within them. Let your hearts become the tabernacle for the living God, pure and undefiled. I call you to repentance My dear ones, that I may come to each one and dwell therein. When I am present peace enters in and the soul exults. In turn I heap My blessings and graces upon you in abundance, and the soul is empowered to progress in virtue and holiness. In turn I find great pleasure in these souls and bring to them the union of My Spirit with theirs. In turn the Spirit enfolds them in blessed renewal. Thusly do we work to sanctify the soul and bring it to its eternal glory. Therefore, My child, tell to My people to be My tabernacles from whence is My light a beacon for all who are in darkness. Let My presence in you, as living tabernacles, bring hope to the forlorn and peace and charity to the hopeless. Be what I ask you to be. Thus say I the Lord God. That is all. (See message of 2-5-94).

(Mother Mary speaks): Call My children home. Open the churches. Let My Jesus be present to all who seek him.

THE ERA OF PEACE

I wish to speak, little one. In My name say: Peace to My people. Speak with My tongue and tell My people I came to bring salvation to mankind. I come now through the triumph of Mary - virgin undefiled - in bringing salvation history to its culmination, *to establish the history of the Era of Peace.*

Oh My dear ones, if you would but believe that beyond the strife is the sublime union of mind and spirit in perfect harmony with the harmony that is the inheritance given by the hand of the Creator -- one bread, one body, one Spirit in the Lord Jesus Christ. A house united is a house built upon the foundations of truth and faith whose members are one in body, spirit, and soul in the unity of the one God. Come, My children, come to the reunion which marks the beginning of the New Age of Grace that awaits you following the tribulation of the end time. Thus say I the Lord God. That is all. (See 2-18-94)

1-22-94 PRACTICE OF ABORTION CONDEMNED

Dear little child of My heart, speak and tell to My people on this day which marks the anniversary of the slaughter of the innocents that is called abortion, that there can be no effort spared to end this abominable holocaust. These innocent babes are your brothers and sisters who, by your indifference, suffer the humiliation of barbaric martyrdom at the hands of those who have forsaken the sanctity of even their own lives. These slaughtered victims, sacrificed on the altar of perverted self-interest, cry to Me in their agony, and I hear them. This great evil shall not go unchallenged, and the day of justice is not withheld from those whose hands are covered with the blood of their helpless victims. For too long have I endured these barbaric executioners; therefore, *this day I tell you that any who permit, support, advocate, or engage in this abomination from hell stand condemned before My justice. The blood of the innocent must be expiated. Those who remain silent will be judged for their silence.* Each one will be called to account and only those whose voices and hands are raised in defense of My beloved but voice-less children will be spared My wrath. Thus say I the Lord God.

2-3-94 There are those who will seek to silence My faithful ones. They (the faithful ones) must not remain silent.

2-5-94 THE TABERNACLE WILL BE DESECRATED
First Friday Eucharistic Adoration - 2:45 p.m.

I wish to speak, little one. Remember I am always with you. My people must understand this for in the *days ahead many will not know My physical presence. The tabernacle will be desecrated, and the image of the one who would be God will be placed therein. This body given for your salvation will repose no more in the holy temple.* Receive Me into your hearts, My loyal ones, that I may dwell in the tabernacles made ready to receive Me in this time of preparation before the final desecration. Then will you become My dwelling places until My triumphant return as the King of Glory. Prepare a place for Me in your hearts, for the Beast of Iniquity destroys the temple, the dwelling place of the Lord your God. It is so. Thus say I the Lord God. (See message of 1-7-94).

Second message - 10:30 p.m. I wish to tell you more, little one. *My people must understand the urgency contained in My words. Unless they understand, and they must understand this grave warning which I now give, they will acquiesce to the abomination that My Church has become in My eyes.* Truly I say to you, I have not abandoned you, you have abandoned Me and turned My Church into a den of corruption, a pagan temple. The veil is again torn asunder and My Church is divided. It hangs upon the cross of apostasy, and heresy, and blasphemy. As My beloved Mother stood at the foot of My cross, so too do My faithful stand at the foot of the crucified Church carrying within their hearts the seeds of truth by which will I restore My kingdom to the glory of its triumphant God. I have spoken. That is all.

2-18-94 THE ERA OF PEACE

This day I wish to speak of a matter most dear to My heart. In My name speak and tell to My beloved children that what dawns upon the horizon of human history is the coming of the era of peace in which all will be united in truth and faith and love. *Speak joyfully of this era for My people must keep hope in their hearts during the dark hours of their purification. Do not ponder the events of the purification, but rather find comfort in the promise of the restoration of the kingdom of God in the affairs of human creatures.* You must not lose sight of the magnitude of My love for you, nor must you falter from My truth which the Father has revealed to you in the Word of scripture. There is but one Word; there is but one Church; and where there are now many there shall be but one as I intended from the beginning. I speak to you these words from the fullness of My love for you that you may know I am God and that what I speak to you shall be so. Thus say I the Lord God.

2-23-94 **I DO NOT SUFFER THE FOOL**

Take up your pen, I wish to speak, little one. In My name speak these words: I say this day that My people must not be lulled by a false sense of security. Remember My words that when all are speaking of peace will I come on a sudden. What peace can there be unless hearts are converted in love of God and thereby, love of neighbor? Do not ancient hatreds still smolder in the hearts of mankind? Have not renewed antagonisms given voice to the status of civil strife and social upheaval? Have not My children given vent to their spiritual poverty in abhorrent deeds that cry to heaven for vengeance? My people, and all are mine, there can be no peace for you spurn peace for the glorification of individual rights. You have deceived yourselves in thinking that compassion permits sinful and evil deeds, that power is virtue, and strength is self-will. This is foolishness, and I do not suffer* the fool.

Thus say I the Lord God: Repent of your foolish ways; seek truth that you may no longer be deceived. Receive My Word into your hearts that you may turn in truth to true knowledge and true peace in the Lord God Jesus Christ. Then will true peace return to the world. I have spoken. That is all.

* Tolerate, allow.

3-7-94   YOU HAVE YOUR CHOICES

I wish to speak, little one. Most recently I have brought My people urgent warnings of impending catastrophes. *I wish to say this day that your future depends on your response to My warning which I have brought to your attention.* Do you think that I will withhold My justice before your defiance of My laws which bring order and holiness if you would but return in love to their practice? Think you not of the consequences of your defiance? Do not close your eyes to the great evil that you accept as necessary in order to bring about the revolution of the godless society. Look about you. What you see is only the beginning of a society which knows not its God. Think very hard, My people, of what your world will be like if My enemies succeed in stilling My voice in the affairs of men. My enemy is the Anti-Christ. If you refuse My urgent warning, then you will suffer the consequences of what you choose. *You have your choices, My people - for good or for evil, for life or for death, for My mercy or My justice.* Choose wisely, for I grant what you choose. I have spoken. That is all.

3-17-94   A HEART CONFORMED TO MY WILL IS A HEART CONFORMED TO MY LOVE

Thank you for coming to Me this day, little one. Take up your pen for I wish to speak. I wish to say this day (that) heaven and earth, the handiwork of My love, stand poised on the threshold of a time when all of creation will unite in My love. So many of My faithful ones long with ardent desire to be united to Me in love. If you love Me and seek always to do My will, then we are united in love. Far too many speak their love for Me but seek their own will before mine. A heart conformed to My will is a heart conformed to My love. Turn your gaze from contemplating your own self-image and look into the heart of your God if you wish to know of the love which I seek from you. It is not a word on the tongue but rather a flaming passion, an all-consuming desire for communion and for the possession of that which is loved. This, My

210

people, is how I love you. This is how I wish you to love Me. Then will we be united in one love . . .

3-24-94 YOU TALK, TALK TALK

I wish to speak, little one. In My name tell to My people that I, the Lord God, speak from a heart filled with yearning for the restoration of a life of grace within the souls of all who profess My name. So many profess My name but live as though I do not exist. YET I DO EXIST! If I do not exist, then there is no salvation. Do you not understand that it is your hearts I seek, not the words that give the lie to what the words profess. You talk, talk, talk, but believe not in what you say. What you profess is a mockery of what it means to follow Me in faith and obedience. I do not want hollow words and cold hearts. Was My passion a hollow gesture? No! It was an agonizing act of infinite and passionate love. Passion is no lifeless, hollow, and meaningless emotion; it is an all-encompassing desire flowing out of the depths of the soul, and does not find rest until it possesses what it desires. I wish to awaken in you this passionate desire to know Me and to possess Me. I have given you all that you need for this union between us. How is it that you would refuse that which can fill the passionate desire in your hearts that nothing else can fill: it is I your God. Think in it My people - only I can fill your emptiness. I wish to give you the graces that will restore you to My loving mercy, but you do not ask. Hence it is that I plead - ASK! I will open My heart of mercy to you. So say I the Lord God.

3-31-94 CALVARY IS LOVE
Holy Thursday Evening

Thank you for coming to Me this night, My little one. This is an infamous night, a night of betrayal, a night of bitter anguish. My spirit recoils from the fearful deeds that are soon to fulfill the will of My Father. My body quakes in revulsion, and I cannot contain the groans that escape My tortured spirit. I find no comfort, I am alone in this suffering, for I know that the cup must be drained to the last drop. It is the cup of your salvation and no man can drink of this cup but I. Only I! Only pure love can overcome sin, and only pure love can triumph over evil. Only God-love can repair for the downfall of God's sublime human creatures. I see all of time from the beginning to the end. I see the multitudes who are lost to the kingdom. I see each sin that has been committed, is committed, and will be committed to the end of time. Do you understand that if the cup had been taken from Me, if I had refused to drink the bitter dregs, for all eternity you would never know the presence of the God who loves you even to die for you. That is what sin accomplished.

Now I accept the cup of death to give you the cup of life - My body and My blood for your salvation. Accept My gift of life. I offer it freely and completely to the last drop of My blood, to My last breath. Love begins the journey to Calvary. Love suffers all for you. Calvary is love. Come to My love.

4-20-94 YOU HAVE FORGOTTEN THE FIRST COMMANDMENT

I wish to speak My little one. I am Jesus Lord, only begotten of the Father. Stay with Me, My beloved ones, in silence and meditation. You experience now My call to interior life in the Spirit.

The powers of Anti-Christ grow bold in their efforts to dismantle My Church. Slowly but surely the foundation upon which My Church was founded is subjected to the chisel of the false teachers and the heresy of modernism. These shepherds listen to the dissonant voices and seek to please these faithless apostates rather than affirming the statutes and precepts which are the foundation for My truth. They betray My faithful ones in the name of progress and persecute, by their indifference, those who remain firmly committed to the Church of Peter. I am displaced. My people, you have forgotten the first commandment - "I am the Lord thy God, thou shall not have strange gods before thee." I will not permit these strange ideologies and divisive egoism to be placed first above Me. *NO! I SHALL NOT PERMIT THIS.*

However strong this new church My seem, it will collapse upon itself for it is founded upon lies, deceptions, false doctrines, and the egos of those who seek only their own importance and power.

I ask you, My faithful ones, to pray unceasingly lest you also fall victim to these strange gods promoted under the guise of renewal. True renewal does not destroy the foundation and the structure thus, when the dismantling of the Church seems complete, the seeds of truth and faith being nourished by the care of the Mother, the Woman, will flower in the new Era of Peace. Remain steadfast, My people, and remember that I am God, and the gates of hell will not prevail. Mine is the triumph. Thus say I the Lord God.

4-29-94 DEATH IS EVERYWHERE

I wish to speak, My little one. Heretofore I have been urgently warning and calling to My people - *RETURN TO ME, CONVERT YOUR LIVES, REPENT OF YOUR SINS.* Hereafter I must speak with sorrow in My heart because My message has been spurned. Poor children of the fallen Eve, from all ages has the Father provided for His people. In every generation He has raised up loyal and faithful leaders of His people. In every generation He has raised up those who foresaw events for future generations; events linked to His justice, events linked to His mercy. In those ages of great evil He raised up prophets to warn of His wrath before unrepentant creatures. So too, in this age has He raised up a loyal and faithful shepherd of the flock (Pope John Paul II) who has heroically defended My truth before the whole world. He has raised up mystics and seers who have seen what will befall mankind before My coming in power and glory. He sends out His prophets and apostles of this age to recall you to mercy if you are to be spared His justice. I gave My life for your salvation. My Mother and the heavenly host work tirelessly to restore closed hearts to the mercy of their God. All is for naught.

The world and its inhabitants are on the brink of self-destruction. Mankind becomes more entrenched in hatred. They are demented creatures, filled with demons, blackened with the slime of hell. DEATH! Death is everywhere. My people, My glorious people created in grace and beauty, are recognizable now only as vicious, unthinking, unloving animals who slaughter each other as no more than worthless garbage. They have turned from Me and rejected Me, thus they cannot love each other as I commanded. They know not love. And so will the destruction of mankind continue, and I sorrow for this generation for it has made its choice. Thus say I the Lord God.

5-6-94 **I EXTEND TO YOU MY INVITATION**
First Friday of Eucharistic adoration

Take up your pen now, I wish to speak. Tell to My people I am the Lord God. In My presence does one find a place of refuge from the world. Remove yourself from the world when you come before My presence and rest your frenzied activities in the peace and stillness of My merciful love. Unless you cease from your activities and still the turmoil of your lives, you cannot find refreshment where all is chaos. Come before Me, for one hour spent in peaceful contemplation of My loving presence is My gift of love, My gentle touch upon your soul, My living gaze upon your heart. Seek peace where peace is — in My Eucharistic Presence. I extend to you My invitation. When you ask of Me I answer. Won't you please respond to what I ask of you? I am Jesus Lord. I await your coming.

Thus is the wisdom of the ages: that all must know their God united in His mercy, subject to His justice.

Come to Me little one, for I wish to speak a message of great urgency. I am Jesus Lord, Son of the Father and Son of Mary. In My name say:

The hour is upon you when all children of the Father's creation must relinquish their pride and in humility seek pardon for their many sins. Do you not see, My brothers and sisters, that if you continue to sin with impunity, greater evils will befall mankind to the very destruction of the whole world. I tell this to you and so many scoff at My words, persecute those who bring you this word in My name, and fall deeper and deeper into the depths of hell from whence there is no return. I speak in a loud voice and I say unto you who are in danger of eternal hellfire, by the grace granted to you by the prayers of the faithful on your behalf, *OPEN TO MY URGENT CALL. SEEK FORGIVENESS, REPENT WITHOUT DELAY.*

My faithful ones, pray urgently for lost souls. So many will perish unprepared in the days to come. Be merciful to your brothers and sisters and pray, and pray, and pray. *I CALL LOUDLY, I SPEAK URGENTLY, I WARN YOU COMPELLINGLY - MANKIND IS RUSHING HEAD-LONG TO SELF-DESTRUCTION AND ANNIHILATION.* The pit is open and the fires (of hell) reach higher and higher to claim the harvest of evil. Do thou human creatures of God-Father, God of justice, God of mercy, understand that the end will come on a sudden, and the state of your soul will be sealed for all eternity? Pray with Me, daughter of My Heart:

"Almighty and loving Father accept from My hands the prayers of your faithful servants. Touch the hearts, and ears, and minds of those hardened in sin and unrepentent in pride. Grant that they may respond to your touch, hear your voice, and accept your offer of mercy. Grant your faithful servants an abundance of grace to persevere in prayer in response to your request. And if it be your will, remove your judgment against us. Thank you, Father, for hearing your suffering children. Amen."

215

My dear one, I am Jesus Lord. I wish to speak. In My name say: There is no power on earth greater than love. Love can transform even the most hardened sinner. Do you doubt this? Why so? To love is also a choice.

† When have you reached out your hand in mercy and forgiveness?

† When have you turned your eyes outward to see the grave injustices committed against the weak and helpless?

† When have you prayed for other than your own needs?

† How often have you sought your own comfort and turned a blind eye toward those who suffer in body, mind, or spirit?

How often have you refused the cross of love and sought only the easy path? If you choose the easy path, you do not walk with Me, and if you do not walk with Me, you do not know the true meaning of love. Even the dumb animal responds to the love of its master, yet My own creatures of intelligence and reason reject Me who am the source of love.

It is not so difficult to understand: you reap what you sow. If you do not sow My love, you sow your own emptiness and reap a harvest of desolation. If you are empty, you have nothing to give, and you seek to fill your own lack. Return to Me My beloved ones, and let Me fill your emptiness with My love. Then will you be able to sow love, and love will transform the world.

Thus say I the Lord God: Seek ye not the spirit of the world but seek ye the Spirit of love and truth.

OPEN THE DOORS OF THE CHURCHES
First Friday Eucharistic adoration

Now I wish to speak a message to My people. In the name of the Lord Jesus Christ and by the power of the Holy Spirit say to My people these words:

Such is the time in which you live that only My supernatural intervention can turn you from total annihilation. *This is why I plead urgently for the restoration of My Eucharistic presence in the churches. Where I am welcomed I bring abundant graces and blessings upon those people and places where I am so honored.*

I speak to the shepherds of My flock - *OPEN THE DOORS OF THE CHURCHES AND LET MY PEOPLE COME TO ME.* Would you continue to deny them the opportunity to reap the benefits of knowing Me more intimately? *PLEASE, LET MY PEOPLE COME TO ME.*

Dear little child of My heart, when you speak My word to My people, ask them to petition their priests to open the churches; ask them to come to Me each day; ask them to support, by their presence in the church and by their prayers, their priests and pastors in this request. Come to Me. Fill the churches. Hear Me and answer Me. This is My wish.

6-3-94 **SEEK TO BE AS THE LITTLE CHILDREN**

Thus is the word of the Lord spoken: *This day marks the beginning of calamities.* Now does it begin. Invoke the name of the Lord Jesus Christ and call upon the mercy of the living God. I hear and answer those who call My name. I am the Living God.

Now say: Holy Lord, Living God, Eternal Unity, blessed be your name. Blessed is He who speaks in the name of the Lord, who dwells in the paradise of the holy presence of God. Blessed too are those of gentle spirit and happy heart, for they are filled with the Spirit of God. The wise man and the learned must become as the little child whose heart is happy in its simplicity and wholly trusting in the love and care of its parents. The childlike soul receives with joy the loving embrace, the stern rebuke, and the unconditional love of its parent, the Triune God. There is no fear, but simply the trusting acceptance of the care of its Creator-God. Seek to be as the little children who rest in peace and security upon the bosom of the Father who provides for their every need . . . Thus say I the Lord God.

7-1-94   A MESSAGE TO THE PEOPLE OF THE UNITED STATES
First Friday Eucharistic Adoration

On this day which marks the beginning of the month which celebrates the independence of a people, I wish to speak a message for the United States. In My name proclaim this word:

My dear children, you have lost sight of what true freedom means. You have become a nation of people seeking only pleasure and material possessions. You are ruled by your passions and governed by the laws of instinct and ego. You have sold your souls; you have become a faithless people, a people subjected to unjust laws, corruption, violence and death. You wallow in self-pity and look for solutions everywhere except in the One who is the solution to every ill and every evil. This once mighty nation will continue its fall from grace until it turns once again to firm faith in the one God of all. Faith, prayer, conversion of lives and lifestyles according to My commands given for all ages, and repentance for your unspeakable sins will open My heart of mercy and cleanse this nation so it may once again shine with the splendor of its founding intentions: peace, justice, faith and freedom for all its inhabitants. What you celebrate now is not freedom and independence, but slavery of body and spirit subjected to the agenda of proud and ruthless and corrupt influences whose goal is a godless society. This people follows this agenda like sheep led to the slaughter; unthinking, uncaring, hopelessly following

218

the liars and deceivers to a utopia that is only a mirage. *Please, dear people of the United States, return to faith, return to prayer, repent lest His nation suffer the same fate that so many nations of the world now suffer.* I am the Lord God. I am your hope and your salvation. I have spoken. That is all.

7-9-94 PRIDE IS THE SOUL OF REBELLION

Take up your pen, My little one. I wish to speak. This day I speak to warn My people. For the last time I speak words of warning. Very quickly now do events unfold as has been foretold. Still, most people fail to recognize the truth of prophecy and continue to follow the false god of intellectual dishonesty. Pride is the soul of rebellion. For lo these many years the word of God finds no dwelling place in the hearts of men, thus does mankind find itself lost in the dark byways of sin and evil, apostasy and heresy. Oh My people, you have been warned innumerable times of what will befall you if you continue upon this path of self-destruction. Even now, as the events of your chastisement quickly unfold before you, you fail to understand their portent and continue in your stubborn rejection of My words of warning. How you grieve Me! How you grieve Me! Is there not even the tiniest flicker of love in your heart for the One whose heart is pierced over and over again by your indifference, your callousness, your coldness? Do you not understand that the grief I suffer at your rejection is the grief you will suffer for all eternity, for you have turned your face from My face of love. It is so, and thus I grieve for My lost children. Thus say I the Lord God.

7-12-94 I WARN YOU! I WARN YOU! I WARN YOU!

I wish to speak this day a stern warning to My people. In My name tell to My people My urgent plea to restore their souls to purity without delay. **CONFESS YOUR SINS IMMEDIATELY! DO NOT DELAY!** Seek refuge in prayer, consolation in My Heart of mercy, serenity of spirit in the serene heart of Mary, our Mother. *I WARN YOU! I WARN YOU! I WARN YOU! WOE TO THOSE WHO IGNORE MY WARNING.*

It is come. The time of desolation is now:

† Desolation in nature,

† Desolation in the heart of My church,

† Desolation in the spirits of those who have relinquished their souls to depravity and evil,

† Desolation throughout all of creation.

Speak, child, of the desperate condition of mankind. My people, you must know that these are the desperate hours of your purification when all must be renewed in the cleansing fire of My justice. Not one creature, not one grain of salt will remain untouched. Therefore, children of the Father, know that I come to claim the kingdom of the just. I am their God, and they shall know that I gather them into the New Age of Grace as the anointed ones of the New Jerusalem. Thus say I the Lord God.

7-25-94 BECOME MY BEACONS OF LIGHT

Take up your pen, My little one, I wish to speak. In My name begin this word. Say to My people: I am the Lord God. I Am Who Am. I who Am am with you through the darkest hours. My presence lights the darkness. You who follow Me walk surely through the darkness. It is always so for those who love Me. Love is the light that conquers darkness. *Become My beacons of light whose rays illuminate the darkness reaching out to those who wander blindly and aimlessly searching for what only can be found in My Presence. If I am the Safe Harbor, you My dear ones, must be the guiding lights that mark the true course to life eternal.* See to it that your light shines steadily in faith for those who have lost their faith, in truth for those who follow the lies of

220

the false teachers, in hope for *the coming of the Age of the Glory of God.*

8-2-94   **THE DAWN OF PEACE BREAKS ON THE HORIZON**

(Mother Mary speaks): Hear Me now, daughter, I wish to speak. I am the Mother who wishes to speak. In the name of Jesus, My Son, speak this message which I bring to My beleaguered children everywhere. Speak and say: Dear children, as your Mother who loves you, find solace and comfort in My presence among you. I come to bring you tidings of great joy. The Father permits Me to tell you that the dawn of peace breaks upon the horizon of your suffering generation. Though your suffering intensifies, and the prophecies for this age are yet to be fulfilled, I come to bring you My motherly assurance of the dawning of your liberation from the chains of Satan which have held you in His bondage. *The links grow weaker, and soon now, very soon, the chains will snap and His power over this sad generation will be broken. As the suffering of your purification grows more intense, know that your deliverance is near. Turn to Me in this vale of tears, and I will pour forth upon you the graces that will bring you safely through this darkest trial into the light of the triumph of My Immaculate Heart: the light of My Son in all His power and glory.* Thank you, My children, for remaining faithful to My call.

8-5-94   **I AM PEACE AND I AM ALWAYS WITH YOU**

Now you may write My Words, My little one. Children of the Father, I address you this day in the Spirit of My Infinite Mercy. Set aside your fears, for My Mercy sets you free from the terrors that fill your thoughts and surround you like a vile vapor. Peace is My gift to those who remain steadfast in their reliance upon My loving care for their every need. Remain fixed in submission to My will for you. In the days to come, the people of the earth shall be subjected to great sufferings, chaotic conditions, death and heretofore

221

unknown diseases. All will be in turmoil, yet My Mercy shall fall like a mantle upon the hearts of My faithful ones, and peace shall follow them in every trial of this dark age. My Peace is with you, for I Am peace and I Am always With You. ... Thus say I the Lord God. That is all. Thank you for coming to My Presence this day.

8-11-94 I AM A JEALOUS GOD
During Eucharistic Adoration.

I wish to speak, My little one. This is what I wish you to speak to My people this day. In My name say: I am the Almighty God and My Word is for all ages. Tell My people I am a jealous God, a God who desires to be the center of each heart. I do not tolerate the false gods and strange idols which have replaced My *dominion over all My creation. I bring My child before you to recall you to My Infinite Mercy, to My Living Presence, to My promise of justice, if you do not take heed of My warning.* Please, My dearly beloved, return to Me with your heart, and soul, and mind. Let nothing separate us. This is My passionate desire. I, the Lord God, ask this of you. That is all.

8-23-94 PEOPLE — WAKE UP!

My dear children, come to Me My children, for I am the Holy One of Israel who leads you through the desert of a faithless and hopeless world order. Death is the agenda and the watchword of this order. Do you not see that it is man himself whose policies of infanticide (abortion), genocide, suicide, fratricide, and homicide bring about his own destruction? **People Wake Up! Wake Up I tell you, for you are being duped into bringing about your own destruction.** The days are coming when you will have no choice in whether you live or die, whether you procreate or

222

remain childless, whether you walk in the light of faith or in a Godless hell on earth ruled by those who call themselves the masters of the universe. Children! I call you My children. My poor, dear children you are so lost, so blind to your fate, so helpless and so hopeless.

I can speak no more now, for My sorrow for you is so great. I must let you go knowing what awaits you. You have chosen death over life; you have given yourself over to the merchants of death. So be it. I, the Almighty God, continue to hold My judgment against you. ... Thus say I, the Lord God.

8-30-94 FLY TO ME QUICKLY

Now must My children take heed of the prophets in their midst.

"Speak Lord for your servant is Listening"

In My name speak and say to My people - **THE GLORY OF GOD** — thus is My Word spoken to you. Fly to Me quickly. Fly on wings of faith. The mighty wind that is My Spirit carries you to the safe shelter which I am for all those who seek refuge in My care. Come quickly. Make sure that you have prepared well in prayer, knowledge of the word, and the sacraments, for the days to come are filled with every lie, every deception, every cruelty, and many will falter and fall from My Grace. Evil abounds everywhere, yet you must not be lured by its false promises. So great is My Love for you that I speak repeatedly to warn you of your danger and to lead you on the lighted path. I do so again. Come My little fledglings, and let Me show you how to soar as the mighty eagle high in the sky away from the danger of faithlessness and hopelessness. Come — perch on My strong shoulders as I carry you through the darkness of the storm that rages all about you. Sing your praises to the God who brings you out of darkness into the light of His

223

presence. Believe in Me, Trust Me, Come to Me. I am surely your help and salvation. Thus say I the Lord God.

9-2-94   LOVE RESIDES IN THE TABERNACLE
First Friday Eucharistic Adoration.

I will speak quickly this day, My little one. This day in My name tell to My children everywhere that love resides in the tabernacle. I am Love and I am present. If you wish to know love, come each day before My presence. My people no longer come to pay Me homage. Their days are filled with the concerns of the world - they cannot even find five minutes to spend with Me. They pay homage to the things of the world. Now must My children come to My presence. I wish to fill them with peace and with love. I wish to embrace them and hold them tenderly to My heart. I wish to pour out of Myself upon them, for **I AM WHO AM HAVE ALL THAT THEY NEED, AND SO FEW COME TO CLAIM THEIR INHERITANCE.** Here I am children, come and find your joy and your peace. Thus say I the Lord God.

9-10-94   YOU SHALL STAND BEFORE ME AND BE JUDGED

I wish to speak this day a message to all My people everywhere. In My name say these words: Hearken to My voice for I tell you that most of humanity is not prepared to stand before My justice. Yet, great numbers will soon stand before Me sooner than anyone knows, and they will not find entrance into the Kingdom. Oh how you deceive yourselves and think there is no sin. But, I tell you your sins cry to heaven for vengeance, and justice is mine say I the Lord God. How you shall wail and weep when now you laugh and trample My truth under the foot of your unbelief. Yes, I say, you shall weep and wail and groan under the weight of your sins, and My justice shall prevail. Laugh now, weep later, but then it shall be too late.

Now is the time of mercy granted for repentance. *I am God. Believe this or not, I say I am God. I exist, and you shall stand before Me and be judged.* The wise shall take heed. Thus say I the Lord God.

9-17-94 AWAKEN LITTLE SEED

I wish to speak. Hear Me well daughter, no one can come to the Father, except through the Son.

The Kingdom of God is like the mustard seed planted in the rich soil of faith. Awaken little seed, it is time for the triumph of Christ the King. Come forth little sprout, for now must the light that is Christ the Lord warm the soil and the air (so) that your tender shoot grows strong in the light of His truth. He is the faithful Son who keeps secure the inheritance of the Kingdom of His Father. He comes to receive the fruits of the sturdy plants which faith has nourished and grace transformed. Thus is the Father's Kingdom maintained and made abundantly fruitful, and your inheritance is held secure. Seek the light of Christ for He is the light of your inheritance who keeps you secure and maintains you in His loving care for the time of your harvest into the kingdom of the father. Thus say I the Lord God. That is all.

10-7-94 WHAT IS REJECTED CANNOT BE GIVEN.

I wish to speak My little one, please take up your pen. If there is one thing My children must know in this time of great trial, it is that I love them beyond measure. Still, while My love is all merciful and all encompassing, My children believe that I will not judge their sinful and evil deeds. This is a fallacy, for while My love is never withdrawn from them, it is they who withdraw from Me, rejecting My love. Thus, they fail to understand that what is rejected cannot be given. Because it cannot be given does not mean that I do not love them; it means they have refused what is theirs and turn instead to those deeds which bring My judgment against them, (and) foolishly believing that a loving God will not hold them accountable for their failure to love. I tell you that while I am a God of mercy, I am also a just God, and those who refuse My love will know My justice. Thus say I the Lord God. That is all.

10-13-94 MY PEOPLE HAVE FORGOTTEN ME
During Eucharistic Adoration

I wish to speak My little one. You see here an empty church. My people have forgotten Me. I stand in solemn splendor alone and forgotten. Where are My people? I call to them, and they do not respond. How can I bless them if they shun My presence?

On this day which celebrates the anniversary of My Mother's presence at Fatima, I tell you that the fulfillment of the prophecy is not yet accomplished. Great suffering will yet come to the world because My people fall from truth, and prayer, and conversion as My Mother has asked of you in all of Her many apparitions which I permit. My people, I implore you constantly — *Come Back to Me* . . . Let Me love you and heal your wounded spirits. **COME TO ME IN MY EUCHARISTIC PRESENCE. PRAY THE ROSARY. CONSECRATE YOURSELVES TO OUR TWO HEARTS. RETURN TO TRUE FAITH AND TRUST IN MY CARE FOR YOU.** I have said this so many times, yet My children continue to leave Me in growing numbers and thus, prophecy is fulfilled and great suffering is your state. Foolish children - the easy way is to do as My Mother and I ask. You choose the difficult way of My judgment against you, and so you suffer what you choose.

Persevere My little remnant. Hold fast to My truth, keep strong in My faith, and follow Me in the light of My true church guided by the chosen one of the Lord God, My Pope of the end times (John Paul II). Thus, you are preserved for the glorious reign of Christ the

King in the new era of peace. Hold fast to the hand of your Mother, Mary, whose Triumph is near.

Yea, Glory and Praise to the Almighty Father, by whose hand is everything accomplished according to His Word. Thanks be to God. I have spoken My Word. That is all.

10-20-94 "THIS IS MY BODY, THIS IS MY BLOOD"
During Eucharistic Adoration

I do wish to speak now, My little one. In My name, say these words to My people: Reflect, My people, upon the Mystery of Redemption. My suffering and death was necessary in the Father's plan to restore fallen mankind to eternal salvation. Do you not understand that I would not be fully present to you in this Eucharistic Bread Had I not assented to this will of My Father? If I say "This is My Body, This is My Blood", it is so for I Who Am do not lie. Who is the liar? It is the one who denies that I am God, the one whose feeble mind cannot accept that I can do all things even to being fully present in the host of the Eucharist and the wine of the cup. Surely, I can do all things and surely I am here present as I have said. Oh you of little faith, for it is lack of faith that keeps so many from recognizing their King of Kings and Lord of Lords in the Eucharist. Neither did those who condemned Me and crucified Me recognize in the poor and humble carpenter their God and Savior. It is no different today — they could not see their God in My human manifestation; you cannot see your God in My Eucharist manifestation. They left Me then; so many leave Me now. Truly I say unto you, I am Jesus Christ, true God and true man, and no one who comes to My presence is ever forsaken. Come, children, in faith accept that I am here. I open My arms wide to receive you and embrace you. Come, fill the church. Sing your praise to the Almighty God who dwells here with you. Come!

10-29-94 I AM THE TRIUMPH OF MARY

I wish to speak, My little one. Please take up your pen and begin. In My name say these words:

Hail the Almighty God who comes to bring you tidings of great joy. Soon you will celebrate My coming into the world as the Infant Son of the Mother, virgin undefiled. But I tell you this day that the Son of Glory, God Incarnate, and ascended from whence He came, returns in power and glory as the Triumph of the Immaculate Heart of Mary. I am the Triumph of Mary. From the moment of My conception in Her virgin womb, she has been the instrument by which mankind has come to receive its Lord of Lords and King of Kings. Now I wish you to know that My Second Coming, which is imminent, is the fulfillment of the Word of God spoken in Genesis — "I will put enmity between you and the Woman and between your seed and her seed" (Genesis: 15).

I, Jesus, Am the seed come forth from the Woman, Mary, and My triumph is the destruction of the seed of sin and evil; the seed of the power of satan to destroy the inheritance of the Son; and My return as God of Mercy, God of Justice. I who am Love have conquered My adversary, and the reign of peace commences. I have said it, it is so. Thus say I Almighty, Triumphant Son of the Father and Son of Mary, Jesus Christ, Eternal God.

11-7-94 LIFE AS YOU KNOW IT CANNOT CONTINUE ON ITS PRESENT COURSE

Be still My little one, for I wish to speak My word. In My name say these words: Today, My children, I call you to fervent prayer. Life as you know it cannot continue on its present course, lest there be no life remaining save for the few who survive the holocaust of worldwide population cleansing. You must understand that this diabolical scheme is meant to rid the earth of all that is good and noble, all that is holy, all who are faithful to My truth. Should this plan succeed, every means of killing will be utilized to rid the earth of all but the diabolical agents who seek to rule the world. *My people you have the power to stop the madness. You must stop it!*

Increase your prayers, increase your daily mortifications, hear and understand what I tell you in this warning. *Do not turn away from truth! Do not remain passive and disbelieving, but open to what I tell you and recognize the great danger inherent in all schemes to control life. These are schemes of massive death heretofore unknown in the history of man.* They are cloaked under the mantle of false compassion masquerading as justice. True compassion, true justice, flow from My command to love your God first above all else, and your neighbor as yourself. *Killing is not the answer to man's crisis of spirit; it is the love of God practiced in charity that is the answer.*

Therefore, My children, you must turn to Me wholeheartedly and accept that only in My love will mankind find its strength to withstand Satan's last assault to gain for himself the Father's creation. See to it that He shall not succeed. See to it quickly. Thus say I the Lord God.

11-17-94 MY COMING IS A SOLEMN OCCASION

I wish to speak, My little one. Thank you for responding to My call. In My name I wish you to say to My people these words:

Solemnly do I speak, for My coming is a solemn occasion. I come as your King, I come as your Judge. All of heaven waits with baited breath, for it knows that the time is near when all of creation will sing forth **THE GLORY OF GOD.** Then will they join their voices to this song and all of creation, seen and unseen, will be united in the one presence who is the Triumphant, Almighty God. Then shall there be peace and joy, and all that went before will be no more. Truly I say, this is a solemn occasion, for all will be in awe of the Mighty God who comes in glory and orders all things according to the will of the Father. Yes, My dear ones, awesome is your God and no knee shall remain unbent or head unbowed at My Coming.

Praise to the Almighty God and Father who orders all things rightly. Thus Say I the Lord God. That is all.

12-9-94   **THERE IS A LIGHT IN THE WORLD**

Embrace Me, child, with every part of your being. Now let us begin this message which I wish to speak to my people. In My name you are to say these words:

Peace to You. With great tenderness and gentle yearning, I look with compassion upon the suffering of those caught in the web of lies that hold them bound in error and confusion. There is a light in the world who leads you in truth, if you would but listen. *Surely, I say to you, this light is My light, for it is granted to him to lead My church in this time of great danger. He teaches in My name and acts by My hand. Recognize in him My own authority. I have placed upon him My royal scepter, the diadem of My eternal priesthood. This one who serves me so diligently, is the voice crying in the wilderness (Luke 3:4) of your apostasy.* Truly I say unto you his voice shall not be stilled until the man of righteousness appears. Trust in this beloved son of mine, for it is I who speak with his voice. He too is my beloved son in the order of the priesthood of my only begotten son, Jesus, eternally God, eternally priest. Thus say I, eternal father. Hear him and believe, and you shall be led to reunion with the truth that sets all people free from bondage to falsehood and deception. The light shines in the darkness (John 1:5), and the

230

light sets you free. That is all that I wish to speak this day. Thus say I the Lord God. Praise and thanksgiving to the Almighty God.

(This message refers to John Paul II).

12-31-94 I OFFER YOU MY HEART OF MERCY

I wish to speak to you this message which is for all My people. In My Name say thus:
Thou who dwell upon the earth hear what I say, for unless you turn aside from unrestraint human passions, the lust of your hearts, the pride of your intellects, the idolatry that consumes your soul, that which must perforce continue the cleansing of all of creation will not abate in the coming year. Sorrow and lamentations will be heard in every area of the earth. Man's inhumanity will grow in proportion to His increasing apostasy and his rejection of those commandments I have ordained to bring order into the affairs of men. Violence, death, catastrophes and diabolical cruelty will increase on a scale heretofore unknown in the affairs of mankind. My people must understand that it is they themselves who are the perpetrators of these heinous deeds, thus it is that so long as they continue upon these paths, so must I hold my judgment against them. And so it will continue, for My people are stubborn people and their hearts have turned to stone. Mercy they do not understand, thus life becomes mercilessly brutal and justice for all can find no foothold. Still, I continue to call all to My self. I offer you My Heart of mercy and reach out My hand to each and everyone. **WOE TO THOSE WHO REFUSE ME; YOU SHALL NOT SURVIVE THE FINAL HOLOCAUST.** Thus say I the Lord God that is all.

231

Appendix I

Prayers received within the context of the messages:

† Mighty Spirit of God inflame us with love for the wisdom of God. Let our souls thirst for the truth. Let us drink to the full power of God's holy Word. Guide our steps to the seat of perfect knowledge that we may know and understand the perfect truth that is our God. Almighty and everlasting God, we place ourselves in your loving hands. Teach us, oh Lord. Strengthen us, keep us free from the errors of the Evil One. Thy truth be ever in our minds, our hearts, and our mouths. Let us live the truth of our Lord, Jesus Christ. Amen. (10-16-90)

† Mighty God, eternal Father, Son, and Spirit, grant your children the comfort of your compassionate heart. Hear, Oh Lord, our voices calling you. We plead to you to rescue us from our oppressors. Deliver us, Oh Lord. Rescue us, Oh Lord. We, your children, come humbly before you and beg your mercy. Hear us, Oh Lord. Your people call your name. Amen. (4-10-91)

† Almighty God and Father, let your Spirit come upon your faithful servant. May the power of the most high God bring truth and wisdom. May all your people respond to the power of the Spirit. Help us, Oh Lord, to be strong and faithful witnesses to your mighty presence. Help us, oh Lord, help us. (Private message 5-11-91)

† Oh Spirit of the mighty God, fill our hearts with joy. Let our throats proclaim that Jesus Christ is Lord. Oh Spirit of the living God, we call on you to open our hearts to the Word. We pray, oh Spirit of love, for love to transform us. May we accept, as little children, the gentle touch of the hand of the Father upon our fevered brows. Oh kindly Spirit of the Lord God, favor us with an abundance of your gifts that we may serve

you and our neighbors for your greater glory. Amen. (7-30-91)

† Dear Mother of My heart, I come before you with trust that you will hear your child. I offer you My heart with love for those of My brethren who do not love and honor what is sacred and holy. Open your compassionate heart to My pleas on their behalf. Grant them the grace of conversion. Touch their hearts with your motherly love. I, your humble child, ask this for the salvation of souls and the grater glory of God. Amen (8-27-91)

† Holy Lord God, by the power of your Spirit, through the intercession of the Mother of Mercy, open the eyes, the ears, and the mouths of those who refuse to acknowledge that you alone are God and deserving of our love and adoration. We ask this with confidence in your love, with trust in your care for all of your children, and with faith that you will hear and answer us. Oh Father of goodness and mercy, we praise you, we thank you, we love you. Our tongues proclaim your holy name. We look to the promise of your glory. We listen for your voice. Have mercy on us, we pray. Amen. (7-13-92)

† I come before you My merciful Jesus and offer you (one act of mortification to be left to the individual) in reparation for My many sins which bring so much suffering to your merciful heart. I come humbly before you and acknowledge that I have sinned. Grant Me your grace to confess My sins to those of your priests who have your power to forgive My transgressions. My God, My God, I beg your mercy. Remove your judgment from Me. Amen. (Private messages 9-19-92)

† Spirit of truth, Spirit of the Living God, thou who restores and refreshes us and makes all things new, come and fill us with your holy presence. Speak to us that which will renew us and fortify us in every trial. Come Holy Spirit, take possession of our darkness that we may become children of the light, holy and faithful

233

people of the Lord God, Jesus Christ. Praise to the Holy Trinity, Three-in-One through whom is salvation given in the name of the Father, Son, and Holy Spirit. Amen. (5-19-93)

† **O Sanctissima, o Purissima, the fairest Queen of Heaven, you who prepare the way for the coming of the triumphant Son in His resplendent majesty, pray for us in the hour of trial. Oh Mother of the Incarnate God grant us your protection and deliver us from the powers of evil. Grant that we may know the love of your Son and the everlasting joy of heaven. Amen.** (11-2-93)

† Almighty and loving Father accept from My hands the prayers of your faithful servants. Touch the hearts, and ears, and minds of those hardened in sin and unrepentant in pride. Grant that they may respond to your touch, hear your voice, and accept your offer of mercy. Grant your faithful servants an abundance of grace to persevere in prayer in response to your request. And if it be your will, remove your judgment against us. Thank you, Father, for hearing your suffering children. Amen. (5-19-94)

Index

1990	Date	Page
First Message	9-10	1
The World is in Great Danger	9-27	1
Hear the Words Spoken Through My Prophets	9-28	2
I Desire to Save All My Creation	10-1	2
Return to Your God -- Come to Me	10-2	3
Proclaim the Name of the Lord	10-3	3
I Come to Lead You Back to Everlasting Love	10-4	4
You Evil Announce My Justice	10-4	4
Receive My Last Warning	10-6	5
My Mother is My Perfect Creation — Life is a Sacred Trust	10-7	5
My Peace is a Gift — I am Truth	10-8	7
Let All the Earth Rejoice	10-9	8
Do Not Delay in Responding to Your God	10-10	9
My Message is Urgent — Pray for My Mercy	10-11	9
My Justice Cannot be Denied	10-12	10
Pray for My Pope — Beware of the Evil One	10-13	10
The Glory of God Radiates Throughout the Universe	10-14	11
Mighty Spirit of God Inflame Us	10-16	12
It is Done	10-17	13
Change Your Hearts	10-18	14
I Am What You Seek	10-19	14
I Have Waited so Long For You -- My Wrath Overflows	10-20	15
You Have No Other Need But Me	10-21	16
I Am the Commandment of Love	10-22	17
Become My Holy People	10-23	18
I Am the Living God	10-24	19
Mary the Mother	10-25	20
Come to the Bread of Life	10-26	21
What is to Come is the Abomination of Desolation	10-27	21
Blessed are They Who Move With the Spirit	10-28	22
I Come to Bring You Peace	10-29	23
Man is Made in My Image	10-30	24
He Has Proclaimed the Holiness of His Handmaid	11-1	25
No Other Idols, No Other Images Will I Permit	11-4	26
I Am Peace . . . I Am the Calm Refuge	11-6	26
Soon the Evil One Will Appear	11-7	27
Pray!	11-8	28
No Prayer Goes Unanswered	11-9	28

1990 *continued*...**Date** **Page**

I Call You to Conversion and Repentance 11-12 29
Your Sins Destroy You 11-13 30
To Priests -- My Church is in Disarray............................11-15 31
There Must be no Compromise with the Evil One............11-16 32
The Hour is at Hand for Your Deliverance........................11-18 32
The Triumph of Our Holy Mother is at Hand...................11-20 33
It Begins...11-22 34
So Humble a Servant, So Powerful a Mother...................11-23 35
To Priests 11-25 36
What Men Have Reaped on Earth, So Shall They
Reap for All Eternity...11-26 37
Let My Love Melt the Coldness of Your Hearts 11-27 38
I Am the One God of Heaven and Earth 11-29 39
The Power of the Rosary Surpasses the Power
of the Evil One 12-1 40
My Time of Mercy Ends 12-1 41
Pope John Paul II...12-2 42
Drink of the Cup 12-3 42
You Are Chosen People of the Spirit............................12-5 43
The Time of Trial is at Hand 12-6 44
My Enemies are Powerful 12-7 44
Allow My Love to Transform Your Hearts 12-9 45
Be Living Witnesses of My Truth..............................12-10 45
Man Will Destroy Himself 12-11 46
Why Do You Deny Me? 12-13 47
Repent! 12-14 47
I Restore What has Been Lost in Sin and Evil 12-18 48
I Call you to Holiness 12-19 49
The Three-in-One Beckon you to Come to
Their Saving Grace...12-28 49
Do Not Be Blind to the signs I Place Before You................12-29 50
Guard Against the Abomination of Abominations............12-30 51

1991   **Date** **Page**

The People of the Earth Must Convert Their Lives............1-4 53
I will no Longer Permit the Suffering of My Mother............1-9 54
I Speak Out in Just Anger 1-10 55
Repent All you Peoples of the Earth 1-14 56
There Can be No Peace Until There is Peace
in Each Heart...1-15 56
My Command is the Law of the Universe 1-22 57
I Am a Just God 1-23 58
This is My Last Warning to Sinful Man 1-24 59
Mother Mary Speaks 1-26 60

1991 *continued* ....Date Page

Trust in My Mercy, Trust in My Love 1-29   61
Follow in My Footsteps 2-1   61
A New Heaven and a New Earth Shall I Create 2-3   63
To Priests 2-8   64
God the Holy Spirit 2-16   65
All Creation Rightly Gives Me Praise 2-18   66
Pick Up Your Crosses 2-19   67
This Short Time is Granted for Conversion
and Reparation 2-26   68
I Am the Lord God 2-28   69
Make Reparation for Your Many Sins...............3-1   70
Seek First the Kingdom of God —Turn to My Mother 3-8   71
Holy is the Name of the Lord God Almighty......................3-10   71
Come Close, My Children — Do not be afraid...............4-3   73
The Time for Your Conversion is Short 4-6   74
Now is the Time of Your Witness.......................4-10   76
You Must Not Remain Silent!..........................4-12   77
I Call Each One 4-22   77
Do Not Be Deceived by False Prophets 5-2   78
Stand Firm Against the Evil One 5-4   79
Abortion 5-15   81
The Glorious King Rules Victorious in His Creation 5-22   82
Have Mercy on Your Loving God 5-30   83
Honor My Sacred Heart 6-8   84
I Am Preparing You 6-18   85
All that is Holy is Attacked 6-29   86
Become the Ripe Fruits 7-3   87
I Call you to Repentance.................................7-11   88
I Speak to You Through My Little Child 7-12   89
I Come! 7-23   89
The Time is Urgent.......................................7-25   90
Those of You Who Remain to the End I Protect
in a Special Way...7-26   91
Pray for the Salvation of Souls.........................7-27   92
I Ask you to Pray Seriously the Rosary Before My Image ..7-28   93
Meditation for the Sorrowful Mysteries of the Rosary 7-28   94
I Will Permit the Devastation of a Large Area of the Earth 7-29   94
Learn From my People of Old............................7-30   95
I Do Not Revoke My Judgment.........................8-7   96
You Do Not Pray Enough.................................8-10   97
What is to Be Will Be.....................................8-11   98
Let the Judgment Commence 8-12   99
Let Your Tongues Proclaim the Glorious Mother 8-15   100
These are the Signs of Your Time.......................8-19   101
Pray to Me Through the Immaculate Mother.................8-23   101

1991 continued ....**Date** **Page**

Pray Seriously, My Children 8-27 102
. . . Their Faith is but a Dying Ember 8-29 103
Personal Messages..9-5 103
Keep Alive the Faith 9-20 104
Take Upon Yourselves Voluntary Acts of Reparation 9-21 105
When All Seems Lost Will I Come in Power and Glory 9-23 106
The Spirit of Renewal is Come 9-25 107
Renew Yourselves . . . in the Fire of Divine Love...............9-26 107
All Are Created Equal in My Image 9-27 108
Without Me you are But Helpless Babes 10-3 108
Make Many Acts of Penance 10-5 110
I Call You Urgently to Repentance 10-11 110
Do Not Scorn Your Crosses 10-17 111
Love 10-24 112
Meditation for the Joyful Mysteries of the Rosary.............11-9 112
Pray Thus 11-12 113
I Call you to Sincere Efforts of Repentance 11-19 114
I Am Infinite Being 12-3 115
Have Your Lamps Ready..12-4 116
The Time Foretold by the Prophets is Now 12-9 117
Be Born Again in the Fire of the Spirit 12-10 118
Personal Message...12-20 118
I Announce to you the Reign of Peace and Justice 12-24 119
That Which is Unclean Must be Made Clean.....................12-31 120

1992   **Date**   **Page**

There is Not One in All the Earth Who Does Not Offend Me ..1-6 121
I Only Am God..1-15 123
Woe to Those Who Reject My Mercy 1-20 123
My Creatures Destroy Themselves Without a
Second Thought 1-22 124
Your Faithfulness is Rewarded 1-23 125
When You Call My Name, I Answer You 1-25 125
Stand in Readiness to Greet Your King 1-27 126
Prepare Well..1-28 127
Why Do You Grieve Me So? 1-29 127
Make Your Homes Havens of Peace 2-19 128
Mother Mary Speaks 2-21 129
The Fullness of God's Power 2-23 130
Mine is Not an Idle Promise 3-5 130
Cursed is This Generation of Evil Doers..........................3-8 131
I Who Am Love Am Rejected 3-19 132
You Are Lost in the Maze of Human Endeavor 4-2 133
. . . The Beginning of the End 4-7 134
These are the Seed on the Barren Ground 4-7 134

1992 *continued* ....**Date** **Page**

Turn Your Hearts to Prayer 4-12   135
The Hour of Mercy is Soon to be Withdrawn 4-15   135
The Lord God Does Not Enter Where the Door is
Closed Against Him 4-20   135
There is Still Yet a Little Time to Respond to the Call
of the Mother...4-21   136
Medjugorje 4-22   137
Celebration of Divine Mercy...4-22   137
You Have Been Seduced by Lies and Deceptions..............4-25   138
My Truth is My Word..4-27   140
How is it That You no Longer Know Me?............................4-29   140
Continue to Pray 5-7   141
The Triumph is Life Over Death..5-16   142
You Are Crucified by Your Own Sins..................................5-20   143
My Mother's Heart is Full to Overflowing With Grief.........5-28   144
They are judged Unworthy Stewards..................................6-9   144
I Let Fall the Sword of My Justice.....................................6-11   145
Forgive! 6-24   146
Mother Mary Speaks 6-25   147
The Church of Satan 6-25   147
I Speak to you a Stern Warning 6-30   149
Your Suffering is Not in Vain 7-7   149
Soon I Cease to Call 7-13   150
I Tell You Clearly that I Come 7-17   151
Those Who Possess Life Possess Me..................................7-21   152
Message for the United States (Abortion) 7-22   152
All is Evil, All is Darkness..7-30   153
Now I Am the Grieving Mother 8-1   153
Love One Another with My Love.......................................8-4   154
The Time of Great Peril Quickly Approaches 8-11   154
I Do not Wish to Chastise 8-23   155
I . . . Ask . . . Sincere Acts of Penance and Reparation 9-15   156
My Faithful Priest-Sons Must Be Strong..........................9-20   156
Listen!...9-22   157
Delay No Longer 10-5   158
Be My Obedient Priests 10-11   158
See How I have Prepared for your Flowering?..................10-20   159
See How I Love You 11-1   160
United States 11-3   160
Let a New Life of Love Begin 11-11   161
Be Disciples of Peace...11-15   161
No Portion of the Earth Will be spared.............................11-19   162
My Faithful ones, Your Numbers Diminish 11-22   163
Before the Fatima Statue...12-11   164
Prepare! Prepare! Prepare! 12-22   164

1993

	Date	Page
You Are My Seeds of Hope	1-1	165
Seek Not After the World	1-2	166
Let Each Voice Speak My Truth	1-9	166
Before the Triumph Must Come the Suffering	1-11	167
Will you Still Refuse My Mercy?	1-13	167
Be Healed in My Love	1-14	168
Pray For Peace	1-19	169
I Am the Safe Harbor	2-3	169
The Prophecies Must Now be Fulfilled	2-8	170
Seek Ye Not After the World	2-18	170
You See not the Evil	2-22	171
My Word This Day is One of Encouragement	3-1	172
In Suffering is Compassion Born	3-6	172
I Have Heard My People Cry	3-9	173
The Upheavals of Nature are a Sign of the Times	3-15	173
The Woman Clothed in the Sun	3-31	174
Fear Not the Tomb	4-9	175
You Are Created in the Image of Love and Mercy	4-14	176
Become My Disciples of Mercy	4-18	177
The Son of Corruption	4-28	177
Eucharistic Exposition	5-7	178
Where Are your Hearts?	5-11	178
Pray to My Spirit	5-19	179
Meditation on the Joyful Mysteries of the Rosary	5-24	180
Refuse Not the Hour of Mercy	6-1	181
The Star of the Evil One Rises	6-4	182
Teaching on the Book of Revelation	6-9	182
Virtue is Your Strength	6-21	184
The Father Does Not Revoke His Judgment Against You	6-25	185
Heaven is Silent (The Seventh Seal)	7-6	186
The First Trumpet	7-20	187
What Folly to Damn Your Souls!	7-23	188
Forgive One Another	7-31	189
The Harvest of the Earth	8-15	190
So Few Understand My Truth	8-20	190
Fight the Good Fight	8-27	190
The Sounding of the Trumpets	9-1	191
Come to the Refuge of the Sacred Heart	9-3	191
Unite	9-7	192
The Stage is Being Set (for Anti-Christ)	9-19	193
Hell is Eternal Reality	9-29	193
Be Still My People	10-3	194
There Will be Great Suffering	10-6	195

1993 *continued* ....**Date** **Page**
Recall the Words of the Prophet Isaiah 10-15 195
The New Jerusalem 10-26 196
The Mother of All Souls 11-2 197
Pride is the God From Which All Evil Flows 11-5 198
It is Finished 11-13 198
Unjust Laws and Governments............................11-30 199
The Kingdom is at Hand 12-2 200
Come to the Eucharistic Presence.....................12-3 201
The Remnant 12-6 201
REPENT! REPENT! REPENT! 12-7 201
The Second Coming of Jesus............................12-10 202
Repent Now, Immediately! 12-18 203
The Message of Urgent Warning 12-21 203

1994   **Date** **Page**
Be My Oasis of Peace.......................................1-1 205
Be What I ask You to Be....................................1-7 206
The Era of Peace..1-18 206
Practice of Abortion Condemned.....................1-22 207
The Tabernacle Will Be Desecrated 2-5 207
The Era of Peace (continued) 2-18 208
I Do Not Suffer The Fool 2-23 209
You Have Your Choices 3-7 210
A Heart Conformed to My Will is a heart Conformed
to My Love 3-17 210
You Talk, Talk, Talk 3-24 211
Calvary is Love 3-31 211
You Have Forgotten the First Commandment 4-20 212
Death is Everywhere..4-29 213
I Extend to You My Invitation 5-6 214
The Pit Is Open..5-10 215
To Love is Also a Choice 5-19 216
Open the Doors of the Churches......................5-24 217
Seek to be as the Little Children 6-3 217
A Message to the People of the United States 7-1 218
Pride is the Soul of Rebellion 7-9 219
I Warn You! I Warn You! I Warn You!...............7-12 219
Become My Beacons of Light 7-25 220
The Dawn of Peace Breaks on the Horizon 8-2 221
I Am Peace and I am Always With You................8-5 221
I Am a Jealous God..8-11 222
People — Wake Up!..8-23 222

Fly To Me Quickly..8-30   223
Love Resides In The Tabernacle...9-2   224

1994 *continued*..**Date Page**
You Shall Stand Before Me And Be Judged..............................9-10   224
Awaken Little Seed..9-17   225
What is Rejected Cannot Be Given..10-7   225
My People Have Forgotten Me...10-13 226
This is My Body, This is My Blood...10-20 227
I Am the Triumph of Mary...10-29 228
Life as You Know It Cannot Continue on Its
Present Course. 11-7   228
My Coming is a Solemn Occasion..11-17 229
There is a Light in the World...12-9   230
I Offer You My Heart of Mercy...12-31 231

✛✛✛

Earthquakes. Abortion. Crime. Family Breakdown. Corruption. War. Are you reading the

Signs Of Our Times

A "decade of tears." That's what visionaries are calling the end of this twentieth century–and already the prophecy begins to unfold. Earthquakes. Tornadoes. Bizarre weather. Corruption. Crime.War. Signs of the times.

We at *Signs of Our Times* Catholic magazine know there's hope amidst this darkness. Because in these last days a "Woman Clothed with the Sun" has descended from Heaven, revealing secrets of the future and calling for peace. Our Blessed Mother is visiting places such as **Betania, Venezuela; Naju, Korea; Kibeho, Rwanda, and Medjugorje, Yugoslavia**. She comes with a message for the whole world.

She comes with a message for you.

Interested in learning more about Mary's messages? Subscribe to *Signs of Our Times* magazine, and you'll receive four quarterly issues plus special updates reporting on Heaven's revelations and warnings to our world. **Subscribe today for only $18 per year.** ($30 Canadian Subscriptions / $35 other foreign. U.S. funds only).

Also available... The *Signs of Our Times* Binder.
All our issues from 1989 through 1993. Now just $49.95 !
(Just use the order form on the opposite page).

Signs of the Times Apostolate
109 Executive Drive ✳ Suite D ✳ Sterling, VA 20166
Tel (703) 742-3939 ✳ Fax (703) 742-0808

Order Form

❏ **Yes**, I want to be kept up-to-date on all of Our Lady's appearances around the world. I've enclosed $18 to subscribe to *Signs of Our Times* magazine. I understand I will receive four issues per year, plus special updates and reports (Canadian subscriptions $30 per year, other foreign subscriptions $35).

❏ **Yes**, please send me both **SOT Binders, Volumes I and II**, containing all issues of *Signs of Our Times* from April 1989 through December 1993 ($49.95 includes shipping and handling).

❏ **Yes**, please send me the **Sot Binder Volume I** containing all issues of the **SOT** newsletters from April 1989 through December 1992 ($34.95 includes S&H.)

❏ **Yes**, please send me the **SOT Binder Volume II** containing all issues of the **SOT** magazine from January 1993 through December 1993 ($15 includes S&H)

❏ **Yes**, please send me the **Sot Binder Volume III** containing all issues of the **SOT** magazine from January 1994 through December 1994 ($15 includes S&H)

Donations

❏ **Yes**, I want to help spread Our Lady's messages of peace and conversion throughout the world. I wish to donate $_____ per month to become a **Monthly Partner for Our Lady's Peace Plan**.

❏ **Yes**, I want to help spread Our Lady's messages of peace and conversion throughout the world. I've enclosed a one—time donation of $_____ to help your apostolate.

My Name _____

Address _____

City, State, Zip _____

Phone (h) _____ (o) _____

Recipient of Subscription (if different from above)

My Name _____

Address _____

City, State,Zip _____

Phone (h) _____ (o) _____

Payment is by

❏ Check

❏ MasterCard _____ Exp. _____

❏ Visa _____ Exp. _____

Signature for credit card orders

_____

Order today! Send your mail orders to:

Signs of the Times Apostolate,
109 Executive Drive ✳ Suite D ✳ Sterling, Va 20166.
Phone Orders: 703-742-3939. Fax orders: 703-742-0808.

Thunder of Justice
The Warning. The Miracle.
The Chastisement. The Era of Peace.

by Maureen and Ted Flynn
Order Form
"This book has changed my life."

That's been the response of readers of **The Thunder of Justice**. Nearly all are profoundly changed by reading the words of warning and hope given today by Our Lady.

Now you can bring these same powerful words to your friends and loved ones. Share Heaven's urgent warnings and ultimate promise of victory—by sending them their own copy of **The Thunder of Justice**. Use the convenient order form below!

Now let it change your friends.

Order today! Send your mail orders to ***Signs of the Times***, **109 Executive Drive ✳ Suite D ✳ Sterling, Va 20166**. Phone orders: 703-742-3939. Fax orders: 703-742-0808.

❏ Yes, I want to order a copy of Thunder of Justice for $13.95 plus $2.95 for shipping and handling. I have included an additional $13.95 plus $1.00 shipping and handling per book to cover the cost of sending more than one to the same address. **(Spanish available— $14.95 plus S&H)**

My Name _____

Address _____

City, State, Zip _____

Phone (h) _____ (o) _____

Recipient of book (if different from sender above)

Name _____

Address _____

City, State, Zip _____

Phone (h) _____ (o) _____

Payment is by

❏ Check

❏ Master Card _____ Exp _____

❏ Visa _____ Exp _____

Signature for credit card orders

Tribulations and Triumph

Order Form

"New and urgent revelations interpreting today's signs of the times.."

A voice from the American Midwest is now warning us about details of events that will soon overtake the world. This powerful book gives us the messages from Our Lord to an American housewife detailing incredible prophecies concerning the Pope, the Anti-Christ and the glorious era that awaits the faithful.

Must reading for those who want to follow the unfolding events as they take their place in history!

Order today! Send your mail orders to:

Signs of the Times Apostolate,
109 Executive Drive ✳ Suite D ✳ Sterling, Va 20166.
Phone orders: 703-742-3939. Fax orders: 703-742-0808.

❏ Yes, I want to order a copy of **Tribulations and Triumph** for $11.95 plus $2.95 for shipping and handling. I have included an additional $11.95 plus $1.00 shipping and handling per book to cover the cost of sending more than one to the same address.

My Name _____

Address _____

City, State, Zip _____

Phone (h) _____ (o) _____

Recipient of book (if different from sender above)

Name _____

Address _____

City, State, Zip _____

Phone (h) _____ (o) _____

Payment is by

❏ Check

❏ Master Card _____ Exp _____

❏ Visa _____ Exp _____

Signature for credit card orders